Prizing Scottish Literature

Prizing Scottish Literature

A Cultural History of the Saltire Society Literary Awards

Stevie Marsden

ANTHEM PRESS

Anthem Press
An imprint of Wimbledon Publishing Company
www.anthempress.com

This edition first published in UK and USA 2023
by ANTHEM PRESS
75–76 Blackfriars Road, London SE1 8HA, UK
or PO Box 9779, London SW19 7ZG, UK
and
244 Madison Ave #116, New York, NY 10016, USA

First published in the UK and USA by Anthem Press in 2021

Copyright © Stevie Marsden 2023

The author asserts the moral right to be identified as the author of this work.

All rights reserved. Without limiting the rights under copyright reserved above, no part of this publication may be reproduced, stored or introduced into a retrieval system, or transmitted, in any form or by any means (electronic, mechanical, photocopying, recording or otherwise), without the prior written permission of both the copyright owner and the above publisher of this book.

British Library Cataloguing-in-Publication Data
A catalogue record for this book is available from the British Library.

ISBN-13: 978-1-83998-716-8 (Pbk)
ISBN-10: 1-83998-716-2 (Pbk)

Cover Image: donatas1205 / Shutterstock.com

This title is also available as an e-book.

CONTENTS

List of Illustrations   vii

Acknowledgements   ix

    Introduction   1
    Literary Award Culture: Existing Scholarship   2
    A Brief History of Scottish Literary Awards   12
    Book Structure   14

Part I

1. The History of the Saltire Society   21

       Origins of the Saltire Society   21
       The Saltire Society and Scotland's Cultural Renaissance   24
       Publications, Pamphlets and the Shadow of War   28
       Scotland's Second Cultural Renaissance and Calls for Independence   31

2. The Saltire Society Scottish Book of the Year   37

       Earliest Commendations and Awards: 1930s And 1940s   37
       Founding the Scottish Book of the Year Award: 1950s–1960s   39
       The Scottish Book of the Year Award: 1960s–1990s   43
       Highs and Lows: 1990s–2000s   57
       Turn of the Century: 2000s   67
       Making Changes: 2010s and Beyond   70

3. The Saltire Society First Book of the Year Award   75

       Prosperous Origins: 1980s   75
       The Minor Award?: The 1990s   78
       Moving On: 2000s–2010s   88

Part II

4. 'What's This Got to Do with Scotland?': Qualifying Scottishness through Terms of Eligibility — 97

    Prizing Scottish Literature: Terms of Eligibility and Scottishness — 99
    Judging Scottishness — 103
    Quantifying Terms of Eligibility — 106
    Who Publishes Scottish Books? — 109
    The Politics of Publishing and Promoting Scottish Literature — 114

5. Noticing Talent: Michel Faber, James Kelman, A. L. Kennedy, Ali Smith and the Saltire Society Literary Awards — 121

    From First Book to Booker: Scottish Writers and Literary Awards — 123
    Michel Faber — 123
    James Kelman — 125
    A. L. Kennedy — 127
    Ali Smith — 129
    Bumped for the Booker? Literary Awards as Marketing Tools — 130
    The Impact of Winning Awards — 137

6. Not Your Typical Book Award: New Ways of Thinking about Literary Awards — 145

    Current Understandings of Literary Awards Culture — 145
    The Saltire Society Literary Awards and Quantifying Prestige — 148
    Not All Prizes Are Created Equal: Literary Award Hierarchies — 157
    False Equivalence and Literary Awards Culture — 163

    Conclusion — 167

Appendix — 173

Notes — 195

Bibliography — 229

Index — 239

ILLUSTRATIONS

Tables

1   List of nominations for Saltire Society Book of the Year Award 1982 — 51
2   Shortlist for the Saltire Society Book of the Year Award 1982 — 52
3   Nominations for the inaugural First Book of the Year Award, 1988 — 77
4   Number of books shortlisted for the Book of the Year Award, 1982–2019, categorised by Saltire Society's terms of eligibility — 107
5   Number of books shortlisted for the First Book of the Year Award, 1988–2019, categorised by Saltire Society's terms of eligibility — 108
6   Number of Book of the Year Award winners, 1982–2019, categorised by the Saltire Society Literary Awards' terms of eligibility — 109
7   Number of First Book of the Year Award winners, 1988–2019, categorised by the Saltire Society Literary Awards' terms of eligibility — 109
8   Location of publishers of books shortlisted for the Book of the Year Award, 1982–2019, categorised by city (England) — 110
9   Location of publishers of books shortlisted for the First Book of the Year Award, 1982–2019, categorised by city (England) — 111
10 Location of publishers of books shortlisted for the Book of the Year Award, 1982–2019, categorised by city (Scotland) — 112
11 Location of publishers of books shortlisted for the First Book of the Year Award, 1982–2019, categorised by city (Scotland) — 112

Figures

1   Saltire Society Literary Awards judging panels, 1965–2013 — 71
2   Saltire Society Literary Awards judging panel, 2014 — 72
3   Saltire Society Literary Awards judging panels, 2015 onwards — 72

ACKNOWLEDGEMENTS

Like many academic monographs, this book is the result of many years of work and research. At times, the challenge of completing and writing up research has felt insurmountable, but it has been made easier by the support, advice and friendship I have received along the way.

I'd like to thank, first and foremost, Professor Claire Squires, who was an exceptional PhD supervisor and always provided insight, support and reassurance. I would also like to thank the Saltire Society, particularly Jim Tough and Sarah Mason, for their unwavering confidence in my research. Without Claire, Jim and Sarah, this project could not have happened. Thanks, also, to Danielle Fuller, whose advice (and research!) has been invaluable to the development and completion of this work. I would also like to thank the Arts and Humanities Research Council for funding this project. Thank you to everyone at Anthem Press who has been part of making this book a reality, particularly Tej P. S. Sood and Megan Greiving, and to the reviewers who provided enormously helpful comments on the earlier versions of this manuscript.

One of the most joyous aspects of research are the friends made along the way, and I feel incredibly lucky to have met, shared ideas and become friends with some of the most talented scholars in the field, including Melanie Ramdarshan Bold, Alexandra Dane, Christina Neuwirth, Rachel Noorda, Corinna Norrick-Rühl, Simon Rowberry, Will Smith and Millicent Weber. Long may our conference ice cream excursions and BLUNT presentations continue. I'd also like to thank the Media & Gender Group at the University of Leicester, and in particular Jilly Boyce Kay, Jessica Martin, Claire Sedgwick, Paula Serafini and Helen Wood – amazing feminist scholars and women who are a constant source of strength and support.

A number of people have been with me throughout this process, providing much needed respite and friendship, including Ash, Donners, Ian, Isaac, Isobel and Tina. A special mention goes to Anna, whose support and advice has gotten me through some of the most challenging parts of book writing. Thanks to my partner, Zach, whose unwavering support of my research has been invaluable. I would be remiss to not also thank Brie whose calming companionship has brought much comfort during the writing of this book.

Finally, I would like to thank my family – Debra, Derek, Mavis, Derek, Jason, Michael and Rachel. While my family might not have always understood exactly what I do, they have nonetheless remained a constant source of support and much-needed humour. I'd particularly like to thank my mum who has instilled in me the confidence to debate and share my thoughts. This might not be the bestselling novel she keeps bugging me to write, but I hope she will enjoy it nonetheless.

INTRODUCTION

In October 2012, I began doctoral research on the Saltire Society, a Scottish cultural charity, and their series of Literary Awards. I, admittedly, had never heard of the Society or its work before I applied to complete the research, but I had by that point acquired a particular interest in literary prize culture and was keen to delve into it more. My main concerns at the time were 'how and why?' *How* do literary prizes instil value and *why* do they matter so much? Who makes the decisions that make one book the winner and all others runners-up? At what point did they become key arbiters of cultural and literary prestige? These initial questions were influenced by my knowledge of literary prizes at the time, which centred largely on the so-called major literary prizes that most people recognise: the Booker Prize, the Nobel Prize for Literature, the Women's Prize for Fiction and the Costa Book Awards. I went into my research assuming my findings would align with those of other scholars in the field. However, as soon as I started to observe and research the workings of the Saltire Society Literary Awards, I realised that not all prizes are created equal, and the kinds of questions I would be asking would need to change if I was going to fully understand the workings of the Society's Literary Awards.

Due to the nature of the project (an Arts and Humanities Research Council Collaborative Doctoral Award), my research identity was split. On the one hand, I was a 'typical' researcher. I read the existing literature on literary prize culture, spent time in the National Library of Scotland digging through the Society's archives and interviewed key figures in the history of the Society and its awards. On the other hand, I was working closely with the Society in the actual administration and management of their Literary Awards.[1] I arranged judging panel meetings, took minutes at those meetings, informed publishers of submission openings and deadlines, and arranged delivery of submitted titles to judges. The day-to-day workings of the awards informed my research and vice versa. This is, perhaps unsurprisingly, unusual in literary award research. By their very nature, literary awards are organised in such a way as to ensure they are hidden and secret. Rules are established by prize organisers and are to be abided by, publishers select which author's they will submit and judging panel meetings are confidential, with the announcement of winners being treated as a spectacle of surprise. My role, then, gave me access to the hitherto mysterious processes that help literary awards to work, and while that experience was of a very particular prize during a very particular period, it nonetheless shed new light on understandings of literary award culture.

However, before exploring such understandings in more detail through this study, it is worthwhile to spend some time to reflect on the existing academic discourse surrounding literary award culture and where this study is positioned within it.

Literary Award Culture: Existing Scholarship

Despite literary awards playing a central role in UK literary and publishing culture for the best part of a century, significant critical discourse considering their influence and effect upon literature has only really emerged in the latter half of the twentieth century. One of the first book-length studies of a literary award and its cultural impact was Richard Todd's *Consuming Fictions: The Booker Prize and Fiction in Britain Today* (1996), which considered the wider impact of the Booker Prize for Fiction[2] in terms of book sales, author status and 'literary enrichment'.[3] As James F. English has argued, Todd's text is one of the first 'that sets out to understand the powerful and complex role such prizes have come to play in our culture'.[4] Accordingly, Todd perhaps instigated the shift from what English called anecdotal retellings of 'scandalous moments in a prize's history' to a more serious and scholarly assessment of the role of literary awards within the contemporary literary and publishing industry.[5] Since Todd's 1996 book, there have been a number of other book-length examinations of the Booker Prize, or at least largely focused on the Booker Prize, including Graham Huggan's *The Postcolonial Exotic: Marketing the Margins* (2001), Luke Strongman's *The Booker Prize and the Legacy of Empire* (2002) and Anna Auguscik's *Prizing Debate: The Fourth Decade of the Booker Prize and the Contemporary Novel in the UK* (2017). This is not to mention the multitude of articles, chapters and conference papers in which the Booker Prize is a central focus (see, e.g., English, 1999; Cachin and Ducas-Spaes, 2003; Todd, 2006; Norris, 2006a, 2006b, 2006c; Squires, 2007; Pickford, 2011; Driscoll, 2014).

In the midst of these Booker-centric studies, James F. English's influential critical assessment of the significance of cultural awards, *The Economy of Prestige: Prizes, Awards, and the Circulation of Cultural Value* (2005), was published. English's text has since become the go-to study for anyone examining contemporary prize culture. In the *Economy of Prestige*, English provides an authoritative critical history of modern prize culture and a theoretical framework – influenced by the works of Pierre Bourdieu – by which to understand the series of cultural and economic value exchanges that occur within it.⁶ Indeed, our understanding of how contemporary literary awards function relies heavily on the work of Bourdieu, specifically his work on the forms of, and relationships between, capital. Writing in 1986, Bourdieu proposed that there were three forms of capital: cultural, economic and social.⁷ Cultural capital 'describes the forms of extracurricular knowledge that [individuals] from certain backgrounds possess'.⁸ In other words, cultural capital encompasses and reaffirms the notion that an individual's understanding of, and engagement with, culture is influenced by socio-economic status and inherited taste(s). Accordingly, Bourdieu's conception of cultural capital should be 'understood and investigated in the broader context of the ongoing reproduction of class privilege'⁹ since it 'is convertible, on certain conditions, into economic capital [and] *social capital*'.¹⁰ For Bourdieu, economic capital 'is immediately and directly convertible into money'¹¹ and is the 'dominant type of capital'.¹² In terms of literary awards, the most obvious form of economic capital is the prize purse bequeathed to a winner on receipt of an award. However, further examples of the kind of economic capital incorporated within literary awards include the economic investment made by an award's sponsors or financiers, which can often lead to increased visibility for an award and, as a result, a potential increase in book sales. This, in turn, may bring with it an increase in income for the author and their publisher. Bourdieu's third form of capital, social capital, 'is the aggregate of the actual or potential resources which are linked to possession of a durable network of more of less institutionalised relationships of mutual acquaintance and recognition – or in other words, to membership in a group'.¹³ Social capital manifests in a number of ways with regard to literary awards. A prize organisation or its administrators often bring their own network of 'institutionalised relationships'. Martyn Goff, the administrator of the Booker Prize from 1973 to 2006, for example, was the director of the National Book League (which became the Book Trust in 1986) and likely brought existing contacts and connections from this position to his role as Booker Prize administrator.¹⁴ Literary award judges are also involved in a negotiation of social capital with a prize and vice versa, as English explains:

> The prestige of a prize – the collective belief in its cultural value – depends not just on the prestige of the jurors [...] but on their own apparent belief in the prize [...] Our belief in a prize is really a kind of belief by proxy, a belief in these others' belief.¹⁵

Our trust in this 'belief by proxy' is influenced by the kinds of social (and cultural) capital we expect from judges: institutional and professional associations which inform their aptitude for a credible assessment of literature.

Symbiotically, judges accrue further social and cultural capital through their work with the 'stature of the prize guarantee[ing] the honor associated with judging it'.[16]

English has done much to develop Bourdieu's work and its application to cultural awards. He proposes an additional form of capital – journalistic – that accounts for the media coverage – particularly of award scandals and controversies – that is critical for an award to develop a reputation (both negative and positive alike).[17] English also argues that such forms of capital are interconnected in such a way that is specific to cultural awards:

> [Prizes] are the single best instrument for negotiating transactions between cultural and economic, cultural and social, or cultural and political capital – which is to say that they are our most effective institutional agents of *capital intraconversion*. [...] The administrators, judges, sponsors [...] and others involved in a prize are thus themselves to be understood as agents of intraconversion; each of them represents not one particular, pure form of capital, but a particular set of quite complex interests regarding the rules and opportunities for capital intraconversion.[18]

In identifying the specificity of the negotiations and exchanges of capital at play in award culture, English's development of Bourdieu's work has provided a framework that facilitates a more nuanced examination of how cultural, economic, social and journalistic capital coalesce in award culture.

Such intraconversions of capital facilitate, English argues, 'cultural "market transactions"' which are part of a 'collective project of value production' comprising a 'whole system of symbolic give and take'.[19] An overt example of the literary prize as a marketable transaction of culture which demonstrates this 'symbolic give and take' is through their direct application within the literary marketplace. Literary awards are, as Claire Squires argues, one element of the wider marketing campaigns and activities of book production and are an integral aspect of book publishing, contributing to the intensification of the 'commodification of the literary marketplace'.[20] One of the key ways in which such commodification manifests is by way of the paratextual features of an award-winning book, or book by an award-winning author. Squires explains how the cultural kudos that comes with winning the Booker Prize can transform into economic capital through increased promotion:

> The strapline 'Booker Prize Winner' [...] becomes part of a wider marketing mix set to build on the book's achievements [...] Hence, particularly with the bigger literary awards and certainly with the Booker,

floor and window space is given over to displays of the shortlist and the eventual winner.[21]

The level of the successful impact a literary award can have within this 'marketing mix' depends, however, on the promotional activity of the award's organisers and the winning or shortlisted book's publisher.[22] It also depends on whether an award has managed to acquire enough cultural and journalistic capital for this strapline, or an association with said award, to make any economic impact on the book or its author and publisher. As is discussed in the final chapter of this book, far from being an inherent aspect of all literary awards, the value and capital a prize accrues and imparts on its winners/shortlistees is dependent on a range of conditions which many awards lack.

Like English, Squires has also provided key examinations of literary prizes, particularly in relation to their influence on the book as saleable product and on the author as celebrity: 'Literary prizes – and particularly the Booker Prize for Fiction (since 2002, the Man Booker) – increase this commodification and celebritisation, with their success in directing media attention to the book world.'[23] Indeed, Squires argues that it is through such commodification and celebritisation of the book and author that literary prizes, and the agents and institutions behind them, contribute to the construction and circulation of cultural value:

> Through branding, through packaging, through imprints, through bookshop shelving strategies, and through literary prizes, the marketing of literature works actively to create cultural meanings.[24]

Squires's analysis of the central role of literary prizes within the marketing of contemporary literature is particularly significant to this cultural history and analysis of the Saltire Society Literary Awards. As this book illustrates through the example of the Saltire Society Literary Awards, an institution's failure to use a prize to effectively market and celebrate award-winning authors and books significantly diminishes the award's potential to generate exposure for the prize and its winners and, therefore, undermines the prize's ability to contribute to the creation of broader 'cultural meanings'. In the case of the Saltire Society Literary Awards, while there have been periods of the effectual marketing of the Book of the Year and First Book of the Year Awards (most notably when they had major media sponsors, as described in Part I), the Society's failure to consistently promote the awards has not only diminished their ability to 'commodify' and 'celebritise' books and authors, but it has also meant that the Society has struggled to position itself as an arbiter of cultural and literary value in Scotland.

Similarly to Squires, Beth Driscoll has focused on the commercial underpinnings and affects of literary award culture. In *The New Literary Middlebrow: Tastemakers and Reading in the Twenty-First Century*, Beth Driscoll examines the Booker Prize in terms of the literary middlebrow and popular culture.[25] More specifically, Driscoll argues that literary prizes are a 'leading example of the new literary middlebrow' since they are 'reader-oriented, commercial, reverent towards elite culture and reliant on cultural intermediaries'.[26] Like English, Driscoll applies Bourdieusian frameworks to her examination of prize culture, and the Booker Prize in particular, seeking to expand upon the application of Bourdieu's work. Driscoll argues that Bourdieu's comments concerning monopolies of power in cultural consecration and legitimacy extends to prize culture since 'the multiple literary awards that exist at any given historical moment comprise a field in which prizes compete to monopolize the power of consecration'.[27] However, whereas there is often a presumption that such 'power of consecration' would fall to prizes like the Booker Prize, as one of the most well known in the world, Driscoll argues that the Booker Prize's 'acts of consecration are not authoritative and are often undermined by other agents in the field [...] Because of its highly mediated status, the Man Booker Prizes does not produce a definitive assessment of literary value, but keeps literary value a contested and fluid concept.'[28] Driscoll's work is significant also for providing articulations of a so-called hierarchy of prizes, which will be examined in further detail in the final chapter of this book.[29]

Sharon Norris also applies Bourdieusian readings of the Booker Prize, but as well as applying Bourdieu's forms of capital, Norris also refers to his writings on the 'two opposing poles' of the literary field, in *The Rules of Art*, and his insights into 'sponsorship as a form of symbolic violence' evidenced in *Free Exchange*.[30] For Norris, the 'issue of symbolic violence is highly pertinent to the Booker Prize, since those involved with this award, including judges, shortlisted authors, and members of the management committee, tend to be from a particular class'.[31] The capacity of the Booker Prize, and indeed other awards, to participate in symbolic violence is also raised in the work of Alex Dane. Dane argues that 'the inclusion and exclusion of different groups of authors, in the construction of shortlists and selection of the winner, is an act of symbolic violence that seeks to maintain traditional hierarchies of power in the literary field'.[32]

Driscoll however remains unconvinced of the exertion of symbolic violence by Booker Prize judges because the judges are 'unable to present a coherent idea of literary value through consistent decisions that build a recognizable canon of winners'.[33] For Driscoll, the Booker Prize (and literary awards more broadly) embodies the tensions between 'credibility and sales: the ultimate middlebrow dream' and, as a result, fails to effectually exercise the dominance – in terms of literary authoritativeness – we might associate with symbolic violence.[34] Such debates surrounding symbolic violence in relation to literary award culture will be discussed in more detail in the final chapter of this book, in which I present a case for furthering such applications of symbolic violence to the fundamental binary logics of literary award hierarchies.

To return to the existing literature on literary award culture, the Booker Prize was also the topic of a number of articles included in a special issue of *Salzburger Beiträge zur Sprach-und Kulturwissenschaft* published in 2006, including an article by Richard Todd in which he details the genesis of *Consuming Fictions* and considers developments to the Booker Prize and its contemporaries.[35] Also included in this special issue are two persuasive articles by Norris, who 'recontextualises' the Booker Prize, noting that the prize has an 'uncanny ability to mirror the broader circumstances surrounding it' and that the prize's origins can be traced back to a meeting of the Society of Young Publishers in 1964.[36] Norris also discusses the relationship between Scottish writers and the Booker Prize, tackling the issue of the prize's seeming disregard of Scottish authors (discussed in more detail in Chapter 4).[37]

Other critical examinations of the Booker Prize have investigated its role as both a relic of Britain's colonial history and an apparent 'postcolonial literary patron'.[38] In *The Post-Colonial Exotic: Marketing the Margins*, Graham Huggan illustrates how the Booker Prize's original status as an award for British Commonwealth countries and Ireland is intricately entwined with the origins of the prize (it was founded by the British Booker McConnell (later Booker Plc) company who had acquired their wealth through cotton and sugar plantations in Guyana[39]). Before 2014, when the terms of eligibility of the Booker Prize were extended to include 'any novel written by any novelist of any nationality from a UK publisher and published in English',[40] the terms of eligibility meant that the prize, according to Huggan, was 'bound to an Anglocentric discourse of benevolent paternalism'.[41] In a similarly focused examination of the Booker and British imperialism, Luke Strongman provides a more optimistic, but less convincing, argument of the Booker Prize's colonial legacy, suggesting that,

> While it is founded, funded and administered in England and could be said to continue the motives and rhetoric of empire, the Booker, has also fostered the movement beyond the old themes of expansion, profits, rule, suppression and displacement towards a new sense of the energies and relations among various immigrant groups, regions and peoples within Britain and among its former colonies.[42]

Strongman's study, while acknowledging the Booker Prize's colonial history, also commends the prize for its ability to maintain connections and 'continuing commonalities of history [...] among the nations of the former Empire' and is arguably representative of how the prize is considered and discussed more broadly in academic and journalistic discourse: its infamy and renown outweigh its problematic history (and present[43]).[44] Indeed, the Booker Prize is known for courting the media in order to control its image,[45] and this has made it, Anna Auguscik argues, a 'problem-driven attention-generating mechanism', making the prize both the trigger and the subject of media and literary industry debates.[46] In *Prizing Debate: The Fourth Decade of the Booker Prize and the Contemporary Novel in the UK*, Anna Auguscik focuses on the prize between 2000 and 2010. Auguscik argues that, due to the prize's status and ability to generate media speculation each year, such 'attention generation' – which often aligns with other events such as highly publicised publication dates of books in the running and extensive media commentary about the shortlisted/winning authors and judging panel members – has become central to the Booker's identity.

As the literature discussed above indicates, a substantial amount of critical discourse has been focused on the Booker Prize and its negotiations of value(s). Such academic focus on the prize is mirrored in the media and journalistic attention the prize receives, which, in turn, perhaps perpetuates our critical focus on the prize as we investigate the how and why it has become such a literary and cultural behemoth. However, there are a number of studies within the field of literary award culture that have moved away from this concentration of Anglo-centric prizes and literature to develop upon existing knowledge and extend it to examine prizes around the world. Gillian Roberts provides a comprehensive study of literary prize culture in Canada with regard to how prizes, and the authors and books they celebrate, contribute to understandings of national culture and identities. In *Prizing Literature: The Celebration and Circulation of National Culture*, Roberts considers the 'negotiations [of the] national identities' of Sri Lankan–born Canadian Michael Ondaatje, American-born Canadian Carol Shields, Indian-born Canadian Rohinton Mistry and Spanish-born Canadian Yann Martel in 'the wake of their celebration and international attention'.[47] The success and acclaim of these authors, Roberts argues, is 'bookended' by Ondaatje and Martel winning the Booker Prize in 1992 and 2002, respectively, as well as a number of shortlistings for major Canadian and international awards during this decade. Such wins, Robert notes, were demonstrative of 'increasing recognition for Canadian writers whose cultural currency within Canada rose in accordance with celebration outside it'.[48] Similarly, Danielle Fuller, DeNel Rehberg Sedo and Anouk Lang have considered the sociocultural phenomena of literary awards with regard to Canadian literary and reading cultures, particularly in relation to the annual 'Canada Reads' competitions, which see celebrities publicly debate books.[49] The debates are broadcast on television and radio over five days during one week, usually in March, May or April.

Driscoll has written about literary awards in Australia, with specific reference to awards functioning as social media events and their influence upon educational book lists and syllabi;[50] likewise, as previously mentioned, Dane examines the Australian literary field, noting how prizes, and women's prizes in particular, can reinforce 'hierarchies of power'.[51] Emmett Stinson has also observed the negotiations of cultural and symbolic capital between Australia's small presses and the Miles Franklin Award, one of Australia's premier awards.[52]

There are also significant contributions to the field examining non-English-language awards, including Britta Scheideler's overview of the Peace Prize of the German Book Trade that is awarded annually to writers at the Frankfurt Book Fair,[53] and Marie-Françoise Cachin and Sylvie Ducas's article 'The Goncourt and the Booker: A tale of two prizes', which compares the French Prix Goncourt to the Man Booker. Furthermore Ducas's *La literature, à quell(s) prix?* (2013) considers the proliferation of literary awards in France and their impact upon the status of the author.[54] Likewise, Edward Mack discusses literary award culture in relation to the Japanese literary canon and cultural capital in *Manufacturing Modern Japanese Literature* (2010).[55] Mack's work echoes other examinations of major national prizes noting how 'one of the most coveted literary awards in Japan'[56] – the Akutagawa Prize – 'allows actors to influence works [and create] a continuous flow of elevated literary commodities and reinforcing the economy of literary value at regular intervals'.[57] Related to this is work that considers the role of prizes in translation in providing new audiences and readership to unknown writers and their work. This includes Yoshio Iwamoto's 'Japanese view' on the Nobel Prize for Literature from 1967 to 1987,[58] Susan Pickford's article on the Booker Prize and Prix Goncourt which 'compares the circulation and reception of two sets of prize-winning novels in translation',[59] and, finally, Melanie Ramdarshan Bold and Corinna Norrick-Rühl's examination of the impact of the merging of the United Kingdom's 'most prestigious awards for literature in translation', the Foreign Fiction Prize and the Man Booker International Prize, on the enhancement of sales of books in translation in the United Kingdom.[60]

However, while significant in their contribution to the field, very few of these analyses consider, or even mention, Scottish literary awards. Scottish writers have won major prizes, such as James Kelman and his infamous 1994 Booker Prize win for his fourth novel, *How Late It Was, How Late* (1994), and these wins are discussed in some of the analyses discussed above, but such discussions generally focus on the scandal or surprise of Kelman's win (and the subsequent drama it caused among the judges) as opposed to Scottish literature and culture in relation to literary prize culture. Even articles or chapters dedicated to Scottish writers and prizes have failed to effectively acknowledge the work of Scottish prizes. Norris's article 'Scots and the Booker' fails to mention Scottish literary awards. Likewise, Todd's *Consuming Fictions* includes a chapter on 'New fiction from Scotland', which refers to the fact that Alasdair Gray was never shortlisted for the Booker, but that his debut novel *Lanark* won a 'Scottish Arts Council Awards [and] was selected as the Scottish Book of the Year' (it is likely that the latter accolade was referring to the book receiving the Saltire Society Book of the Year Award in 1982).[61]

Accordingly, this book fills a discernible gap in knowledge of how Scotland's oldest literary awards dedicated to Scottish literature have evolved and the influence they have had on Scottish literary culture. Indeed, this book follows the lead of Squires, who argues that:

> the analysis of literary prizes, as one specific example of the 'phenomena' of 'recent cultural history', provides concrete examples of institutions and the rules by which they function (the sponsors, the prize-giving bodies, the eligibility criteria etc.), as well as the ideological contexts both in which they operate and which they also construct.[62]

This study of the Saltire Society Literary Awards, therefore, considers the awards both in terms of the social and political history within which they emerged, and in terms of the ongoing impact they have within Scotland's literary culture.[63] In doing so, it simultaneously locates their position and influence within the broader history of literary prize culture (and aligns their work with other prizes) and carves their own space in that history, facilitating new ways in which to think about contemporary literary prize culture. Using the Saltire Society Literary Awards as a case study, this book will illustrate how the tendency to focus on so-called major awards in literary award scholarship perpetuates a literary award hierarchy in which a prize's success or impact is subject to assessment according to how 'major' prizes work. Yet, such comparisons are fundamentally false equivalences, since each literary award operates according to its own motivations and affecting variables.

With this approach in mind, it is helpful to apply the work of Pascale Casanova to this study.[64] In *The Republic of Letters*, Casanova proposes 'a new tool for the reading and interpretation of literary texts that may be at once, and without any contradiction, internal (textual) and external (historical)'.[65] While Casanova's focus is on the circulation of literary texts, her argument can be valuably applied to a broader study of the interrelations of

INTRODUCTION 11

literary prize culture(s), and in this analysis, literary prizes are treated akin to Casanova's literary 'texts'. In other words, the Saltire Society Literary Awards, and other literary prizes, are herewith considered as 'texts'; and to further our understandings of awards and how they function in contemporary literary culture, it may be useful to consider them in terms of what Casanova identifies as 'internal (textual)' and 'external (historical)' attributes or contexts. A prize's internal, or textual, attributes, for example, might include things such as terms of eligibility, judging processes or sponsors, and it may be useful to think of external or historical attributes and contexts of prizes to be the sociopolitical and cultural environment within which they emerged. In this book, I argue and demonstrate how an understanding or 'reading' of both these facets of a prize (aka 'the text') will enable a more nuanced examination of contemporary literary prize culture. Indeed, one could go as far as to suggest that Part I of the book considers the external/historical aspects of the Saltire Society Literary Awards, and Part II the internal/textual aspects.

To apply Casanova's writings to prize culture further still, her argument against exclusive analyses of texts goes some way to explain how existing understandings of literary prize culture have come to be determined by examinations of a select few prizes. As Casanova notes,

> The persistent tendency for critics to isolate texts from one another prevents them, from seeing in its entirety the configuration (to use Michel Foucault's term) to which all texts belong; that is, the totality of texts and literary and aesthetic debates with which a particular work of literature enters into relation and resonance, and which forms the true basis for its singularity, its real originality.[66]

As this book notes time and again, the Society and its series of awards have continuously struggled to attain and maintain recognition, even within the annals of Scotland's cultural history. This, I would argue, may be due to the isolationary, or exclusionary, way in which prize culture has been examined by both academic and journalistic commentators alike to date. As the texts discussed above demonstrate, it is common for studies to focus solely on a major award and use this as the backbone to an understanding of prize culture generally, when a more comprehensive approach is needed. Casanova also makes this argument in terms of literary works, or texts, but her argumentation can be modified to include literary prizes, too:

> A literary work [or literary prize] can be deciphered only on the basis of the whole of the composition, for its rediscovered coherence stands revealed only in relation to the entire literary universe of which it is a

part. The singularity of individual literary works [or prizes] therefore becomes manifest only against the background of the overall structure in which they take their place. Each work [or prize] that is declared to be literary [or culturally significant] is a minute part of the immense 'combination' constituted by the literary world as a whole.[67]

The purpose of this study of the Saltire Society Literary Awards, therefore, is to examine the prize's singularity in order to reveal its significance 'in relation to the entire literary universe of which it is a part'. An examination of this particular, 'minute part' of literary prize culture facilitates an understanding of the 'immense "combination" constituted by the literary [prize] world as a whole'.[68]

A Brief History of Scottish Literary Awards

Before conducting this micro, or 'minute', examination of the Saltire Society Literary Awards in order to acquire a sense of the macro-machinations of literary prize culture, it is worthwhile to explain the context of the literary prize ecology, or economy, in which the Society's Literary Awards emerged, particularly in terms of other awards for Scottish literature.

Even though Scotland is home to two of the United Kingdom's oldest literary awards – the James Tait Black Memorial Prize and the Hawthornden Prize, both established in Edinburgh in 1919 – the country's literary award history is actually quite sparse. Indeed, the James Tait and Hawthornden Prizes cannot even claim to be Scotland's oldest prizes, since neither are specifically for Scottish writers or books. The James Tait Black Memorial Prize, financed and administered by the University of Edinburgh, confers two awards annually, 'one for the best work of fiction and the other for the best biography' with each recipient receiving £10,000.[69] The Hawthornden Prize, on the other hand, 'rewards works of "imaginative literature" whether prose or poetry'.[70] As of 2017, prize winners received £15,000.

The Scottish Arts Council (SAC) provided grants and awards for Scottish writers and those living in or writing about Scotland through a variety of programmes from the early 1970s. A now-archived website detailing the history of the SAC stated that 'since 1972, the Scottish Arts Council Book Awards have recognised and rewarded excellence in literary fiction, poetry, and literary non-fiction by Scottish authors'.[71] Early winners included Sydney Checkland, who reportedly won the Scottish Arts Council Book Award (henceforth SAC Book Award) in 1971 for *The Gladstones, a Family Biography 1764–1851*[72] (Checkland, incidentally, also received the Saltire Society History Book of the Year Award in 1977), and Charles MacLean, who received the SAC

Book Award in 1972 for *Island on the Edge of the World: The Story of St Kilda*.[73] In the 1986 *Guide to Literary Prize, Grants and Awards in Britain and Ireland* compiled by the National Book League (known as the Book Trust since 1986) and the Society of Authors, there are two entries for SAC Book Awards. One is for the 'Scottish Arts Council Book Awards', detailed as 'a number of awards [which] are given to authors of published books in recognition of high standards in new writing as well as work of established writers'.[74] The awards, worth £750 each, were conferred biannually in spring and autumn; and similar to the Saltire Society's own Literary Awards, the SAC Book Awards required that authors be 'Scottish, resident in Scotland or writing books of Scottish interest'.[75] The other award listed is the 'Scottish Arts Council Publication Award'.[76] A kind of precursor to the Saltire Society's Publisher of the Year Award founded in 2013, the award was given to the 'publisher of the book considered to be a good piece of all-round publishing, in respect of writing, editing, design, production and appropriate selling price'.[77] Worth £250, the prize was open to 'Scottish publishers of books submitted for SAC Book Awards' and was also conferred biannually in spring and autumn.[78] By the early 1990s, however, the SAC Publication Award was no longer listed in the annual *Guide to Literary Prizes, Grants and Awards in Britain and Ireland*. The 1992/93 edition of the guide lists the SAC Book Awards, with an increased prize fund of £1,000 per award,[79] and the Scottish Arts Council Research Grants which were a 'limited number of small grants [...] awarded three times a year to assist writers of professional status to contribute to the cost of researching a book'.[80] The grants, which were 'advertised in Scottish press', were for varying amounts of money 'according to need' for each project.[81]

In the late 1990s, the SAC fortified its literary awards. First, and in a way which would again foreshadow the Society's own award expansion in the mid-2000s, SAC formalised and expanded its book awards to include four categories: Fiction, Poetry, Literary Non-Fiction and First Book. The winner in each category would receive £2,000 and become the shortlist for a £10,000 Book of the Year Award. Second, SAC founded what was reported to be 'the first Children's Book Awards in Scotland for writers for children',[82] the winner of which would receive £5,000.[83] By 2007, the Children's Book Award would be sponsored by Royal Mail until the early 2010s (when the administration of the prize was overtaken by the Scottish Book Trust).[84] In March 2009, the Scottish Mortgage Investment Trust was introduced as the lead title sponsor of the SAC Book Awards. The Scottish Mortgage Investment Trust Book Awards, affectionately known as the SMITs, would increase the prize money to £30,000 and were presented until 2013.[85]

The other major Scottish literary award operating during the 1980s and 90s was the McVitie's Prize for 'Scottish Writer of the Year', founded by the

Book Trust in 1987 and offering a £5,000 prize to its winner. The McVitie's Prize for Scottish Writer of the Year was described as being

> for the best substantial Scottish work of an imaginative nature first published or performed between 1 September and 31 August (a novel, a collection of short stories, poetry, autobiography, theatre, cinema, radio and television scripts etc.) Writers born in Scotland, or who are or have been resident in Scotland or who take Scotland as their inspiration, are eligible. Submissions accepted in Scots, English and Gaelic.[86]

McVitie's remained the lead sponsor of the award until 1996 (by which time the prize purse was £10,000) when sponsorship was overtaken by Stakis Hotels. McVitie's were reported to have withdrawn their sponsorship two months prior to the announcement of the winner because they 'felt [their] investment was seen as wasted and the company's involvement was increasingly becoming seen as embarrassing rather than prestigious'.[87] Some speculated that the sponsor had been embarrassed when the actress Jane Asher, who announced the prize shortlist for 1997, included 'so many references to the sponsor's digestive biscuits' in her speech that 'the audience was reduced to laughter'.[88] The hotel and leisure chain Stakis sponsored the award for a further two years, but the award was permanently terminated in 1998, seemingly due to the negative coverage of the 1998 awards ceremony. The Scottish press were demeaning about the location of the ceremony, describing the event as 'tragically naff' and referring to women employees of Stakis as 'bimbos'.[89] A spokesperson for Stakis commented that the press coverage of the event was 'insulting to both the staff of Stakis and the inhabitants of the surrounding area. We were a Scottish company presenting a Scottish prize and we had the Scottish media attacking us for it.'[90]

Consequently, during the late 1980s and through to the early to mid-2010s, the Saltire Society Literary Awards was one of three major literary awards in Scotland, and in the 1990s, these awards worked together to celebrate the breadth of Scottish literature (discussed in more detail in Part I). However, upon the demise of the SMITs in 2013, the Society's Literary Awards became the longest running and only series of literary awards for Scottish literature to survive.

Book Structure

In a way that mirrors the duality of my own experience in collecting the research for it, this book is split into two distinct halves. The first half, Part I, is a cultural history of the Saltire Society and two of its key literary awards – the

Book of the Year Award and the First Book of the Year Award. It provides a detailed account of the development of the Society, exploring its originations and demonstrating how it was borne during a particularly tumultuous period in history. Part I also provides a history of the Society's Book of the Year and First Book of the Year Awards and their influence within Scottish literature and culture. These histories are deliberately detailed. Unlike many other literary awards, whose histories are as much part of their identity as their annual celebrations, the history of the Saltire Society Literary Awards remains largely unknown. Knowing how the Society's Literary Awards were founded, funded, organised and maintained is key to understanding the influence and impact the awards could, or perhaps should, have. Through a microanalysis of the Saltire Society Literary Awards, I aim to exemplify how such cultural histories are imperative to developing a comprehensive understanding of the impact of cultural organisations and awards on the construction and circulation of value in literature.

In order to make this study concise and to maintain its focus on *literary* award culture, only the Society's Book of the Year and First Book of the Year Awards are discussed in detail. While the Society's other book awards – Research Book of the Year and History Book of the Year Awards – have their own intriguing and important histories, their focus on research-based or largely academic books means they inhabit a very particular space in literary award culture which operates differently to that of awards for fiction and poetry, for example. Therefore, while further research into the mechanisms of prizes for academic writing would be a valuable contribution to the field, this book will not consider these genres in great detail. Squires's definition of 'the literary' has been used to inform this decision. As Squires notes

> a simple definition of the 'literary' might say that 'literary' writing (including literary fiction, poetry and non-fiction) is writing of a certain (high) standard. 'Literary' is then an assurance of quality, a guarantee that what is to be approached here is 'good' writing.[91]

It is the former part of this definition that relates most to how the term 'literary' is being used to describe the Society's *literary* awards (the Book of the Year and First Book of the Year Awards), and this preference of the literary over the academic is not to be considered a value judgement as the second half of the definition argues. The Society's own preference for 'Literary' awards, over, for example, 'Book' or 'Writing', has also informed this leaning towards the use of 'literary'.

Staying on this point of the preferred terminology for this study, after much deliberation about the use of 'prize' or 'award', unless specific to a particular title (i.e. the Women's Prize for Fiction, the Saltire Society Literary Awards), they are used interchangeably throughout this book. This is not in order to evade examining the complexities of such terms, but rather to avoid overcomplicating the discussion at hand. 'Prize' and 'award' are largely interchangeable and synonymous in meaning; therefore, it is unhelpful to become preoccupied with such semantic debates concerning their different value(s).

Furthermore, this study does not examine the intricacies of the expansion of the Book of the Year Award (into the Fiction Book of the Year and Non-Fiction Book of the Year Awards in 2016) and the introduction of the Poetry Book of the Year Award in 2014. The reason this study does not delve into these developments in more detail is twofold. First, due to my embedded role with the Society while conducting research into their Literary Awards, I was part of the team who assessed the existing formation of the Society's Literary Awards in 2015 and decided upon the splitting-up of the Book of the Year Award into two, more distinct categories (for Fiction and Non-Fiction). As a result, not only did this happen at the point when I had largely completed the data collection of this project and had begun writing my findings, but as someone involved in the process of making such changes, I do not have the same kind of distance from this portion of the history of the Society's Literary Awards that would be helpful for a more concerted examination of the choices made during that period. Second, since these changes were only made within the last four to five years, the longer-term impact they may have on the awards – perhaps in terms of their ability to widen opportunities (since there are more awards available for authors to win) or clarify exactly what kind of book is suitable for which category (the expansion of the categories brought with it more specificity for publishers submitting awards) – cannot yet be measured.

The second half of this book, Part II, builds upon ideas established in the literature discussed above and, using theoretical frameworks utilised in such literature, analyses the Society's Literary Awards and illustrates their cultural impact in relation to Scottish literature and publishing. In 'What's This Got To Do with Scotland?' Qualifying Scottishness through Terms of Eligibility, I consider the ways in which the Society's terms of eligibility for their Book of the Year and First Book of the Year Awards relate to wider conversations regarding the categorisation of 'Scottish' literature. This chapter uses first-hand experience, archive materials and interviews with Saltire Society Literary Award judges to examine how the Society's understanding of 'Scottishness' aligns with broader sociocultural debates around Scottish national identity and culture. The second chapter of Part II, 'Noticing talent: Michel Faber, James Kelman, A. L. Kennedy, Ali Smith and the Saltire Society Literary Awards', uses Faber, Kelman, Kennedy and Smith as case studies by which to examine the impact of the Saltire Society Literary Awards, and other literary awards, on an author's career. Following a brief description of each author's 'career in awards', the chapter conducts a paratextual analysis of key books – both award-winning and not – to illustrate how the Saltire Society Literary Awards and other organisations' awards are used as part of what Squires identifies as the 'marketing mix' of a book. Finally, the last chapter of Part II argues that, in order to move the critical discourse surrounding literary awards – and cultural awards more generally – forward, we need to reassess how awards are currently considered and discussed. The chapter questions whether the conceptual frameworks and methodologies by which value and prestige in prize culture are most commonly considered remain relevant when applied to different types of cultural awards. It posits that the prize hierarchies at play – in which prizes like the Booker, the Nobel Prize for Literature and the Oscars maintain the most dominant positions and are used as exemplars of the kind of impact and prestige cultural prizes can have – are exceptions as opposed to the rule(s) of prize culture. As a result, there is a need to move away from considering smaller, perhaps lesser-known prizes like the Saltire Society Literary Awards in terms of evaluations of prize culture legitimised, and based upon, extraordinary prize practice. What is needed instead, as this book illustrates, are more close readings of awards, in which the sociopolitical and cultural context of their emergence is explored and considered as part of the way in which they have acquired, upheld and imparted their own cultural capital and prestige.

Part I

Chapter 1

THE HISTORY OF THE SALTIRE SOCIETY

Origins of the Saltire Society

The Saltire Society was 'formed in 1936 by a group of people who wished to see Scotland take its proper place as a cultural unit'.[1] The Society, a 1939 annual report stated, would 'loo[k] back to the past only to move forward' and that its main concern was 'with the future'.[2] It would 'envisag[e] a new Scotland with a vigorous intellectual life, drawing on the past for inspiration to new advances in art, learning, and the graces of life'.[3] According to George Bruce, the origins of the Society arose from a conversation between the journalist George Malcolm Thomson and politician and academic Andrew Dewar Gibb.[4] Quoting Alison Sheppard's *Memories of the Saltire Society* (a lost autobiographical account by Sheppard), Bruce suggests that Thomson 'found himself shocked by the Scots' and their lack of interest in their own history and culture and 'communicated his feeling to Dewar Gibb'[5]:

> [Thomson] was amazed to find how the English knew about and appreciated in their heritage and how ignorant the Scots were about theirs and how indifferent they were about preserving it. He prodded Dewar Gibb into doing something about it. He also mooted the idea of calling it the Saltoun[6] Society.[7]

It was Dewar Gibb's wife, Margaret Downie, who repeated 'the gist' of this conversation to Sheppard, who was secretary of Glasgow University's Women's Student Union at the time. This story of the origination of the Society's founding is supported by the report of a conference organised by the Perth branch of the Society in 1947, at which Sheppard spoke during a session called 'The Saltire Society: Retrospect and Intentions'.[8] The published report of the conference states that Sheppard, who was by then the Society's honorary secretary, said:

> The Saltire Society came to birth in Glasgow [...] There were present as midwives, three Professors, an author, and an historian. [...] the Saltire Society owed its being to professors.
>
> From the first, certain fixed principles, by common consent, were taken for granted:
> - It was to be a National Society.
> - There was to be no feeling of inferiority. Comparisons with Scotland's southern neighbour were abandoned. International contacts were to be made direct with other countries, and members of the Society were to behave as representatives of a small, but important European country.
> - The primary interest of the Society was in the *future* of Scotland; hence its energy was to be directed to the contemporary scene, to encouraging *living* authors and artists.
> - The aim of the Society was to be inclusive, not exclusive; to unite, not divide. Political, religious, or any other divisions were to be ignored. [...]
> - Rejection of the second-rate was a cardinal feature. It was felt that far too much inferior work was acclaimed, simply because it was Scottish. [...]
> - The grand objective was a richer, fuller life, for all inhabitants of Scotland.[9]

It is worth noting at this point that Sheppard is an oft-forgotten figure in the history of the Society. She was, by many accounts, instrumental in the organisation of the Society in its early years. An essay published in *Scotland's Magazine* in May 1947 acknowledged her as such, stating that although the Society was 'not by any means faultless [...] it has accomplished such effective work [...] largely due to the restless initiative of Alison Sheppard in the earlier years'.[10] Sheppard's status as an influential but overlooked woman in the history of the Society not only replicates the disregard of women's roles in history in general[11] but also echoes historic oversights of women writers in the Society's Literary Awards.[12]

On its founding, the Society was organised as a members' organisation governed by a group of volunteers who managed its activities and decided upon constitutional policies. From the outset, the organisation's structure was intricate. It included a number of honorary presidents (of which there were six by 1939, including 7th Baronet of Luss Sir Iain Colquhoun, writer Eric Linklater, politicians William Power and Sir John Stirling-Maxwell, classical pianist Frederic Lamond, and historian George Pratt Insh[13]); a president, who when present would act as chair at all meetings and have 'a deliberate and a casting vote'; a secretary; a treasurer; and an executive committee.[14] The executive committee included the president, secretary and treasurer and ten other members of the Society, four of which formed 'a quorum of the Committee', with office bearers and committee members being elected each year at the Society's general meeting.[15] Sheppard was elected as honorary secretary in 1937 but, despite being a driving force in the establishment of the Society, would not become an honorary president until 1945.[16]

The Society's membership rose steadily in its initial years. By 1939, it had 371 members. This rose to 420 by early 1942 and increased to 541 a year later. Such surges in membership, which was purchasable for an annual fee of 5 shillings, is quite remarkable given that Scotland had not only been at war since 1939 but had also been suffering from the economic depression that followed the First World War and ran into the Second World War during the 1930s and 1940s. However, such figures did not necessarily equate to income for the Society. A note in the annual report for 1941–42 reveals that 'the number of old members who have failed to pay their subscriptions is rather more than before'.[17] Presuming that this was 'no doubt due to the War', the Society remained optimistic, feeling safe in the prediction that 'peace would bring an immediate and spectacular rise in membership', which it seemingly did: by 1946, membership had increased to 1,725.[18]

Such upsurges in membership indicate that the Society was fairly successful in its ambition to 'stir the mind of the Scottish people,[19] but not everyone was convinced of the Society's impact and contribution to Scottish culture. In an anonymous contribution to *Scottish Journal*,[20] one writer suggested that far from making a significant impact, the Society was not only failing to engage with key figures in Scottish culture (although the writer of the article does not suggest who these key figures may be) but also comprised 'middle-class [but] well-intentioned nonentities'.[21] Writing specifically in reference to the Society's conference held in St Andrews in 1953, the contributor continued, arguing:

> In a small country like Scotland it is ridiculous that such a Society cannot muster and give due place in its deliberations to all the really significant authors [...] and other creative people in our midst. Until it does it can have no real authority. Its deliberations on cultural matters must remain deliberations *in vacuo* unless they are effectively united to the real trends manifesting themselves in our literature, arts, and cultural affairs.[22]

This anonymous reproach did not go unnoticed by the Society. Robert Hurd, the Society's honorary secretary, wrote to William MacLellan, editor of *Scottish Journal* and a member of the Society, contending that, 'for a member of your standing to have allowed a statement of this kind to appear in a Journal directly under your control seems to me quite extraordinary'.[23] In addition, Dr Oliver Boyd (not to be confused with the publisher Oliver & Boyd, with whom the Society would later publish a number of pamphlets and books) wrote a direct rebuke to the article in a later issue of *Scottish Journal*, in which he defends the Society's activities and maintains that it cannot make significant changes to Scottish cultural policy without the assistance of other groups:

> Even though it may not always have spoken as loudly and clearly as it ought to have done, it *has* spoken – and acted [...] If it has not done more, the fault is not all the Society's. It can act only by getting other bodies to act; it is not a Scottish Ministry of Fine Arts – fortunately perhaps; and though it may publish books, it cannot compel people to buy them.[24]

Such correspondence illustrates how this view of the Society as a peripheral organisation – always present, but not necessarily effective or engaged in contemporary debates – occurred early in the Society's history and it has lingered ever since. It was for such reasons that the Society commissioned a report in 2010 to assess the influence and impact of the Society and how it was perceived by those outside of the Society. According to the report, despite there being an 'important and distinctive role for the Society' in Scotland, it had 'a lower public profile than was the case for much of its earlier existence',[25] and there was 'a general lack of recognition on the part of the public of what the Society is'.[26] The report goes on to note that if the Society is known, it is regarded as having a benevolent influence.[27] However, while the Society's impact may at times seem inconspicuous, from its earliest days it has engaged with significant cultural issues within Scotland, and far from existing '*in vacuo*', the Society has paralleled key developments in Scotland's wider cultural and sociopolitical growth, developing interrelationships that continue to this day.

The Saltire Society and Scotland's Cultural Renaissance

The end of the First World War in 1918 brought with it worldwide economic instability that hit Britain hard, with Scotland feeling the full effects of the post-war crisis. Catriona M. MacDonald argues that a 'southward drift of industry' in post-war Britain led to noticeable differences between Scotland and England at this time:

Over-crowding in Scotland was six times greater than England [...] unemployment remained persistently higher than the British average and social performance indicators, [...] showed that the average Scot was in much poorer physical shape than his southern counterpart.[28]

And while T. M. Devine has since argued that 'the inter-war period was not all doom and gloom'[29] for Scots, there is no doubt that the First World War was, as Michael Lynch argues, a 'watershed in the development of Scottish society and its economy'.[30] Such economic issues, coupled with seemingly half-hearted attempts from Westminster to offer concessions to Scotland in the 1920s and 1930s, led to a noticeable rise in nationalist ideologies in Scotland's political landscape.[31] The significance of such events cannot be underestimated when constructing a history of Scotland's cultural evolution during this time. As MacDonald and others argue, this sense of dissatisfaction towards the political status quo of the union not only led to an intensification in Scotland's attitude towards political governance and autonomy, but it also influenced writers and artists who became vocal proponents of political causes.

George Malcolm Thomson – the same George Malcolm Thomson who was said to be part of the conversations that led to the founding of the Saltire Society – was one such writer, becoming infamous for his so-called lurid 1927 book, *Caledonia, Or the Future of the Scots*, a text known for its censorious evaluation of Scotland's social and cultural identity.[32] Thomson's acerbic commentary criticised Scotland's failure to celebrate its art, music and literature and preserve a position as a significant cultural voice in Europe. The influence of Thomson's opinions was seemingly far-reaching. George Bruce argues that it was the expression of such feelings in the previously noted conversation between Thomson and Andrew Dewar Gibb that led to the founding of the Society.[33] According to Bruce, this conversation was the 'chance factor' that acted as the 'stimulus' for the founding of the Society.[34] This story is repeated by George McKechnie in his critical biography of Thomson, *The Best Hated Man* (2013). Following Bruce's lead, McKechnie committed fully to the notion that 'the Saltire Society was a body conceived following an original idea from George Malcolm Thomson'.[35] This is despite the fact that there is no mention of Thomson in any of the Society's own documents from the time.[36]

Thomson's published works, particularly *Caledonia*, illustrate that there are certainly elements to his writing which directly relate to the founding principles of the Society. Most notable of such is his argument that Scottish people are ignorant of their own culture: 'there is not a nation in Europe which knows as little and cares as little about its past as the Scots'.[37] Thomson goes on, suggesting that what little Scottish people do know about Scotland is based upon a 'whole mythology' founded on a 'vague complex of generalisations'.[38]

The Society's annual report from 1939 reveals that, ten years after the publication of *Caledonia*, such sentiments resonated with the Society, with the report declaring that 'the nation that forgets its past is dead', an assertion which led the Society to aspire to 'revive the memory of famous men and to make Scots conscious of their heritage'.[39]

A further significant point Thomson makes in his polemic, which was pertinent both to the Society and Scottish culture more widely in the 1920s and 1930s, is that Scotland had no 'national literature', so much so that even the production of literature in Scotland had stalled:

> There is no literature in Scotland. The country has produced none in the twentieth century, or to be exact, since the year 1901 [...] The publishing of books has been dead in the country for a very much longer period [...] There has been, since the war, one modest and shortlived attempt to create a national publishing house in Edinburgh but this is the only ripple in the stagnant pool [...] The book-buying public [in Scotland] is, as a matter of fact, extraordinarily small.[40]

Thomson's suggestion that the book-buying public was at this time 'extraordinarily small' is likely an exaggeration, based on a conjectural and classist opinion rather than any evidence. The early twentieth century was in fact a turning point for readers and book-buyers in Scotland as the 'move of book retention from public to private spaces', as well as the production of 'less expensive one-volume works, and the rise of paperback publishing', allowed more readers access to literature than ever before.[41]

Thomson, however, was not alone in his strong opinions regarding Scotland's apparent lack of knowledge or pride in its cultural heritage. In the same year, C. M. Grieve, better known by his pen name Hugh MacDiarmid, wrote the 'hastily written' 95-page *Albyn, or Scotland and the Future*, which echoed Thomson's ideas.[42] Believing Thomson's arguments to be 'cogent, but far too pessimistic',[43] in *Albyn*, Grieve argued:

> The forces that are moving towards a Scottish Renaissance are complex and at first sight incompatible. The movement began as a purely literary movement some seven or eight years ago, but out of necessity speedily acquired political and then religious bearings. It is now manifesting itself in every sphere of national arts and affairs.[44]

Such sentiments regarding the broadening of this 'movement' were reiterated four years later when the Scottish author George Blake stated that 'one does not need to be a politician to appreciate the importance of this slow restoration of our self-respect'.⁴⁵ Furthermore, early Society advocate and member Edwin Muir made similar assertions eight years later in the equally controversial *Scottish Journey* (1935). For Muir, Scotland was 'gradually being emptied of its population, its spirit, its wealth, industry, art, intellect, and innate character'.⁴⁶ Such opinions did not, of course, go without challenge. In their history of Scotland published in 1934, Robert Rait and George S. Pryde call Grieve's work 'vitriolic' and its so-called companion volume – Thomson's *Caledonia* – 'discordant'.⁴⁷

What these texts reveal is that the Society's appearance in 1936 was not merely a fortuitous occurrence based upon the opinions of an isolated group of people, but in fact reflected a wider discord in Scottish culture which was being openly discussed by Scottish writers. Suggesting that the context for such 'overt ideological creative writing' developed because of 'concern[s] over the increasingly depressed economic and social condition of Scotland', Margaret Palmer McCulloch notes how 'for the major part of the 1920s [...] the dominant manifestation of the revolutionary objectives of what Denis Saurat had called *le groupe de la Renaissance Écossaise* was a literary one'.⁴⁸ On this implication that Scotland's interwar sociopolitical circumstances influenced Scotland's literary output, McCulloch continues, proposing that the works of Thomson and MacDiarmid 'sought to remind readers of the history and considerable achievements of the fledgling Scottish Renaissance movement, while emphasising how much still had to be done artistically and politically before achievement of its aims could be within sight'.⁴⁹ This 'Scottish Renaissance' saw an intensification in Scottish authors actively participating in party-political debates regarding nationalism that were taking place during the 1920s and 1930s. According to John Foster, this was a new phenomenon, much different to that of past Scottish writers and artists:

> The Scottish Renaissance was [...] something quite different from the Scottish tradition of Stevenson, Barrie or Buchan. Neil Gunn, Edwin Muir, Eric Linklater, Grassic Gibbon, Naomi Mitchison – all identified themselves in some form or other with movements seeking to change the political relationship which defined that tradition: the union between Scotland and England. [...] Some sought formal links with working-class politics – like MacDiarmid [...] Others saw their role more in literary terms [...] All, however, wished to break with a past in which Scottish literature existed as a sub-species of English.⁵⁰

Others have been more tentative in their assessment of the political influence upon the writers and artists commonly included under the 'amorphous' Scottish Renaissance title, with Richard Finlay arguing that a sense of crisis permeated the renaissance in that all knew that something was wrong and that the artistic status quo had to be overturned, yet there was no agreement as to what should replace it. For some it was anarchy, for others a new order, and, probably for most, it signified uncertainty.[51]

Finlay continues to suggest that the 'main achievement of the renaissance was to leave a cultural legacy which has become more appreciated after its demise', but this sells short the work of the organisations founded during this time.[52] Far from being more significant after the fact, the Society, for example, was founded in direct response to the sense of crisis that Finlay suggests permeated Scottish culture at that time.

Likewise, the aims and foci of the organisations established in this interwar period reflected how the longevity of Scottish cultural promotion and dissemination was key. Alongside the Saltire Society, a number of other major cultural bodies were established during this crucial interwar period. These organisations, which remain active to this day, ranged from those dedicated to the preservation of Scottish culture with the intention of making it available to a wide audience, to groups concerned with the conservation of Scotland's cultural heritage and economic developments, including the Scottish Society of Women Artists (est. 1924), the National Library of Scotland (est. 1925), the Association for the Preservation of Rural Scotland (est. 1926), Scottish PEN (a Scottish centre for the international PEN association, est. 1927), BBC Scottish Symphony Orchestra (est. 1930) and the Scottish National Dictionary, the Scottish National Development Council and the National Trust for Scotland (all est. 1931). Despite its absence in most cultural histories of Scotland, the Saltire Society was essential to this 'culmination of a growth of civic and cultural organisations which focused on Scotland's problem[s]'.[53]

Publications, Pamphlets and the Shadow of War

With the outbreak of war in 1939, the momentum of Scotland's cultural reimagining slowed, and national priorities, and those of the Society, were diverted. Politically and socially, 'the Scots were drawn back into Britain by a sense of togetherness'.[54] For the Society, the war brought significant economic difficulties; and by 1944, the Society was warned by its treasurer that it would need to raise the cost of membership or 'eat into its [financial] reserves'.[55] Following a discussion of these options, it became 'obvious that the members of the Society were anxious that the subscription should not be raised' and that the Society would think of different ways to ensure 'prompt payment' of member subscriptions (which included 'instituting a membership drive' and issuing a membership card).[56] Another way in which the Society attempted to raise funds during this period was through the publication of pamphlets and books. Between 1939 and 1965, the Society produced 25 publications, including books, pamphlets, chapbooks and an exhibition catalogue.[57] The Society also produced the literary magazine, *Saltire Review*, between 1954 and 1961.[58] Half of these publications were published and printed in collaboration with existing publishers and printers such as Oliver & Boyd, C. J. Cousland and Sons, and Thomas Nelson and Sons, with such partnerships enabling the Society to limit the risk and expense of publishing books on their own.

The collaboration between the Society and Oliver & Boyd seems particularly fitting given that both parties were interested in disseminating informative documents and texts about Scotland to Scottish readers. Oliver & Boyd, was a key proponent in Scottish educational publishing up until the sale of the company to the *Financial Times* in 1962:

> From the middle of the nineteenth century, Oliver & Boyd's educational and medical lists dominated and provided the basis for strong export revenues. This position persisted until the second half of the twentieth century when the company retrenched to serve the distinctive Scottish educational market.[59]

The fact that Oliver & Boyd's publishing catalogue at this time was focused on instructional materials with export value makes their collaboration with the Society – who were determined to promote Scottish culture both domestically and internationally – particularly timely and an astute move in which both parties could benefit from each other's cultural and economic capital. Oliver & Boyd took much of the financial burden from the Society in their early publications, promising to sustain the production and promotion of the publications while maintaining an equal partnership with the Society and the authors. A 'Memorandum of Agreement between Oliver & Boyd Ltd. and The Saltire Society' from October 1939 referring to the Society's series of 'Scottish Classics' pamphlets states that, as publishers, Oliver & Boyd 'shall publish at their own risk four volumes of SCOTTISH CLASSICS' and, after a deduction of 15 per cent for publishing commission, the profit would be divided equally between the publisher, the Society and the author.[60] In a similar contract from 1947 for the Society's 'Scottish Poets' pamphlets, the publisher not only agreed to fund the production and split the profit equally, but also committed to having 'sole control' of 'advertisement (including the number and destination of free copies), price and marketing of the works'.[61]

Such publishing output is impressive given that the war halted much of the book production in Scotland during this time. Alistair McCleery has noted how the impact of the war was not only felt between 1939 and 1945 but lingered long after and caused 'long-term and structural decline' within Scotland's paper-making and publishing industry.[62] Restrictions on raw materials and paper lasted until 1956, which may offer an explanation as to why almost all of the Society's publications between 1939 and 1960 were chapbooks or pamphlets that were no more than 70 pages long. Despite such restrictions on resources and finances, the Society remained determined to produce and publish content that reflected their aims. Although reeling from a depletion in personnel 'with time to devote for furthering its aims', the Society believed that the war brought with it a time 'propitious for awakening interest in the objectives of the Society'.[63] Suggesting that the war had ignited patriotism among Scots, the annual report for 1941–42 argued that

> never was there a greater and more growing sentiment in Scotland in favour of things Scottish, whether cultural or material; never were people's minds more susceptible to new ideas and unconventional action such as the Society has stood for during the past six years. If the Society can be kept alive during these difficult times, the small flame we are helping to kindle can be fanned in times of peace, until a light will shine out in Scotland at least as bright as that to which we pay homage in Poland, in Czecho-Slovakia, in Norway or in Greece, whose culture and patriotism are the admiration of us all.[64]

The Society's self-proclaimed status as a cultural conservationist with a passion-over-profit publishing model illustrates its attitude towards the democratising intentions of their publications during this time. However, despite such optimistic attitudes, reports from the Society's publication secretary in 1949 reveal that the national 'recession in the book trade' was affecting the Society's publications.[65] While the Society continued to engage with Scotland's literary culture in some capacity through the 1950s, bestowing a number of Scottish Book of the Year Awards (which are discussed in Chapter 2), by the mid-1960s, the Society's Publications Committee was becoming increasingly aware of its inability to sustain its publishing projects. The Publications Committee was frequently turning down or postponing projects during this time because they could not afford to sustain them. In February 1966, it was stated that the committee had agreed that 'unless a commercial publisher was prepared to finance the holding of stocks, the Publications Committee would rarely be able to contemplate anything larger than a small paper-backed pamphlet'.[66]

Scotland's Second Cultural Renaissance and Calls for Independence

Just as the Society was born in the midst of a Scottish literary renaissance, so too was its work in the 1960s and 1970s influenced by Scotland's wider sociopolitical and cultural factors. Many have suggested that contemporary Scottish literature and arts have emerged from a second renaissance in Scotland's post-war cultural identity. Exactly when such a second renaissance occurred is still in contention. In 2002, Michael Gardiner defined the 'First Scottish Renaissance' as being a 'pre–World War Two' phenomenon, with the 'Second Scottish Renaissance' following 'post-World War Two'.[67] Similarly and more specifically, other discourse examining Scotland's second cultural renaissance has suggested that its origins can be traced back to cultural production from the 1960s.[68] On the other hand, Gerrard Carruthers has argued that the emergence of key Scottish writers in the 1970s and 1980s, such as Tom Leonard, James Kelman and Alasdair Gray, delineated the second renaissance.[69] (However, both Kelman and Gray have expressed scepticism of the 'Scottish renaissance' moniker, with Kelman commenting that 'the term is a convenient wat of dismissing the need to talk properly about the topic and to hide a lack of knowledge'.[70]) Alternatively, Douglas Gifford suggests that post-war Scottish fiction can be roughly divided into two groups:

> In the immediately post-war period before 1980, writers tend overall to be deeply pessimistic and ironic regarding earlier romanticism and distortion of Scotland's culture and history. After 1980 [...] the fiction attempts a more positive vision of Scotland, increasingly working in new genres, mingling these in a determined contemporary eclecticism which simultaneously exploits older Scottish cultural and fictional traditions and breaks with them.[71]

Just as the 'First Scottish Renaissance' influenced the shaping of the Society in its formative years, so too did the 'Second Scottish Renaissance' influence, and become influenced by, the work of the Society in the late twentieth century. Far from being exclusive to Scottish literature and fiction, Scotland's second renaissance had a much wider effect upon the arts in Scotland.

As a means of justifying the timeframe by which he is separating modern Scottish literature, Gifford tentatively suggests that the 'change in confidence' in Scotland's post-1980s literature may 'somehow be related to the 1979 Devolution referendum'.[72] Neil Davidson has expanded upon this, suggesting that the post-1980 developments in debates surrounding Scottish culture and national identity correspond to specific political developments in Scotland:

> If it were possible to draw a graph showing the strengthening of Scottish national consciousness over the last 20 years, it could be charted in relation to the Conservative party general election victories of 1979, 1983, 1987 and 1992, and would show the curve ascending more steeply with the announcement of each result. [...] In other words, this heightened sense of Scottishness was not an assertion of primordial being but a response to a particular political conjuncture.[73]

Davidson continues, noting how such correlations between political change and a heightened interest in national identity are interrelated, since 'nationhood is never asserted for its own sake, but always in order to achieve some economic, social or political goal'.[74] Accordingly, just as political happenings had affected the way by which writers had expressed their opinions earlier in the century, political discord and the 'quasi-democratic debacle' of 1979[75] appears to have instigated a change more generally within Scotland's cultural milieu.[76]

The interrelation between Scotland's culture and politics is arguably most aptly evidenced by T. M. Devine's description of the rise of the Scottish National Party (SNP) in the 1970s. Illustrating the complexities of the SNP's success in the UK general election in 1974, Devine suggests that

> few Scots, even at the height of the [SNP's] electoral popularity in 1974, wished to break the Union; the aim was rather to improve it to Scottish advantage [...] The SNP's success [...] was seen as an effective way of drawing attention to Scotland's problems.[77]

Despite the fact that the Society has always maintained it is an apolitical organisation – or 'suprapolitical' as it was described in a document from 1975 – its interests and actions have frequently mirrored those of the SNP.[78] Not only were both organisations established in the mid-1930s, inspired by the post–First World War revival in concern for the preservation of Scottish national identities and culture, but also, as Devine's statement illustrates, the two bodies' ideologies – of improving Scotland and 'drawing attention to Scotland's problems' – complemented each other. Considering Devine's statement within the context of the Society and Scotland's wider cultural environment at the time accentuates the extent to which Scottish political thought reflected, and no doubt influenced, cultural developments.

Following Scotland's failed devolution referendum in 1979, the UK general elections in 1983, 1987 and 1992 – in which the Conservative Party ruled despite Scotland's preference for more liberal parties at the polls (most notably Labour and the SNP) – seemed to accentuate Scotland's lack of power in the United Kingdom's democratic procedures and, therefore, highlighted the suppression of Scottish culture more widely.[79] The after effects of such political tensions have continued throughout the 1990s and 2000s and directly contributed, according to Ian Macwhirter, to the rise of Scottish nationalism in the 2000s and 2010s:

> Scots have voted SNP in recent years, not to celebrate their race or ethnicity or even to define themselves culturally against another nation, but to express their repugnance at another political creed: Conservatism. [...] If the rise of Scottish Nationalism can be credited to any one person, it is the former Conservative Prime Minister [Margaret Thatcher].[80]

As Davidson and Macwhirter have both suggested, the political disorder present in Scotland during the past 40 years has influenced debates surrounding nationhood and national identity (which is discussed in relation to the Saltire Society's Literary Awards in more detail in Chapter 4). According to Gerard Carruthers, from the 1970s to the turn of the century, Scottish writers and artists were no longer concerned with the notion of 'an organic national identity' – an identity which, he argues, 'rested on an over-wrought perception of the country's ever fragmented history'.[81] Rather, Carruthers claims, 'Scotland during the last three decades of the twentieth century has increasingly found a series of 'usable' pasts and presents'.[82] In other words, rather than concentrate on identifying an essential or 'correct' Scottish cultural identity, since the 1980s, Scottish writers and organisations have sought to assimilate the different aspects of Scotland's cultural landscape.

Considering this, it is no coincidence that much of the Society's work has reflected concurrent political developments. In 1977, for example, the Society proposed establishing a working group with other arts organisations to establish a 'Policy for the Arts' in Scotland.[83] This idea, which led to the development of a 'Manifesto for the Arts in Scotland', was directly influenced by the possibility of Scotland's devolution in 1979.[84] Indeed, the Society's Book of the Year Award was founded in between major UK elections: three years after the 1979 referendum and one year before a UK general election in 1983, which led to Margaret Thatcher's second term as prime minister. It could therefore be argued that the establishment of the first award in 1982 was not only a means by which the Society could continue its endeavour to promote Scottish culture, but also an engagement with the contemporaneous debates surrounding national and cultural identity. Accordingly, just as the formation of the Society was a consequence of the sociopolitical conditions of the time, the formal founding of the Society's first literary award in 1982 could be interpreted as a political act responding to Scotland's wider party-political discord.

The Society's work would be subtly intertwined with Scottish politics once again in the 2010s. In March 2013, the Scottish government announced that there would be another vote for Scottish independence in September 2014 (also known as IndyRef). Voters were asked, 'Should Scotland be an independent country?', ultimately voting against Scotland's independence from the United Kingdom, with 55.3 per cent of voters voting no and 44.7 per cent voting yes.[85] While the Society maintained that it held an apolitical position on the party politics of the IndyRef campaign leading up to the vote, it did engage with the cultural debate concerning the referendum and the impact it might have on Scotland's future. In 2014, the Society published two pamphlets: *Nevertheless* by Allan Massie, and *Dreaming Scotland* by William McIlvanney. Massie's pamphlet made the case for a 'no' vote, whereas McIlvanney's explained his reasons for voting 'yes'. The pamphlets were launched at an event 'marking 50 days to polling day' at which both authors read from their pamphlets and discussed their perspectives.[86] When explaining the reason for publishing the pamphlets in a newspaper article which emphasised the Society's position as a 'non-political cultural charity', the Society's director Jim Tough said:

> Much of the political debate around the referendum has focused on practical questions. We wanted to provide an opportunity for some more philosophical thought to be given to the question.[87]

Even though the Society published commentary both for and against Scottish independence, and Tough's comments suggest the Society was aiming to provide balance to the existing political debate surrounding the referendum, it would perhaps be disingenuous to consider their deliberate foray into the IndyRef debate as entirely non-partisan. The publication of the pamphlets was a commercial as well as cultural venture, with the pamphlets selling for £4 for Saltire Society members and £5 for non-members. Furthermore, the holding of an event to mark 50 days until the vote at a central venue in Edinburgh (with substantial audience capacity) is arguably a political act in and of itself, since it was a public acknowledgement of the Society's engagement with the debate. The Society may have refused to come down on one side of the argument, but it did not remain impartial to the vote itself. A fact which perhaps illustrates the impossibility of the Society maintaining its non-partisanship when it is so deeply involved in the arbitration of Scottish cultural value(s).

This is also evidenced in the types of books published in Scotland and in turn celebrated by the Society's Literary Awards post-IndyRef. In 2015, for example, Peter Geoghegan's *The People's Referendum: Why Scotland Will Never Be the Same Again*, and Daniel Gray and Alan McCredie's *This Is Scotland* (both published by Edinburgh-based independent publisher Luath Press) were shortlisted for the First Book of the Year and Non-Fiction Book of the Year Awards, respectively. At the time, one Literary Award judge stated that Geoghegan's *The People's Referendum* 'speaks to the moment eloquently',[88] and a review noted that the 'books strength lies ultimately in reminding us that there is more to Scottish politics and Scotland itself than Yes or No'.[89] On the announcement of the non-fiction shortlist, the judging panel described *This Is Scotland*, a book of photographs and short essays about Scotland, as 'quirky', suggesting that 'the unexpected areas to draw out in the chosen places and the deliberate banality of some of the images counter the too-easy coffee table visions of Scotland'.[90] Both these books are illustrative of the kinds of books published post-referendum that ruminated on Scotland's sociopolitical and cultural discourse, as a review of *This Is Scotland* noted:

> There have been many important books about Scotland published this year. Weighty tomes were required to explain how we had reached a point where the hand of history lay heavy on the shoulders of ordinary men and women. But for many people [...] the referendum must have been but a distant din [...] They were not concerned with offering their tuppence worth to any national or international media outlet that would have them; nor with attending meetings to have their own convictions confirmed [...] For many people, life continued as normal then and it continues as normal now.[91]

This description could also be applied to the Society's own relationship with the Scottish independence referendum in 2014. Despite emphasising its non-political stance and treating Scottish politics as a 'distant din', the Society nonetheless engaged and offered their 'tuppence worth' through its publications and events. Indeed, the Society continues to be intertwined with Scotland's political milieu. In 2015, 2016 and 2018, the Society received varying levels of financial and affiliate support for their events and Literary Awards from Creative Scotland through its Open Project Funding which supports 'artists, groups, and creative organisations based in Scotland who are looking to apply for a wide range of artistic and creative project activity'.[92] As an executive non-departmental public body of the Scottish government, which oversees the awarding of grants and funding to the Scottish creative industries (including the arts, literary and screen industries), Creative Scotland is a fundamentally political – and politicised – institution, and the Society's dependence on this support is therefore inseparable from Scotland's political landscape.[93]

In offering insight into the historical contexts of the founding and evolution of the Society, this overview of Scottish sociopolitical history and culture since the 1930s has illustrated that, since its founding in 1936, the Society has been a product and stimulus of Scotland's cultural landscape. The value of establishing this chronology of events is practical, in terms of establishing the Society's timeline and considering it alongside significant developments in Scotland's recent history, and important in offering an illustration of how a nation's sociopolitical changes are reflected in its cultural institutions. From the beginning, the Society has consistently been affected, both positively and negatively, by events in Scotland more widely. The result has been for the Society to continually evolve in order to engage with new policies, initiatives and events, making it an incredibly valuable resource both in terms of the materials it has produced – which are now artefacts demonstrative of Scotland's cultural history – and as a body whose initiatives have reflected and helped create Scotland's cultural landscape.

Chapter 2

THE SALTIRE SOCIETY SCOTTISH BOOK OF THE YEAR

Earliest Commendations and Awards: 1930s And 1940s

Keen to establish itself as an organisation dedicated to the celebration of Scottish cultural life in its first year, the Saltire Society set to work establishing a number of cultural awards. These included a housing award and an inaugural book of the year commendation.[1] For the years 1936–37, these commendations were awarded to Robert Gore-Brown's biography of the fourth earl of Boswell, James Hepburn, *Lord Bothwell*, and Neil Gunn's novel *Highland River*, both published in 1937 (the Society favoured the term 'commendation' over 'award' through the 1930s and 1940s). The judges for these commendations were the writers and early advocates and members of the Society – Eric Linklater, Compton Mackenzie and Edwin Muir.[2] In 1937, two further commendations were made to Agnes Mure Mackenzie's *The Passing of the Stewarts* (1937), and Robert McLellan's *Three Plays in Scots* (1937). Although there is no archival record of whether Linklater, Mackenzie and Muir continued to act as judges after 1937, George Bruce suggests that the judges remained the same until the outbreak of war in 1939 brought the 'discriminating assessments of the adjudicators' to an end.[3] The Society's book of the year commendations would continue until 1940, with Fred Urquhart's *Time Will Knit* (1938) earning the accolade in 1939, and Edwin Muir's autobiography *The Story and the Fable* (1940) and J. A. Bowie's *The Future of Scotland* (1939) receiving commendations in 1940.[4]

Even in these early years of the Society, there was interest in expanding the range of literary awards and commendations it would offer. The Society's 1937 annual report stated that during their AGM that year it had been suggested that they found a poetry prize which would be 'awarded annually for the more meritorious first work published by a Scot living in Scotland'.[5] It was also suggested that the Society establish an award for 'first novels', but the Scottish journalist, politician and future leader of the SNP, William

Power, argued against instituting more awards for the celebration of literature, suggesting that 'what was wanted for novels was Birth Control'.[6] A comment indicating that Power believed the literary market was already saturated and the Society should not add to this by establishing an award to encourage first-time novelists. It would take another 49 years before the Society's First Book of the Year Award would be founded in 1986.

However, to return to the awards made in the Society's earliest years, it is worth examining the kinds of books the Society commended, since they quite clearly reflected the Society's constitutional commitment of 'restoring Scotland to its proper position as a cultural unit' and 'mak[ing] Scots conscious of their heritage'.[7] The three fiction books celebrated by the Society were highly successful books set in Scotland and dealing with Scottish themes and topics (features that would later become important to the Society's literary award terms of eligibility, as discussed in Chapter 4). Gunn's *Highland River* – which also received the James Tait Black Memorial Book Prize in 1937[8] – is set on Scotland's highland coast, and McLellan's collection of three Scots-language plays (*Toom Byres*, *Jamie the Saxt* and *The Changeling*), set in various stages of Scotland's monarchical and political history, became 'immediately successful and in demand with Scottish audiences'.[9] According to Alastair Cording, the popularity of McLellan's plays ensured the overnight establishment of the 'validity of Scots language as a theatrical medium'.[10] Equally, Urquhart's novel *Time Will Knit*, a drama about the eviction of a working-class family from their Edinburgh home, was a popular text and would be reissued and canonised by Penguin as part of its 'New Penguin Writing' series in 1944.[11]

The non-fiction titles that received commendations from the Society in 1937, 1938 and 1940 were also focused on Scottish subjects, specifically the political and monarchical history of Scotland. Gore-Browne's *Lord Bothwell* explores the life of James Hepburn, the third husband of Mary Queen of Scots, and Mackenzie's *The Passing of the Stewarts* describes the history of the Stewart dynasty in Scotland. This focus on celebrating books concerned with Scotland's past changed with the commendation of Bowie's *The Future of Scotland* in 1940, a book which presented Scotland's current political, economic and social position with the view of advocating 'a policy of progressive planning' in Scotland.[12] This shift in priorities from considering Scotland's past to speculations on its future reflected the outlook of the Society and its work during this period. In a 1939–40 annual report, the Society stated that one of its main concerns 'is with the future' and that it 'envisages a new Scotland with a vigorous intellectual life, drawing on the past for inspiration to new advances in art'.[13] It seems this was the future Scotland that the Society wanted to help create through its earliest commendations of books that furthered knowledge of Scotland's past while also celebrating the possibilities of the future.

The Society's book commendations were not major public affairs. There were no ceremonies nor press releases announcing the news. While there was notice of Gord-Browne and Gunn's commendations in an August 1937 edition of the *Aberdeen Press and Journal* newspaper, there is no evidence of the commendations being promoted outside of the Society's AGMs and annual reports which were only available to Society members.[14] Consequently, even though the Society's earliest book commendations were a means by which the Society could demonstrate its aims, attitudes and support for Scottish culture, the celebration of books was quite an insular practice, indicating that the purpose of the commendations was to, quite literally, commend the author and their work. In other words, it seems the bestowal of cultural and social capital, as opposed to a public and ceremonial celebration of books (which may have drawn the attention of readers and the publishing industry), was the intention of the Society's earliest commendations.

Founding the Scottish Book of the Year Award: 1950s–1960s

The cessation of the commendations in 1940 aligned with the Society's reduction in personnel following the outbreak of war and a reduction in book production across the United Kingdom. The introduction of paper rationing in March 1940 meant that 'competition for paper was fierce',[15] and UK publishing production, already difficult to measure, 'became still more indeterminate during the war years'.[16] With fewer books published, and the country's collective focus on the war effort, the Society took a break in making book commendations, and it would be over ten years before the Society began rewarding writers and books again.

During a meeting of the Society's Publications Committee in Edinburgh, October 1953, it was noted that a 'Book of the Year Award' was proposed during a Society conference held in St Andrews earlier that year.[17] The Publications Committee agreed that 'this matter should be held over for discussion at the next meeting' which took place in February 1954. It was at this meeting that historian and former Saltire Society president (1939–1948) J. W. Oliver, Publications Committee honorary secretary Alison Cairns, and rector of the University of Glasgow and Society committee member Tom Honeyman devised an outline for a Book of the Year award:

> After discussion it was agreed to recommend to the Council: (One) that an award might be made to the 'person', publishers, author, editor

or journalist, who contributed most to Scottish Literature during the year; (Two) that the award, which should take the form of a money prize, should be made within one year of the first announcement of the scheme but not necessarily from year to year thereafter – possibly every second year, and (Three) that it should be made by an *ad hoc* Committee appointed to the purpose.[18]

This outline describes something that might be more akin to an award for a contribution to Scottish literature, rather than for a single book, and does not quite align with the 'Book of the Year' designation which was being used to describe the venture.

More members of the Society's Publications Committee attended a later meeting in June 1954 to discuss these proposals, including the historian and author Agnes Mure Mackenzie, who was made an Honorary President of the Society in 1942 (and received a Saltire book commendation in 1957), and author George Scott-Moncrieff.[19] During the June meeting, it was proposed that the prize should 'take the form of a shield or plaque', be made 'annually as a commendation rather than a prize' and that the 'panel of judges [should] be selected by the Publications Committee'.[20] It was also suggested that 'an offer of publication would be […] the most helpful form of prize or award', but this suggestion was never taken forward in subsequent meetings and has not been offered as a form of prize by the Society to date.[21] The committee also proposed that five 'subjects' should be eligible for the prize, 'namely History and Biography, Drama, Fiction, Poetry and Belles Lettres' and that 'the judge should be an expert in the particular field in which the award happened to be made in any one year'.[22] The committee suggested the quite unconventional idea that the award, while bestowed annually, should 'cover a period of five years', either to ensure an extensive range of titles would be eligible for the award or, if it was to be awarded for an oeuvre or contribution to literature (as the above outline had described), that it encompass a number of years' work by an individual or publisher. However, in a meeting in December 1954, the author J. M. Reid 'advised against spreading the award over a period of five years' because, he argued, the award would then 'resemble the P.E.N. "Niven" Award'. Reid is likely referring here to the Frederick Niven Award, which was founded in 1949–50 by Pauline Niven (the widow of the Canadian author Frederick Niven) and presented triennially.[23] Funded by donations made by Pauline Niven, the award was administered by the Scottish Centre of International PEN. The final Frederick Niven Award, which came with a cash prize of £500, was made in 1984 (for the years 1980–83) and given to Alasdair Gray for his novel *Lanark* (which would also win the Saltire Society's

Book of the Year Award in 1982).[24] To avoid confusion, and perhaps comparison, with the Frederick Niven Award, Reid 'recommended that the award should be an annual one for the "Scottish Book of the Year"'.[25] Such detailed discussions of the logistical administration of the awards, and their potential impact upon authors and the Society, suggests that the Society's Publications Committee was taking the founding of this new award for literature industriously. The meeting minutes reveal that the Publications Committee and the Society's Council were keen to establish a literary award that effectually supported and celebrated the winning author and books while also upholding distinct literary merit and critical acclaim, hence the preference for experts in the respective fields to judge the books and the reference to 'belles lettres'. Notwithstanding these in-depth discussions about the establishment of this Book of the Year Award, there appears to have been no reference made to the similar awards made by the Society in the 1930s, indicating that this new award was not considered a continuation of the commendations the Society had made 20 years earlier, but an entirely new venture.

Suggestions for the 'ad hoc committee' of judges who would select a winner for the award were tabled at a meeting in March 1955[26] and included English literature lecturers Walter Keir and William L. Renwick, historical novelist and academic Dr Janet M. Smith, and a Mr Hogben.[27] Keir, Renwick and Hogben accepted the offer to form a subcommittee to 'deal with matters pertaining to the award', but Smith declined the invitation to join the panel, and the writer and historian J. M. Reid, who had advised on the prize in the previous year, accepted a position on the subcommittee in her place. The predominantly academic composition of the judging panel implies that the Society's Publications Committee either placed particular value in the expertise of researchers and teachers of literature and history, or that the committee members were socially and professionally connected to academics in Scottish literature and history – or, indeed, both. This is important because, not only did the makeup of the Society's Literary Award judging panels remain largely academic for decades to come, which was perhaps a kind of legacy of this initial judging panel, but it also reveals the kinds of social and professional network of the Publications Committee and the judges. To apply Bourdieu here, the Society's earliest Book of the Year Award judging panel(s) reflect the social capital or 'institutionalised relationships of mutual acquaintance and recognition' of those involved.[28] This early praxis of Saltire Society Literary Award judges being embedded in researching, teaching, writing and publishing about Scottish literature would continue well into the twenty-first century.

Following the formation of the panel, details of the Society's Scottish Book of the Year Award were announced in the Society's annual report for 1954–55 and received some coverage in a Scottish national newspaper, with a one-line piece in the *Scotsman* stating, 'The Saltire Society have approved a scheme for an annual award for the best piece of work in any of the following categories: History and biography, drama, fiction, poetry, and belles lettres.'[29] However, the initial momentum building around the Society's Scottish Book of the Year Award would soon be stalled by a series of unfortunate events. The death of Agnes Mure Mackenzie in February 1955 appears to have delayed the progression of the award during this period. As a key member of the Publications Committee (having attended her last committee meeting only eight months before her death), a previous recipient of the Society's earliest book commendations and an Honorary President of the Society, the loss of Mackenzie no doubt altered the dynamics and priorities of the Society and its Publications Committee. Moreover, her death inspired the Society's executive board to suggest the founding of another award for 'a published work of Scottish historical research' in tribute to Mackenzie (this would become the Society's History Book of the Year Award). As a result, the Publications Committee were distracted by the organisation of this new award.[30] The Scottish Book of the Year Award was delayed further still because the ad hoc committee convenor Hogben had been ill throughout 1956, meaning that by January 1957 the committee had not yet met to discuss the award: well over a year since the Society had publicly announced the founding of the award. The patience for such (albeit unavoidable) delays wore thin, and at a meeting in late January 1957, it was agreed that 'the other three judges – Professor Renwick, Dr. Keir and [Mr Reid] – might make up and compare their respective selections for the Award in the meantime'.[31]

The winner of the Society's first Scottish Book of the Year Award was finally revealed in early November 1957. The three judges selected Edwin Muir's seventh poetry collection, *One Foot in Eden* (1956). Publications Committee meeting minutes from Wednesday, 6 November 1957, record that 'the Judges had given the Saltire Literary Award for 1956 (the first to be made) to Dr. Edwin Muir's book of poems "One Foot in Eden"' and the prize to be conferred to Muir was 'a specially bound copy of the winning book'.[32] This was the first mention of what form the physical prize element of the award would take.

The delay in presenting the 1956 award to Edwin Muir had a knock-on effect in the presentation of the Scottish Book of the Year Award in subsequent years. The decision to confer the 1957 award to George Hay's *The Architecture of Scottish Post-Reformation Churches* (1957), a 'handsome and well-produced' review of ecclesiastic architecture in Scotland, was not made until late 1958.[33] The Society's annual report for 1957–58 did not mention Hay's award win, presumably because it was decided after the annual report was released. Instead, the 1957–58 report reiterated Muir's 1956 award, stating,

'The award itself is to take the form of a specially bound copy of the book [and] after some difficulty the Committee hope that they have found a design which can be repeated each year.'[34] However, the annual report for 1958–59 also fails to note Hay's 1957 award, but does report that the 1958 award was given to Stuart Piggott's *Scotland before History* (1958), an essay about Scotland's prehistory.[35] The report noted that a 'bound copy of *One Foot in Eden*, which won the first Award, has been presented to Mrs Edwin Muir', following Edwin Muir's death in January 1959. This meant that Muir received the prize for his award nearly two years after it was conferred to him. Following the 1958 award, there were no other Saltire Society Literary Awards conferred until the Book of the Year Award was re-established in 1982.

The Scottish Book of the Year Award: 1960s–1990s

During the 1960s and 1970s, the Society's Publications Committee concentrated on the production, as opposed to celebration, of Scottish literature. Throughout this period, the Society published a number of books and pamphlets – such as *Scottish Book: A Brief Bibliography for Teachers and General Readers* (1963) and *Voices of Our Kind: An Anthology of Contemporary Scottish Verse* (1971) – as well as the short-lived literary journal *New Saltire*, printed between 1961 and 1964. The Society was also active throughout the late 1970s and early 1980s in trying to stimulate cultural policy reform and the promotion of the arts in Scotland. While the Society's interest in literary awards seems to have stalled (though the Agnes Mure Mackenzie Memorial Award for Scottish Historic Research was awarded, sporadically, through the 1960s and 1970s), it was one of the most active members of the Society's leadership, Paul Henderson Scott, who would spearhead the new age of the Society's Literary Awards.

A former diplomat, Scott was one of the key figures in the Society's activities between 1977 and 1994, acting as convenor of the Society's Publications Committee and secretary of the 'Manifesto of the Arts in Scotland' committee (ca. 1980). Speaking in 2013, Scott recalled that the re-establishment of the Society's Book of the Year Award was a relatively simple process:

[At] the very first meeting I attended [as a member of the Saltire Society Council] they said [...] 'Is there anything you think the Saltire Society ought to start doing that we haven't been doing?' I said yes, certainly, you ought to start an award, a book award, and the reason for that was that Scotland was producing very many excellent books [...] very good poets and very good novelists, and so on [...] But the odd thing is that there's no body that actually recognised them [...] with nothing to recognise their productions and to celebrate them so [...] the committee agreed with this and said 'As long as you can raise the money, let's go ahead and do it'.[36]

Scott gave a similar account of the return of the Society's Scottish Book of the Year Award in an article titled 'Behind the awards' in the Spring 1991 issue of *Books in Scotland*. In the article, Scott reiterated the Society's longstanding connection with Scottish literature, suggesting that a literary award seemed like an obvious means by which the Society could continue its support for Scottish writers:

> Literature has always been important to the Society [...] So why was there no book award, especially at a time when Scottish writing was in a very flourishing state? The Council of the Society readily approved proposals which I put to them in 1981 and almost at once we found a very generous and helpful sponsor in the Royal Bank of Scotland.[37]

As with the other revivals of the Society's Book of the Year Award over the years, Scott made no reference to former incarnations of the earlier commendations and awards for books that the Society had bestowed. This is a significant point, given that that Society has continually struggled to articulate a coherent narrative of the history of its literary awards. Having a secure sense of such history would not only make it easier for the Saltire Society to substantiate claims of prestige, which are in part shaped by a prize's repute and longevity, but it would also enable the Society to project a clear sense of identity for the award (such issues are discussed in more detail in Chapter 6).

Scott proved a force to be reckoned with and quickly secured sponsorship for his proposed Book of the Year Award from the Royal Bank of Scotland (RBS) in summer 1981. Scott restated the ease by which he raised the financial support for the award, stating that he approached the Bank of Scotland, who, despite apparently liking the idea, were unable to commit to financial sponsorship. He then discussed the idea with RBS, who 'agreed immediately to do it'.[38] In fact, Scott claimed that during RBS's period of sponsorship, the *Scotsman* newspaper also approached him to ask if they could take on the sponsorship of the prize once RBS's support ceased. Such interest in the Society's Book of the Year Award suggests that a new literary award for Scottish literature was considered a ripe sponsorship opportunity by several major Scottish businesses. This corresponded with a growth in sponsorship of the arts during this period more broadly. As Mark W. Rectanus has noted,

The rapid growth of sponsoring during the 1980s and 1990s was facilitated by an increasing awareness of new definitions and uses of culture within the contexts of everyday life. This process of redefining culture was in part driven by corporations themselves and mediated through advertising and promotion. Reconfigurations of everyday culture and cultural identities (e.g., gender, ethnicity, or nationality) were shaped by and circulated within media that produced, packaged, organized, and disseminated culture for expanding global markets (e.g., cable and satellite television).[39]

While it would be safe to assume that RBS, as one of the largest banks in Scotland, did not necessarily need further promotion as an 'everyday' corporation, they may have sought a kind of 'reconfiguration' in terms of their connections with other forms of 'culture and cultural identities' that an association with literary awards might provide. Indeed, as Driscoll synopsises, 'symbolic capital is important to corporations because it can be used to reposition a company's reputation'.[40]

Correspondence between Scott and RBS's assistant public relations officer, Gordon Fenton, from August 1981 illustrate the terms by which such sponsorship was secured. In a letter to Scott, Fenton notes:

> I have obtained agreement for the Bank to become involved with the Society in the proposed Literary Award Scheme. The conditions would be as follows:
>
> 1. Agreement on a title for the Scheme. I suggest 'The Royal Bank – Saltire Society Scottish Literary Award Scheme'.
> 2. Agreed title to be placed on all Press Releases and other related communications, as well as the band to be placed round the winning book.
> 3. We agree to sponsor the Scheme to the extent of £1,000 in each of the next three years, i.e. a total of £3,000, with the option to review at the end of that time.[41]

Scott appears to have accepted this proposal with immediate effect, but the title of the award 'scheme', as Fenton called it, would be changed between this correspondence and the press release announcing the new award distributed three months later in November 1981. The press release described the award as 'The Saltire Society and Royal Bank Scottish Literary Award', as opposed to the original suggestion from Fenton which foregrounded the name of the sponsor.[42]

Within a month of receiving Fenton's confirmation of support from RBS, Scott began approaching people to become judges and nominators for the award. In September 1981, Scott wrote to the critic and editor of the *Scottish Literary Journal*, Thomas Crawford; the Scottish writer and civil servant James Allan Ford; the poet Edwin Morgan; and the founder of the *Literary Review*, Dr Anne Smith, to invite them to be members of the 'Saltire Society and Royal Bank Scottish Literary Award' judging panel.[43] In the letter, Scott notes that RBS had agreed to sponsor the award for £1,000 per year for three years and that it was his intention to announce the scheme in mid-November 1981, with the first prize presented in October 1982.[44] Scott also set out the criteria for the award, formally identifying, for the first time in the history of the Society's Literary Awards, exactly what was meant by the term Scottish Book of the Year:

> The term, 'Scottish Book', would include any book by an author of Scottish descent or living in Scotland, or a book by anyone which deals with the work or life of a Scot or with a Scottish problem, event or situation. The book might therefore be poetry, a novel, play or other work of imaginative literature, or biography, literary criticism or a study of any Scottish issue. Books on history would not be excluded, although works in which the main emphasis is on original historical research will continue to be the special province of the Agnes Mure Mackenzie Award.[45]

Scott continued, explaining how books fitting the criteria of eligibility noted above would be nominated and judged:

> (a) The literary editors of leading Scottish newspapers and the editors of magazines and reviews in Scotland, which are concerned with literature, will be invited to act as the nominating body for the reward. They would be asked by the end of October each year to nominate a book which in their view merits consideration for the award from among the books reviewed in their pages during the preceding twelve months.
>
> (b) A panel of three or four members (who would be distinguished writers, critics or academics) will be appointed [...] to consider these nominations and make the final decision. In addition to the Book of the Year, they might award smaller prizes to one or two additional books which they considered deserved commendation. They would have the right to withhold the awards in any year they considered that no book reached the required standard.[46]

Scott also wrote to literary editors and reviewers of Scottish journals and newspapers, including *Chapman*, *Cencrastus*, the *Glasgow Herald* and the *Scottish Review*, explaining the new award and asking if, in principle, they would be willing to provide nominations for the award.[47]

The terms and conditions put forward by Scott for the administration of the award, including requesting nominations from editors and reviewers of literary journals, not only illustrate how thoroughly considered and well planned the Society's new award was – as already noted, previous embodiments of the award were often haphazardly founded and organised, with little to no external public relations regarding the awards being distributed – but they also reveal that Scott was clearly trying to establish the Book of the Year Award as a well-considered *quality* award from the beginning. In prohibiting open submissions and restricting nominations to recommendations from literary editors and reviewers, Scott produced a layer of selection for the awards, assuming that literary reviewers and editors would submit books which they had already read and appraised. Likewise, in declaring that the judging panel would consist of '*distinguished* writers, critics and academics' (emphasis added), Scott asserts that the individuals chosen to judge the award would be highly qualified and accomplished, implying that the decisions they make will be nonpareil, since they are experts in their respective fields.

However, not everyone was convinced that such a method of nomination and adjudication was the best way in which to survey Scotland's yearly literary output. John Arnott, a senior producer at BBC Radio Scotland, wrote to Scott on 19 October 1981, questioning the nomination method:

> Are you convinced that this is the best method of nomination? I can understand that you do not wish to be deluged with titles as you might be if, [...] nominations were open to all. [...] At present it is basically an editor's choice. Would it not be more attractive, and comprehensive, if it were initially a critics' choice, open for nomination by anyone who had published literary criticism or review in that year?[48]

Arnott also indicates that he felt individual producers of the BBC's book programmes could not nominate books, since such nominations would inevitably be seen as 'the BBC nomination', going against the BBC's constitutional requirement to remain 'ever-impartial'.[49] Arnott's concerns were well founded, particularly given that two of the judges Scott had invited to join the first judging panel were also editors of literary journals: Tom Crawford was the literary editor for the *Scottish Literary Journal*, and Anne Smith was the founder and editor of the *Literary Review*. Such circumstances increased the risk of nominations coming from a relatively small pool of reviewers. Indeed, as Squires has argued, book reviewers and reviews 'have their role [...] in both judging literary quality and selling books. The former role sees it as one of the early points of (potential) canon formation.'[50] Requesting book reviews with nominations, then, arguably provided a kind of pre-adjudication sifting process by which the judges could acquire a sense of the quality of the nominated title from the review. While there is no record of the reply, if any, Arnott received in response to his concerns, Scott nonetheless would still be explaining and defending the Book of the Year nomination process a decade later. Writing in *Books in Scotland* in 1991, Scott openly defended the nomination procedure favoured by the Society, illustrating the pragmatic benefits of the process:

> Nomination by literary editors has two purposes. First of all it throws the net wide by including in the selection process most of the people involved in the reviewing of books in Scotland. On the other hand, it is a safety valve to exclude the scores of books which are not seriously in the running. We want to protect our judges from the superhuman task of reading, or pretending to read, every new book that appears. At the same time we do not want to miss any book which deserves consideration.[51]

Scott's argument that asking literary editors to provide nominations 'throws the net wide' and includes 'most of the people involved in the reviewing of books in Scotland' in the nomination process for the Society's award seems disingenuous for two reasons. First, Scott's fellow judge, Douglas Gifford, wrote that he wished the panel received '*more* nominations' for the awards, months after the publication of Scott's article.[52] Second, the majority of nominations received for the Book of the Year Award at this time came not from external parties but from the panel itself. In 1987, for example, 25 books were nominated for the Book of the Year Award, but only five of these nominations came from outside the panel: the literary journals *Leopard*, *Chapman*, *Lines Review* and the *Edinburgh Review* all nominated one book each, as did the *Glasgow Herald* newspaper.[53] Likewise, in 1990 and 1991, 32 and 35 nominations for the Book of the Year Award were received, respectively, but 70 per cent of the nominations for these years came from the panel. In addition, a number of nominations in 1990 and 1991 came from Scottish Television (STV) and the *Scotsman* who were co-sponsors of the Book of the Year Award by this point.[54]

This trend would continue into the mid- to late 1990s, and it was during this time at which nominations from publishers began to appear, although there is no recorded explanation as to why nominations from publishers were accepted from this time onwards. In 1996, of the 55 books nominated for the Book of the Year Award, 15 per cent came from the literary editors of newspapers or editors of literary journals, 18 per cent came from publishers and 67 per cent came from the panel, which at the time included Angus Calder, Ian Campbell, Douglas Gifford, Joyce McMillan, Isobel Murray and Derick Thomson (see the appendix for a full list of judges by year).[55] A similar pattern emerged in 1998, with 22 per cent of nominations coming from publishers (although this was 13 nominations from only four publishers), 73 per cent of nominations from the panel and only 5 per cent of nominations from the editors of literary journals.[56] The incremental increase of nominations from publishers and the decrease of nominations from editors of literary journals between 1996 and 1998 continued until the Society stopped recording exactly who made nominations after 1999. By 2010, although the Society continued to request nominations from 'literary editors, publishers and producers of book programmes in radio and television', the majority of entries came from publishers.[57] In 2015, the Society changed the wording of the Book of the Year Award entry form (which was also separated into Fiction and Non-Fiction Book of the Year Awards from 2015 onwards) to state that nominations were *only* accepted from publishers.[58]

To return to the origination of the Book of the Year Award in 1982, however, Scott appears to have been aware of the importance of acquiring media coverage of the award, organising a midday press conference for the launch of the award at the Society's offices in Edinburgh on Tuesday, 17 November 1981.[59] Ninety guests were invited to the event, with invitees including the poet Norman MacCaig, assistant producer of the BBC's 'Books Now' programme Elinor Aitken, Walter Cairns of the Scottish Arts Council, publisher's consultant David Fletcher, and literary editor of the *Scotsman*, James Seaton.[60] The official press release that accompanied the launch of the award confirmed the judging panel for the first Saltire Society and RBS Literary Award would be Thomas Crawford, David Daiches (who was a late addition to the panel), James Allan Ford, Edwin Morgan, Paul Henderson Scott and Anne Smith.[61] It also noted that the judging panel 'might award smaller prizes to one or two additional books which they considered deserved commendation' and that the panel 'would have the right to withhold the awards in any year when they considered that no book reached the required standard' (although, to date, the panel has never withheld a Book of the Year Award).[62]

News of the launch of the award was announced in the *Scotsman* and the northern edition of the *Daily Telegraph* on Wednesday, 18 November 1981, as well as in *Books in Scotland, Business and Finance in Scotland* and the *Glasgow Evening Times*.[63] Correspondence from writers and publishers enquiring about the award indicates that the launch of the award was successful in generating interest. Many of the letters the Society received (some of which were forwarded from RBS, who also received correspondence relating to the award) enquired as to the 'ground rules [and] conditions'[64] of the award and asked for an 'entry form'.[65] Such enquiries demonstrate how, initially, there was some expectation that the nomination process for the award would be an entirely open one.

Despite this concerted and public announcement of the Book of the Year Award in late 1981, Scott would not formally request nominations for the award until eight months later. In early August 1982, Scott wrote to the members of the Book of the Year Award judging panel and a number of literary reviewers and editors, including the editors of *Akros*, *Books in Scotland* and *Cencrastus*, and the president of the Scottish Publishers' Association,[66] calling for their nominations for that year's Scottish Book of the Year.[67] Scott ended the note thanking the nominators for their help, and reiterating that it was hoped that the award would 'encourage Scottish writers and draw attention to their work'.[68] As Table 1 illustrates, the Society received 11 nominations in August and September 1982, with Alasdair Gray's *Lanark* (1981) receiving 2 nominations from Norman Wilson, the editor of *Books in Scotland*,[69] and the editorial committee of *Cencrastus*.[70]

Of the 11 books nominated for the inaugural Book of the Year Award, 5 were non-fiction, history or biographies, three were novels, 2 were collections of poetry and 1 was a collection of plays.[71] William Buchan's memoir, *John Buchan* (1982), was the only nomination to come directly from the book's publisher and arrived two months before Scott requested nominations from his group of literary editors and critics. Unusually, three of the books nominated by *Scottish Literary Review* editor Thomas Crawford – Corson's *Notes and Index to Sir Herbert Grierson's Edition of the Letters of Sir Walter Scott*, Kinsley's *The Poems of William Dunbar*, and Davies and Watts's *Cunninghame Graham: A Critical Biography* – were all published in 1979. While these books appear anomalous in comparison to the other books nominated and published between 1981 and 1982 – and, as will be discussed shortly, the eligibility of 'older' publications was questioned by a member of the judging panel – Scott's original criteria of eligibility for the awards did not actually specify that the books should be published in the preceding 12 months. The 'procedure of selection' decided upon by Scott and RBS's public relations officer Fenton stated that 'by the end of October each year [literary editors are] to nominate a book [...] from among the books reviewed in their pages during the preceding twelve months'.[72] This criterion indicates that the key date to be taken into consideration when deciding upon a book's eligibility for the award is the date at which it was *reviewed*, not the date on which it was published. Furthermore, since, as Crawford explains in his nomination letter to Scott, the 'review supplements' for the *Scottish Literary Journal* were 'years behind with their reviewing', it seems inevitable that the

Table 1 List of nominations for Saltire Society Book of the Year Award 1982

Author	Title	Publisher	Nominator	Publication date
Buchan, William	*John Buchan*	Buchan and Enright (London)	Fiona Carlisle, *Buchan and Enright*	1982
Calder, Angus	*Revolutionary Empire: The Rise of the English-Speaking Empires from the 15th Century to the 1780s*	Jonathan Cape	Sheila G. Hearn, *Cencrastus*	1981
Corson, James C.	*Notes and Index to Sir Herbert Grierson's Edition of the Letters of Sir Walter Scott*	Oxford University Press	Thomas Crawford, *Scottish Literary Journal*	1979
Dunnett, Dorothy	*King Hereafter*	Michael Joseph	Cuthbert, *Aberdeen Press and Journal*	1982
Gray, Alasdair	*Lanark*	Canongate	Sheila G. Hearn, *Cencrastus*; and Norman Wilson, *Books in Scotland*	1982
Hart, F. R. and Pick, J. B.	*Neil Gunn – A Highland Life*	John Murray	James Seaton, *Scotsman*	1981
Kinsley, James	*The Poems of William Dunbar*	Clarendon Press	Thomas Crawford, *Scottish Literary Journal*	1979
McLellan, Robert	*Collected Plays Vol 1*	John Calder	J. K. Annand, *Lallans*	1981
Smith, Iain Crichton	*Selected Poems, 1955–1980*	MacDonald	Trevor Royle, *Lines Review*	1982
Toulmin, David	*Hard Shining Corn*	Paul Harris	Robert Jeffrey, *Sunday Standard*	1982
Davies, Laurence and Watts, Cedric	*Cunninghame Graham: A Critical Biography*	Cambridge University Press	Thomas Crawford, *Scottish Literary Journal*	1979

Table 2 Shortlist for the Saltire Society Book of the Year Award 1982

Author	Title	Publisher and publication date
Dunnett, Dorothy	*King Hereafter*	Michael Joseph, 1982
Gray, Alasdair	*Lanark*	Canongate, 1982
Hart, F. R. and Pick, J. B.	*Neil Gunn: A Highland Life*	John Murray, 1981
McLellan, Robert	*Collected Plays Volume I*	John Calder, 1981
Smith, Iain Crichton	*Selected Poems 1955–80*	MacDonald, 1982
Toulmin, David	*Hard Shining Corn*	Paul Harris, 1982
Davies, Laurence and Watts, Cedric	*Cunninghame Graham: A Critical Biography*	Cambridge University Press, 1979

nominations made by the editors of the journal would be for books published in the years preceding 1981.[73] Crawford's seemingly ineligible nominations were commented on by other members of the literary panel. In a handwritten note responding to the news of the nominations, Edwin Morgan wrote: 'As regards the list, by the way, I have some doubts about HARD SHINING CORN (1972) and CUNNINGHAME GRAHAM (1979) [*sic*] being called 'Book of the Year'! What year?'[74] However, despite Morgan's observation that David Toulmin's collection of short stories, *Hard Shining Corn*, was originally published in 1972 and was in fact rereleased in 1982, the book *was* shortlisted for the inaugural award, adding further confusion as to how the judges accounted for the eligibility of books nominated and shortlisted for the award in its first year.

The shortlist for the inaugural Book of the Year Award (as shown in Table 2) selected from the nominations illustrated in Table 1 was announced in a press release from RBS on Wednesday, 13 October 1982.[75]

Not only do the Society's records indicate that these 7 books were the only books of the 11 nominated which Scott requested from publishers for the panel to read, but they were requested just two weeks before the public announcement of the shortlist was made. Writing to the publishers of the shortlisted books on Friday, 1 October 1982, Scott requested six copies of books that had 'been nominated for consideration as the first Scottish Book of the Year'.[76] This short, two-week timeframe between Scott's request for books from publishers and the public announcement of the shortlist implies that either the judges had already read the books, or Scott knew the books that were selected for the shortlist before requesting them and that the judges would only need to read the books included on this shortlist. While this system seems unorthodox in comparison to the current literary awards nominations procedure followed by the Society – by which publishers are asked to send copies of nominated books two to three months before a shortlist announcement in order to enable plenty of reading time for the judges – it is possible that Scott and the judges relied heavily upon the nominators to *only* recommend award-worthy books (as discussed earlier). When prompting literary editors and reviewers for nominations in August 1982, Scott requested that nominators also send a 'photocopy of the review' of the books they were nominating.[77] A number of these reviews were written by the nominator themselves with one review submitted alongside a nomination of Alasdair Gray's *Lanark* written by future Saltire Society Literary Award judge and eventual Literary Award judging panel co-chair Douglas Gifford.[78] Perhaps, then, Scott and his fellow judges put so much trust in the recommendations they received from literary editors that they created and publicised a shortlist from the titles before they had even read them.

Further correspondence between Scott and the nominators during this period is revealing. While seven nominators wrote a letter, which detailed their nomination with an accompanying review of the selected book, only Crawford and Cuthbert Graham went into great detail to explain and justify their selections. After 'careful consideration', Graham, a journalist and reviewer for the *Aberdeen Press and Journal*, nominated Dorothy Dunnett's *King Hereafter*[79] and enclosed a copy of his own review in which he described Dunnett's novel as being 'profoundly moving'.[80] Acknowledging that 'it may seem unusual to recommend a book which is a historical romance or fantasy', Graham defends his nomination noting that 'after all it was the historical fiction of Sir Walter Scott which introduced the entire genre to European literature'.[81] Graham continues this defence, stating:

> It seems natural that we should give credit to a revival of this esteemed tradition. In making such an award to Mrs. Dunnett incidental acknowledgement would also be made of her five 'Lymond' novels [...] [Dunnett's] book as a whole gives abundant evidence of very deep and wide research and it conveys to the reader a very vivid feeling for the whole period and way of life in the Scotland and the Europe of the eleventh century.[82]

In defending the novel's genre, Graham reveals that he believed particular genres of fiction ('historical romance or fantasy') would not be taken seriously for the award or might even be ruled out because of their form or style, unwittingly foreshadowing the kind of debates about the literary value and merit of genre fiction which the Society's Literary Awards – and many other book awards – have to this day.[83] It also shows how he positioned his selection in relation to the major Scottish writer Sir Walter Scott, perhaps in order to further legitimise his decision.

The presentation of the 1982 Book of the Year Award was made just six weeks after Scott requested copies of nominated books for the judging panel, a timeline which again indicates the panel had little time to read – or reread – the seven books shortlisted for the award. On Tuesday, 16 November, RBS issued a press release announcing that Alasdair Gray was awarded the inaugural 'Saltire Society and Royal Bank Scottish Literary Award' for his debut novel *Lanark* at a ceremony held at the RBS offices in Edinburgh.[84] The press release stated that 'the panel of judges was impressed by the high standard of entries and was also conscious of the difficulty of judging between works of fiction, drama, poetry and biography' (a difficulty acknowledged throughout the history of the Society's Book of the Year Award).[85] The release also noted that, on making the announcement of the winner, Literary Award judge David Daiches said that '*LANARK* was unanimously considered by the judges to show a remarkable imaginative power which gave a new dimension to the modern Scottish novel'.[86] During the ceremony, Dorothy Dunnett was 'commended' for her 'powerful and persuasive historic novel', *King Hereafter*, which was 'based on deep research', and Robert McLellan's *Collected Plays* received 'a special mention in overdue recognition of McLellan's great contribution to modern drama in Scots' (there is no evidence to suggest that Dunnett and McLellan's commendations came with any monetary or physical prize).[87] Comments from the award sponsor, RBS, came from the company's executive director Jack Kirkland, who stated that he had 'been aware that The Saltire Society have for some time been anxious to introduce such a Literary Award and we at The Royal Bank are happy to join them in fulfilling this desire'.[88] Kirkland continued, noting that RBS was 'attracted to the aims of the Award insofar as it provides recognition for a Scottish author or a book with a Scottish theme. We are particularly pleased that this Award acknowledges the work of writers, [whose] contribution to the Arts is so often forgotten.'[89]

The ceremony, and resultant press release, indicates what the Society wanted their Literary Award to represent. In selecting *Lanark*, which was described as 'unconventional'[90] and was compared to James Joyce's *Ulysses* on its publication,[91] the judges appeared to be celebrating and awarding innovation and experimentation. However, the commendation for Dunnet's historical novel reiterates the Society's appreciation of texts demonstrative of traditional Scottish literature, history and research, echoing the kinds of texts the Society had rewarded in the past. Furthermore, the commendation for Robert McLellan's *Collected Plays* is stated to have been grounded upon 'overdue recognition' for McLellan's overall 'contribution' to Scottish literature, as opposed to the specific book nominated for the award. The singling out of these three texts and the explanatory cases made for their selection mirrors the Society's constitutional aims of 'look[ing] to the past only to move forward' and 'seek[ing] to revive the memory of famous men and to make Scots conscious of their heritage'.[92] In endorsing both *Lanark*, an experimental and thoroughly modern novel, and *King Hereafter*, a historical novel based upon Scotland's monarchical history, the Society's Literary Award judges encapsulated the duality of the Society's self-proclaimed role of being both conscious of Scottish tradition *and* modern developments. Likewise, in commending McLellan's work, the judges explicitly stated that they did indeed seek to 'revive the memory' of his work.

Newspaper reports of the 1982 awards ceremony described Gray, who was present to accept his award, as 'a man of few words'.[93] According to one report,

> Alasdair rose from his seat, said: 'Thank you', and sat back down again! His brevity was commended by the society's chairman, Paul Scott, but at a reception afterwards [Gray] confided in me that he had, in fact, had a longer speech in mind. He had written two sentences but, at the last moment, decided to cut down even that. 'Really, just a waste of words. A heartfelt "thank you" says it all.'[94]

This particular report of the inaugural Book of the Year Award ceremony continues, making a particularly interesting, yet erroneous, critique of the Society:

> In announcing the award Professor David Daiches [...] commented that the panel of judges had been impressed by the high standard of entries, but that 'Lanark' had been a unanimous choice. [...] Strange as it may seem it has taken nearly half a century to award that first literary prize. When the [...] Society was founded some 50 years ago one of their aims was to establish a 'Scottish Book of the Year' award, but they never got round to it until the Royal Bank stepped in to offer £1000 for each of the next three years.[95]

Exactly where this inaccurate assertion about the Society's failure to found a book award (and the insinuation that the newly instated Book of the Year Award was instigated by RBS) comes from is unclear. The publication of such incorrect information – in an article about the Society's inaugural Book of the Year Award ceremony, no less – is once again demonstrative of how the Society's failure to clearly articulate its literary award history impeded effectual reporting and promotion of the Book of the Year Award.

Following the presentation of the 1982 award, there was little respite for Scott and the Book of the Year Award. Just eight weeks later in early 1983, Scott invited a new group of people to become the judging panel for the award. Scott wrote to Angus Calder (who was longlisted for the 1982 award), Ian Campbell, Douglas Gifford, Allan Massie and Isobel Murray on Friday, 14 January, to invite them to be on the judging panel for the Book of the Year Award in 1983. In this letter, Scott assured everyone that 'the nomination system limits the number of books which the Panel has to consider and the task is not therefore too onerous'.[96] All but Massie agreed to join the panel, with the writer and civil servant James Allan Ford remaining on the panel in Massie's place.

It is unclear exactly why Scott decided to change the panel following the 1982 award. While this indicates that Scott was attempting to instil the establishment of a fresh judging panel annually, the fact that several of the people who became judges in 1983 went on to serve as judges for many years – with some remaining on the panel for two or three decades – undermines this. After joining the panel in 1983, Calder was on the panel for 16 years, leaving in 1998; Murray was a member until 2005; Gifford served on the panel until 2010; and Campbell was a member of the judging panel until 2017. The only member of the 1983 panel who did not continue as a judge was James Allan Ford. Further cementing the established status quo, once Scott stood down from his position as convenor of the Society's Literary Awards judging panel in 1994, Gifford and Campbell took up the position of co-chairs, alternating the role year on year. On Gifford's departure, Campbell took up the post exclusively until he stepped down and was replaced by the former literary editor of the *Scotsman*, David Robinson, in 2016 (although in Robinson's first year Campbell was a 'shadow' chair alongside Robinson).[97]

Another important feature of the judging panel established in 1983 is that it was a predominantly academic group. Campbell, Gifford, Murray and Calder were all academics who specialise in Scottish literature. Campbell wrote extensively on Victorian and modern Scottish literature; Gifford published works evaluating twenty-first century Scottish literature; and Murray edited a number of editions of Oscar Wilde's poetry and short fiction, as well as editing the work of Naomi Mitchison and writing a biography on the Scottish author Jessie Kesson.[98] Similarly, Calder was a historian, who published works discussing Britain's political history as well as editing works by writer Hugh MacDiarmid.[99] While not an academic, James Allan Ford still had substantial literary credentials in Scotland. He was the author of five novels,[100] President of Scottish PEN from 1980 to 1986 and a trustee of the National Library of Scotland.[101] As already discussed in relation to the Society's Book of the Year Award, in selecting this particular group of people, who held numerous scholarly and professional credentials as well as publications relating to Scottish literature, Scott was trying to instil a reputation for the award as an authoritative indicator of quality Scottish literature, and was drawing from, or relying on, the panels' academic, cultural and social capital – and the Society's legacy in largely academic panels – in order to do this. Scott has since repeated that this was part of his motivation when founding the award. In 2013, Scott stated that the award's 'initial purpose was not just to encourage the writers and pat them on the back, but it was to draw attention to the fact that Scottish literature was serious and important', and the selection of judges demonstrated this.[102] As both English and Driscoll have argued, judges bring with them their own social and cultural capital that can be shared with, and bolstered by, their association with an award. As Driscoll explains (quoting English),

> Judges, through their own symbolic capital and through their chosen winners, are significant determinants of a prize's reputation and influence on the field. English is perceptive on this point: 'it is the first axiom among prize administrators that the prestige of a prize is reciprocally dependent on the prestige of its judges'.[103]

Accordingly, the way in which the Saltire Society Book of the Year Award was administered in the early 1980s, particularly in terms of the nomination and judging processes, was inherently connected to its purpose as a response to what Scott perceived as a systemic lack of interest in, and appreciation for, Scottish literature. The nomination procedure and judge selection in the early award's early years, then, aimed to legitimise the Society's claim to be an arbiter of Scottish literature.

Highs and Lows: 1990s–2000s

The Saltire Society and Royal Bank Scottish Literary Award continued as an annual award, awarding authors such as Edwin Morgan, Tom Leonard, Norman MacCaig and Muriel Spark, until RBS withdrew their sponsorship in 1987 (see the appendix for a full list of Scottish Book of the Year Award winners). In a letter sent to the Society on Monday, 11 May 1987, M. G. Keohane, the head of group public relations at RBS, stated that '6 years support of the [Book of the Year] award could be viewed as reasonable' and indicated RBS's intention of ending their sponsorship of the award.[104] The Society's President and former literary award judge and Book of the Year Award winner, David Daiches, was disappointed and seemingly surprised by this news. Writing to RBS's chairman Sir Michael Herries in July 1987, Daiches asked whether it would be possible for RBS to reconsider its decision, noting that the Society would be 'deeply sorry' to lose 'this unique and important award'.[105] Although Daiches's response came two months after the letter from RBS, his suggestion that losing RBS's support would lead to the loss of the award indicates that the Society was not in a position to take over covering the cost of the award upon themselves. In his response, Herries reiterated that the decision to withdraw sponsorship was 'only taken after considerable discussions and deliberation by the Executive of the Bank'.[106] Herries stated, however, that there 'may be other ways in which [RBS] may be able to help you' and requested a member of the Society's offices to contact him for more information.[107]

Paul Henderson Scott soon began pursuing other avenues of sponsorship and, by December 1987, he was already in discussions with the *Scotsman* regarding a potential sponsorship deal. In a letter to a representative from the *Scotsman* sent on Wednesday, 2 December, Scott stated that he was 'naturally very pleased that there is a possibility that the *Scotsman* might take on the sponsorship of the Saltire book award'.[108] He continued, stating that he felt the Society could 'ask for [a] no more suitable sponsor' and that the two organisations could 'work together very effectively to develop the award as an important part of the Scottish literary scene'.[109] With this letter, Scott enclosed a selection of press releases from past years and information about the financial cost of sponsorship of the award:

> Initially the award was for £1,000, but the Royal Bank increased this to £1,500 three years ago. The only other costs have been £200 annually [...] towards the expenses of administration [of] the award ceremony. The members of the Awards Panel have given their services free [...] we have kept administrative costs to the bare minimum.[110]

In highlighting to this potential sponsor that the administration costs of the award had been kept to a 'bare minimum', Scott sought to make the award seem like a valuable financial investment. He demonstrated this further by comparing the Society's award to the 'MacVittie [*sic*] award' which, Scott claimed, 'is a good deal more lavish than this'.[111] The award Scott was here referring to was the McVitie's Prize for Scottish Writer of the Year (a brief history of which is given in the Introduction of this book). When Scott wrote this letter in 1987, the prize fund for the McVitie's Prize was £5,000, which was doubled to £10,000 in 1992. Scott also wrote that a 'P.R. firm has been paid [by McVitie] to handle the publicity and they have been entertaining on some scale' and that he believed the McVitie's panel members 'have been paid a fee'.[112] However, Scott assured Allan that he did not believe it was necessary for the Society's award to 'emulate any of this'. Instead, Scott proclaimed:

> After fifty years of award schemes in various fields, a certain prestige attaches to the Saltire name which more than compensates for a lot of

P.R. razamataz [*sic*]. The award might be increased in value to keep up with the Joneses, but I do not think that this is essential.[113]

Such correspondence reveals how Scott framed the cultural and economic value of the Society's award – at least when discussing the award with a potential sponsor – in comparison to a similar award for Scottish literature. The McVitie's Prize for Scottish Writer of the Year was, in fact, remarkably similar to the Society's Book of the Year Award. Moreover, like the Society's award, the announcement of the McVitie's Prize was made in November, with journalists often coupling the winner announcements of each award in single articles or features about Scottish literature more broadly.[114] However, Scott argues that the key difference between the Society's award and the McVitie's Prize is the fact that the Society has the experience of 'fifty years of awards schemes', experience which, in Scott's opinion, carries with it a cultural kudos and prestige especially afforded to the Society precisely because of its longevity.[115] The fact that Scott articulates his opinion of the Society's award to a potential sponsor in this way was a deliberate accentuation of the Book of the Year Awards' established cultural value as a means of eschewing concerns regarding the financial commitment anticipated from the sponsor.[116]

Scott wrote to the Book of the Year judging panel – which still included Calder, Campbell, Gifford and Murray, and additional judges Derick Thomson (who joined the panel in 1984) and Alan Taylor (who joined in 1987) – in early February 1988 to tell them that the *Scotsman* had 'offered to sponsor the Book of the Year Award from the current year onwards'.[117] The terms of the sponsorship, Scott continued, would 'remain as last year with an award of £1,500' and an additional £1,000 for a Scottish New Writer of the Year Award for 'the author of the best first published book'. This award for 'the best first published book' would evolve into the Society's First Book of the Year Award, which is discussed in more detail in Chapter 3.[118] Four months later, the *Scotsman*'s then editor, Magnus Linklater (who became the President of the Society in 2011), was also 'prepared to act as one of the judges'.[119] Records suggest that it was the *Scotsman* who suggested that Linklater become a judge for the award, and Scott was seemingly open to the suggestion, despite the obvious potential conflict of interest this could lead to. However, despite this suggestion, there is no evidence to suggest that Linklater did in fact serve as a member of the judging panel between 1988 and 1989.

The *Scotsman* continued to be an active, and opinionated, sponsor in these early months. In December 1988, Simon Berry, the features editor for the *Scotsman*, wrote to Scott to make a number of suggestions regarding the Book of the Year Awards' schedule, stating that he hoped Scott would 'be able to persuade the [judging panel] of the wisdom of the changes'.[120] These 'changes' included

> a change in the timing, so that winners are announced in early *January* and the *shortleets in mid-November* (n. b. the Whitbread shortlist this year was Nov. 8th) [*sic*]. This will allow your panel a little more time to select the winners, and we can promote the shortleets more effectively to the book trade over Xmas. [...] The shortleets will be nominated by literary editors (a maximum of 2 in each category) and the Panel from all titles received for review by Oct. 31st 1989; the Panel might be extended next year by an extra member who is an imaginative writer, also one member might become due for retirement each year (with the possibility of being invited back in future years).[121]

Berry's suggestions are noteworthy because they indicate that he has spotted the kind of structural problems with the award – most notably the lack of rotation of judges – that would continue to plague the Society and its Literary Awards for many years to come. Furthermore, in mentioning the practices of the well-known Whitbread Awards (now known as the Costa Book Awards), it seems Berry is trying to offer an example of best practice which, he suggests, the Society might want to imitate to maximise the impact of the award. This correspondence reveals how much consideration the *Scotsman* was putting into its sponsorship of the Book of the Year Award, and hints at some of the sponsor's trepidation as to whether the Society was really optimising the potential for the award. Significant, too, is the suggestion that the awards could be more effectively marketed to the book trade since, as Driscoll argues, 'the very structure of the literary prize render it a suitable media object'.[122] Indeed, the profile-raising potential of awards is often considered to be one of their key attributes for sponsors in particular.

These suggestions, however, were not taken on board by Scott and other members of the judging panel. Writing to the panel on Wednesday, 21 December 1988, Scott explained Berry's proposal to change the timeline by which the Book of the Year Award was organised.[123] While he acknowledged that the movement of the announcement of the winner from November to January would 'give us more time [and] enable the Award to make the maximum impact during the main book buying season', Scott expressed apprehension with the proposal to change the closing date for nominations to 31 October, stating that it would 'run the risk of making us work in too much of a rush', since, according to Berry's suggestion, the shortlists for the award would be announced in mid-November.[124] While Scott's concern about this quick turnaround from submission deadline to the announcement of a shortlist is understandable, the fact that he did not suggest negotiating the submission deadline date with his fellow judges suggests he was not keen on rescheduling the award's timeline at all. Berry's suggestions received mixed reviews from the panel. Derick Thomson[125] and Isobel Murray[126] wrote to Scott and indicated their concern with arranging a panel meeting to select a winner in January, with both suggesting that organising a post-Christmas and New Year panel meeting would be extremely difficult.

Scott also noted how the *Scotsman* were 'considering the introduction of a new category for books on poetry', but Angus Calder was not convinced that this was a good idea:

> I'm a bit worried about the idea of a special award for poetry *criticism*, if that is what 'books on poetry' means. I'd be against a special award for books of poetry, since it would presumably ensure that the main prize always went to a work of prose. I'm glad that the award has been given in the past so as to acknowledge the excellence of much recent Scottish verse, and wouldn't want to see poetry 'ghettoised'. The Whitbread doesn't do that, nor does the W H Smith.[127]

Although the confusion as to whether this new award would be for a book *of* or *on* poetry was cleared up by Scott, who confirmed it was for a 'book of (not on) poetry', Calder's response is nonetheless interesting.[128] First, it was the second time that a proposal for a separate award for poetry was made. As discussed earlier, in the Society's 1937 annual report, it was suggested that an award for poetry be founded, but this suggestion was never pursued. Second, Calder's response to the idea of a new award for poetry indicates that he favoured the Book of the Year Award's open remit which pitted books of (or on) poetry against all types of writing, including prose. This resistance to so-called 'ghettoising' particular forms of writing by creating specific awards has also been expressed on a number of occasions by the Society and its Literary Award judges in relation to Gaelic language books. While concerns have been raised by the panel as to whether the adjudication of Gaelic language books alongside English or Scots language books is fair, since the number of judges who can read Gaelic is limited, there has always been reluctance to create a separate award for Gaelic writing precisely because of this perceived 'ghettoisation'.[129] Finally, Calder's letter revealed how the Society's Literary Award judges did not have a full understanding of other literary awards. Calder's disinclination towards a new award for poetry is partly based on his belief that the Whitbread (Costa) Awards did not award books in multiple categories, but this was incorrect. Since the founding of the Whitbread (Costa) Awards in 1971, it has included three awards: poetry, biography and novel. It also introduced children's book and first book categories in 1972 and 1975, respectively. In fact, the multicategory setup of the Costa Book Awards was used in a 2014 report to exemplify how the Society's Literary Awards may be better organised.[130] This report, along with the introduction of a Poetry Book of the Year Award in partnership with the Scottish Poetry Library in 2014, led to a complete restructuring of the Society's Literary Awards (which is discussed in more detail presently).[131]

On Tuesday, 1 March 1988, Scott wrote to the entire judging panel stating that 'the proposals in my letter of 21 December 1988 have not been generally welcomed'.[132] However, Scott continued to state that the *Scotsman* wanted to 'announce the new arrangements fairly soon' and that they had made 'two additional suggestions [...] that John Prebble should be invited to join the Panel after the short leet [*sic*] stage [and] that there should be some rotation in the membership of the panel'.[133] The judges had quite divergent opinions on these suggestions. According to Calder, the introduction of Prebble – a historian, journalist and documentarian well known for his research in Scottish history – was an 'excellent idea – raising [the awards'] profile, and also bringing in someone who is not involved in Scottish literary politics like the rest of us!'[134] But with regard to the rotation of the panel, Calder was 'agnostic', arguing that 'continuity of the panel membership indicate[d] the commitment of all involved'.[135] Isobel Murray also felt that adding Prebble to the panel following the shortlisting stage sounded 'fine' and that rotation of the panel seemed 'very reasonable', although she acknowledged that she 'enjoy[ed] and valu[ed] the yearly experience' of reading for the award.[136] Ian Campbell, on the other hand, was against both the inclusion of Prebble and introducing regular rotation of judging panel members, stating:

> I see no real advantage in a new member joining us at the leet stage – quite the reverse – but if the Scotsman put it forward strongly it seems unnecessarily obstructive not to accept gracefully. [...] Some rotation is no bad thing; though I think [...] that it has worked well with the stability of membership building up some expertise and some experience of the ground rules, the actual experience of running a competition like this, among people who have come to know one another. [...] There would be a case for keeping the same group a year or two longer, I think. Our range is such that an impartiality is not so difficult to achieve.[137]

Although Campbell suggests that some rotation 'is no bad thing', he in fact goes on to explain why he feels the 'stability' of the panel over the years has been beneficial to the award (such panel stability has also been associated with the oft-professed 'integrity' of the Society's Literary Award judging panel members, which is explored in Chapter 6). This – along with Campbell's preference to avoid inviting Prebble to join the panel after the shortlist was already decided (although he was seemingly willing to capitulate on this for the sake of a good relationship with the *Scotsman*) – indicates that Campbell was in fact reluctant to change the Society's Literary Awards judging panel. As the longest serving judge and former chair of the Literary Awards panel, Campbell's hesitancy to modify or develop the Society's Literary Awards is perhaps the main reason why panel rotation was stunted, and the general administration of the prize did not really change or develop. As will be discussed here and in relation to the Society's other literary awards, when Scott retired from the panel and took a lesser role in the Society's activities, Campbell and co-chair Douglas Gifford only ever sought to maintain the management of the Society's Literary Awards as opposed to seeking developments which may have advanced the awards and their role and standing in Scottish literature. Even though the Saltire Society Literary Awards judging panel spent months discussing whether John Prebble should be invited to join the panel, and the lack of rotation of existing panel members, through 1989, little changed in the organisation and adjudication processes of the awards between 1989 and 1994 (when the *Scotsman*'s sponsorship of the awards ended). There was, however, a major change in how the award would be sponsored during this period.

In 1990, STV became a joint sponsor of the Society's Book of the Year and First Book of the Year Awards, alongside the *Scotsman*. The prize funds for each was increased to £5,000 (from £1,500) and £1,500 (from £1,000), respectively. Writing to congratulate Sorley McLean, the winner of the 1990 Book of the Year Award, in January 1991, Scott stated that the award was 'sponsored by *The Scotsman* and *Scottish Television*'.[138] Scott also informs McLean that the awards ceremony, which was held on Thursday, 31 January 1991, would be 'covered by radio and television'.[139] Two years later, STV and the *Scotsman* were still sharing the sponsorship of the awards and were seemingly alternating the presentation of the Book of the Year Award, or the so-called main award. In a letter to Kathleen Munro, the Society's administrator, written in January 1993, Ian Campbell noted that 'STV are anxious that it's "their turn" to present the main award'.[140] Although STV and the *Scotsman* were seemingly co-sponsoring the awards in the early 1990s, there is little to suggest that there was any interaction between the two organisations regarding this relationship. It seems all organisation of the sponsorship criteria, including the negotiation of the alternating presentation of the Book of the Year Award, was facilitated through the Society. In February 1994, however, the managing director of STV, Gus MacDonald, wrote to the editor of the *Scotsman*, Magnus Linklater, and the editor of the *Herald*, Arnold Kemp, questioning whether – as sponsors and promoters of Scotland's various literary awards – they could 'perhaps co-operate to pull them together into an event which becomes the Booker of the north of the Border'.[141] This idea of the awards being brought together to create a kind of Booker Prize event equivalent in Scotland is important for two reasons. First, it brings to the fore issues raised in the introduction of this book and dealt with in more detail in Chapter 6 regarding the use of the Booker Prize in the media, in academic literature and by prize administrators and sponsors themselves as a benchmark by which to measure and compare literary prizes. This, as discussed in Chapter 6, contributes to a literary prize hierarchy which creates unfair expectations based on exceptional prize circumstances, such as the level of media coverage and renown prizes like the Booker Prize acquire. The second reason why Kemp's suggestion is important, and it is related to the first, is the fact that there is an insinuation that the three existing prizes for Scottish literature would need to be brought together to have the chance of generating the kind of public profile and interest that the Booker Prize manages on its own, a point which once again reiterates the idea of a literary prize hierarchy.

Two weeks after receiving Kemp's letter, Linklater forwarded the proposition to Paul Henderson Scott, stating: 'I don't know what your reaction would be to this but we could not possibly take it any further if the Saltire Society was unenthusiastic', indicating the Society's role in this venture was important.[142] Linklater continued, suggesting that

> the advantages would be a higher profile, more money etc. The disadvantages might be a diluting of the Saltire involvement. It might be better not to rule it out altogether at this stage but to make a few more enquiries to see what might be involved.[143]

In response to this proposal, Scott wrote to Linklater and the head of public affairs at STV, David Whitton (who had already contacted Scott to say that STV were 'quite keen to explore' this idea), noting that he had 'long thought that there would be advantages in one combined award which might attract more attention than the present diversity'.[144] Scott continued, hypothesising as to how such collaboration might work:

> [The award] could perhaps have a number of categories (say fiction, non-fiction, poetry and first book) to reduce the difficulty of making rational choice between books of very different kinds. In fact, when [United Biscuits (UB)] launched the McVittie [sic] Award in close imitation of the Saltire Award, I suggested [...] that we should combine forces. For their own commercial reasons, they preferred to go it alone. They argued (and it is a fair point) that a diversity of awards was good

for Scottish writing because it meant that more writers had a chance of recognition. Possibly UB might not be more interested in co-operation because they have lost the support of the BBC and their recent awards have not been well received.[145]

These comments indicate that Scott believed the founders and sponsors of the McVitie's Scottish Writer of the Year Award may have used the Society's Literary Awards as an exemplar when establishing the award. The similar terms of eligibility of the two awards meant there was often crossover of shortlisted and winning authors and – while open to the suggestion of merging the Society's Literary Awards with the McVitie's Prize and the Scottish Arts Council's literary awards – Scott made it clear that the Society was unwilling to compromise its own methods of adjudication: 'the Saltire method of judging has produced results which have met with general approval and I suggest that this tried and proved format should be maintained'.[146]

Members of the Society's Literary Awards judging panel were much more sceptical of this proposal. Writing to Kathleen Munro in March 1994, Derick Thomson, who had been a member of the panel intermittently since 1985, questioned the motives of STV's proposal and suggested that they should be dropped as a sponsor altogether:

> I have little doubt that STV are looking for a high-profile, down-market situation, with a smaller financial input from their company, and small regard for the ultimate literary consequences. [...] What STV proposes, it seems to me, might make better TV but [does] nothing to enhance the real value and purpose of the Saltire awards. Might it not be better to look for a new sponsor, especially since the Scotsman seems supportive of the Saltire's individual position?[147]

Echoing Scott's prioritisation of the Society's administration and adjudication, Thomson also stated that he 'hope[d] the Saltire Society [would] not easily surrender its prestigious prize, and well-considered methodology'.[148]

Despite the concerns raised by the panel members, by July 1994, David Whitton was writing to Scott to confirm STV's co-sponsorship of the Society's Literary Awards for the upcoming year.[149] The plan, as described by Whitton, was for a pre-recorded 'Book Award programme' to be broadcast on STV on St Andrew's night in November 1994.[150] An invitation to an Evening of Book Awards confirms that the combined ceremony – which included the announcement of the winner of the 1994 McVitie's Scottish Writer of the Year Prize (Janice Galloway's *Foreign Parts*, 1994) and the Society's Book of the Year Award (George MacKay Brown's *Beside the Ocean of Time*, 1994) and

First Book of the Year Award (Andrew Crumey's *Music in a Foreign Language*, 1994) – took place on Monday, 28 November, in Edinburgh and was broadcast on STV on St Andrew's night (Wednesday, 30 November 1994). There is no documentation to provide exact reasoning for the Society's final decision to be involved with this award's night, but the Society might have believed the benefits – and journalistic capital – of this kind of exposure and collegiality would outweigh the potential negative effects of the Society's Literary Awards being overshadowed or presented in a 'down-market' way.

It was fitting that the 1994 Saltire Society Literary Awards would receive so much coverage, since it would be the last year that Paul Henderson Scott acted as convenor of the Society's Literary Awards panel. This role was handed over to Scott's fellow judge, Douglas Gifford, who had been on the panel since 1983. When writing to Gifford to thank him for taking on the role, Scott also revealed that STV had withdrawn their sponsorship for the Society's Literary Awards, but that Derick Thomson had secured funding of £1,500 for the First Book of the Year Award through *Gairm*, a literary magazine co-founded and edited by Thomson.[151] STV, it seemed, were still interested in helping to promote the awards and confirmed that they intended to include the announcement of the Society's Book of the Year and First Book of the Year Awards at another televised awards ceremony in November 1995.

Gifford's tenure as chair of the Society's Literary Award panel was shared with Ian Campbell, with the men establishing a system by which they would alternate assuming the role each year. Accordingly, Campbell became chair of the panel to the 1996 awards. As part of the handover to Campbell, in January 1996, Munro wrote to Gifford and Campbell to highlight some of the areas of the Society's Literary Awards that required attention. As well as confirming sponsors for the awards, Munro also noted that 'the procedure for selection is a farce: *we* need to work on this' and suggested that the chair should 'find out names of Literary Editors or equivalent' and 'send information [about the awards] to them'.[152] Munro's frustration stemmed from the fact that the nomination and selection process had become bloated and confused, with the introduction of nominations from publishers in the early 1990s only adding to the confusion. In 1995, for example, all but one of the 35 nominations made for the Book of the Year Award had come from the members of the panel or sponsors, despite the fact that nominations were meant to be coming from publishers and literary editors.[153] Munro, Gifford and Campbell worked to resolve this for the 1996 awards, and the imbalance in nominations for the 1996 Book of the Year Award was moderately improved: of the 55 books nominated for the 1996 awards, 37 came from panel members, 10 came from publishers and 8 came from the editors of literary magazines or the literary section of newspapers.[154]

As well as making some progress in the expansion of the narrow field of nominators for the Book of the Year Award during 1996, Campbell was keen to improve the marketing of the awards. In a letter to Munro, Campbell notes a series of issues that were raised at a meeting of the Literary Awards panel, which once again evidenced the propensity to compare the success of the Society's Literary Awards in relation to other prizes. Campbell notes that the panel felt

> the publicity for the short leet, its announcement and its general visibility round the bookshops is disappointing compared to the McVitie prize. We should investigate ways of raising money to try to do more to draw the Saltire award to public attention, in bookshops and in newspapers, radio and TV.[155]

A method of mitigating this, which Campbell admitted was inspired by the McVitie's marketing campaign, was through the production of posters and stickers 'bearing the Saltire award shortlist message'.[156] Campbell's comparison to the McVitie's Prize, and his aim for the Society to replicate this, indicates that the McVitie's Prize was effective in its marketing and promotion, utilising techniques such as 'produc[ing] stickers for book covers [...] and also prepar[ing] point of sale material for retailers' use in bookshops'.[157] There is, however, no evidence that such suggestions led to a concerted marketing campaign from the Society for the Literary Awards in 1996, and stickers to promote the Saltire Society's Literary Award shortlists would not be introduced until 2014.

Turn of the Century: 2000s

Campbell was right to be concerned about the visibility of the Society's Literary Awards. The publicity boost the Society's Literary Awards had received during the mid-1990s via the televised broadcast of the awards began to peter out by 1997. Moreover, the loss of the *Scotsman* as a key sponsor in 2000 signified the beginning of a sustained period of uncertainty and financial difficulties for the Society's award.[158] Between 2000 and 2004, the Society failed to secure sponsorship for the Book of the Year Award and used their own reserves to absorb the cost of running the award and the prize purse, which still stood at £5,000. In 2004, the Faculty of Advocates, an Edinburgh-based independent body for Scottish legal advocates and QCs, took over the sponsorship of the Book of the Year Award,[159] providing the Society with £8,000 – £5,000 for the award prize, £2,000 towards the cost of the awards ceremony and £1,000 towards the administration of the award.[160] This partnership came to an end three years later in February 2007. Echoing the earliest Book of the Year Awards presented by the Society in the 1930s and 1950s, this period of sporadic finance and general instability continued through the late 2000s and into the early 2010s, with the Society covering the costs of the Book of the Year Award in the years it could not secure sponsorship. The major difference being that, unlike in the earliest years, when the awards would be stalled or put on hiatus due to a lack of monetary reserves and few personnel to help run the awards, by the 2000s the Society's Literary Awards were arguably so well established and recognised as part of Scotland's literary events calendar that the Society was perhaps obliged to continue bestowing Literary Awards despite significant financial backing.

The lack of financial support for the award throughout the 2000s was such that in 2009 the Society sent a statement, under the title 'The Scottish Book of the Year Axed', to all 'interested parties' (including Society members, publishers, journalists and writers) asserting that without financial backing the Society's Book of the Year Award would not be able to continue:

> Unless the Saltire Society finds financial support for its Scottish Book of the Year Award before March 2009, there will be no award presentation in 2009.
>
> We are desperately looking for a company, organisation or individual who would be willing to support this prestigious award for the next three years. We are open to suggestions and would greatly appreciate constructive help.[161]

This call to action was more successful than the Society may have anticipated, with the Scottish government stepping in to offer financial aid to the Book of the Year Award as part of Homecoming Scotland 2009, a programme of events held throughout Scotland in 2009 to encourage the Scottish diaspora. A Scottish government news release from November 2008 notes that the Culture Minister Linda Fabiani announced that the Society was to be given £25,000 of 'Homecoming Year sponsorship' for the following years' awards, increasing the prize fund for the Book of the Year Award to £10,000.[162] As part of this partnership, the Society created a subcategory of the Literary Awards, titled the 'Homecoming Award'. A government press release about the Homecoming Year campaign quoted Fabiani as saying:

> Scotland's rich heritage of literature and language is enjoyed by people all over the world, many of whom have developed their love and appreciation of this country from books about Scotland or written by

Scottish authors. This reflects one of the main themes of next year's Homecoming [...] The year of Homecoming will provide a unique opportunity for visitors to join in the celebration of all the great things Scotland has given to the world. So it's appropriate that for 2009 a special Homecoming award is being created that will enhance the profile of Scottish literature around the world.[163]

This goes some way to explaining how the government viewed the contribution the Society's Literary Awards could make to the Homecoming campaign, and the Homecoming shortlist certainly was representative of books about Scotland or written by Scottish authors. Five authors were shortlisted for the award: Robert Crawford's Robert Burns biography, *The Bard* (Jonathan Cape, 2009); Seamus Heaney's *The Testament of Cresseid and Seven Fables* (Faber, 2009), a modern English translation of work by the Scottish makar poet Robert Henryson; the radio and stage play *The Lamplighter* (Bloodaxe Books, 2008) written by Jackie Kay and broadcast on BBC Radio 3 in 2007; Esther Woolfson's *Piano Angel* (Two Ravens Press, 2008); and *A Passion for Nature: The Life of John Muir* by American historian Donald Worster (Oxford University Press, 2008). Two of these authors, Robert Crawford and Jackie Kay, had already won Saltire Society Literary Awards. Kay received the First Book of the Year Award in 1992 for her poetry collection *Adoption Papers*, and Crawford won the Research Book of the Year Award in 2007 for *Scotland's Books: The Penguin History of Scottish Literature*. Crawford would also go on to receive the Society's Book of the Year Award in 2009 for *The Bard*. Worster's *A Passion for Nature*, on the other hand, would go on to receive the £30,000 Scottish Mortgage Investment Trust (SMIT) Book of the Year Award in 2010, and Woolfson's *Piano Angel* was longlisted, alongside 156 other books, for the Impac Dublin Award in 2009.

The Scottish government's support for the Society's Literary Awards lasted for one year, and in 2010 the Society was once again left without the financial aid to sustain the Book of the Year Award. In the autumn of 2010, the Society launched an appeal, akin to what would now be recognised as a crowdfunding campaign, inviting its members to make donations towards the Book of the Year Award. The donation request form sent to Society members described the history of the award to date, testifying that '28 years on, the Saltire Society's Book of the Year Award is regarded as among the leading awards of its kind in Scotland' and asked members if they would 'help the Society sustain this vital award in 2010 and beyond'.[164] The campaign raised £2,870 towards the £10,000 required by the Society to run the Book of the Year Award.[165] The majority of donations ranged from £10 to £100, but there was one large donation of £1,000 from an anonymous donor.[166] Although this appeal failed to raise the full amount, the 2010 Book of the Year Award went ahead as usual, with the winning author, James Robertson, receiving £5,000 for his novel *And the Land Lay Still* (2010). However, this fraught, and somewhat unsuccessful, method of subsidising the award only sustained part of the award in 2010 – and the next year the Society was once again seeking new sponsorship, raising the amount sought from £10,000 to £12,250.[167]

Making Changes: 2010s and Beyond

The Society's failure to secure long-term funding and significant coverage for the Literary Awards was, it seemed, indicative of their difficulty in effectively publicising and sustaining its work more broadly, and concerns surrounding the future of the Society as a whole came to a head during this period. In March 2010, the Society commissioned its then chairman, Rt Hon Lord Cullen of Whitekirk, to conduct a strategic review of the Society's activities. The purpose of this review, published in 2011, was to assess the status of the Society, particularly in terms of its impact and public profile. One of the key issues identified in the report was the fact that the Society, and its suite of prizes, 'face[d] increasing competition from other newer awards which offer larger monetary prizes'.[168] A reference, perhaps, not only to major national awards like the Booker Prize and Costa Book Awards but also to other awards for Scottish literature, like the SMIT Book of the Year Awards, which offered four category winners – for fiction, non-fiction, poetry and first book – £5,000 and an overall winner, selected from these four winners, an additional £30,000.

The report of the Saltire Commission made a series of recommendations for the Society, with Cullen noting that 'we would not have made the recommendations […] if we had not been convinced that there is an important and distinctive role for the Society'.[169] The most significant recommendation made pertaining to the Literary Awards was that the Society 'should regularly review its awards, and consider whether there should be awards in additional areas'.[170] This suggestion was applied a few years later in 2014 when the administration and sponsorship of the Society's Book of the Year Award changed. Since 2014 (up until the time of writing), financial support for the Literary Awards has come largely from Creative Scotland. This partnership transpired a year after Creative Scotland discontinued its own series of literary awards – the SMIT Book of the Year Awards – in 2013 (see the introduction for more on these awards). The SMIT became the title sponsor of Creative Scotland's (then the Scottish Arts Council) literary awards in 2009, and the awards included Fiction, Non-Fiction, First Book and Poetry Book of the Year categories.[171] Creative Scotland's investment in the Society's Literary Awards was astute, since it enabled them to continue supporting Scottish literature through prize-giving without having the responsibility of prize administration,

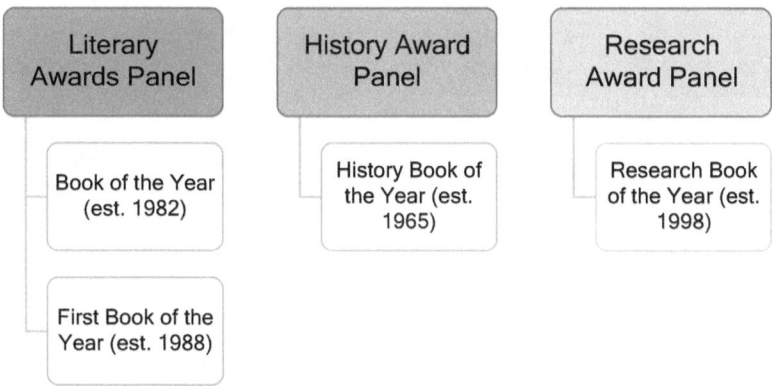

Figure 1 Saltire Society Literary Awards judging panels, 1965–2013

the management of which remained with the Saltire Society. This new financial support, along with the introduction of the Scottish Poetry Library as sponsor of a separate Poetry Book of the Year Award in 2014, made it possible for the Society to change the way in which their literary awards were structured.

Since the introduction of the Society's Research Book of the Year Award in 1998, the Society had presented four prizes within its suite of Literary Awards: Book of the Year, First Book of the Year, History Book of the Year, and Research Book of the Year. The Book of the Year and First Book of the Year Award longlists, shortlists and winners were decided by the Literary Awards panel, with the History and Research Book of the Year Awards each having its own judging panel (see Figure 1).

The introduction of the Poetry Book of the Year Award in 2014 brought with it a new judging panel specifically for the award. Since poetry had originally been included within the remit of the Book of the Year Award (or First Book of the Year Award for debut titles), the Society decided to retitle the Book of the Year Award to Literary Book of the Year Award to encompass the fiction and non-fiction books that would still be considered under this category (see Figure 2).

The winner of each category – including Literary Book of the Year, First Book of the Year, Poetry Book of the Year, History Book of the Year, and Research Book of the Year – received £2,000 and, much like the SMIT Book of the Year Awards, the category winners for each award became the shortlist for the 'overall' Book of the Year Award, the winner of which received an additional £10,000. However, by 2015 it was decided that the Literary Book of the Year Award should be expanded yet again, leading to the creation of

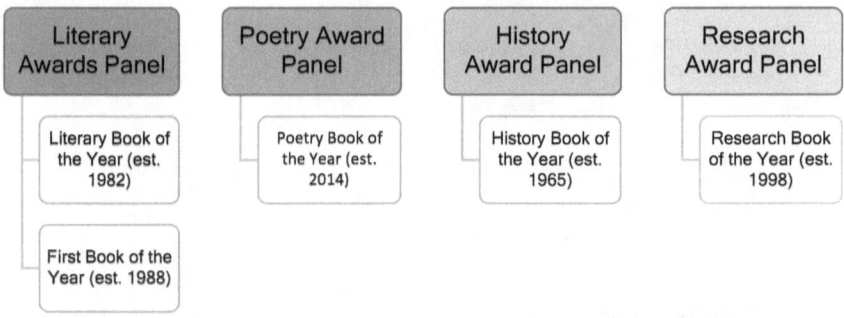

Figure 2 Saltire Society Literary Awards judging panel, 2014

Figure 3 Saltire Society Literary Awards judging panels, 2015 onwards

two new categories: Fiction Book of the Year, and Non-Fiction Book of the Year. As illustrated in Figure 3, while the categories for the Society's Literary Awards were expanded, the judging panel set-up remained largely unchanged. Furthermore, although the category winners have received £2,000 each year since 2015, the prize fund for the 'overall' Book of the Year Award winner has diminished year on year. In 2015 the Book of the Year Award winner received £8,000 in addition to their £2,000 from the category win; this was reduced to £6,000 in 2016 and £3,000 in 2017. This once again rose to £6,000 for the 2018 award.

THE SCOTTISH BOOK OF THE YEAR

Given the inconsistent history of the Society's Book of the Year Award, during which, at its peak, it received significant financial and commercial support from sponsors like STV and RBS and, at its lowest, the Society implored with members to donate money to sustain the award, the most recent variations in the financial reward offered by the Saltire Society for the Book of the Year Award in the mid- to late 2010s are perhaps unsurprising. The Society has had to adapt its longest-running book awards over the years in order to maintain a sustainable presence within Scottish literary culture. Coming from confused and, at times, disorganised beginnings, the Society's Book of the Year Award has evolved into a 'major cultural milestone in Scotland's year', as one publisher put it.[172] While, as the subsequent chapters will illustrate, the Book of the Year Awards' vulnerabilities are not unique, of all of the Society's Literary Awards it is the one with the longest history, being reincarnated and saved from obsolescence over and over again. The determination of the Society's personnel and judges to keep the award going over the years is what has made it the award what it is today. As other prizes for Scottish literature, such as the McVitie's Prize and the SMIT Book of the Year Awards, have come and gone, the Society's Book of the Year Award has defied the odds and endured. Yet, this history goes largely unknown. The Society has never effectively exploited this history of survival to create a cohesive narrative or identity for the award. Even though the Book of the Year Award no longer exists in the form in which it was originally founded, the fact that the current Literary Awards are heirs to this decades-old saga is critical to their current identity and status within contemporary Scottish literary culture. Unlike many other literary awards, what has made the Saltire Society's Literary Awards 'cultural milestone[s]' in Scottish literary and publishing culture is not their wealth or notoriety but their tenacity and longevity. However, as will be discussed in Part II, such longevity is not necessarily enough to sustain a prize's cultural, social and economic capital(s).

Chapter 3

THE SALTIRE SOCIETY FIRST BOOK OF THE YEAR AWARD

Prosperous Origins: 1980s

The founding of the Society's First Book of the Year Award was arguably the most significant, and certainly the most longstanding, development made possible by the prosperity the Society was experiencing through sponsors in the late 1980s. It was the introduction of the *Scotsman* as sponsor of the Book of the Year Award in 1988, following the cessation of Royal Bank of Scotland as sponsor in 1987, which brought the First Book of the Year Award into existence. Writing to the Book of the Year Award judging panel in February 1988 to inform them of the introduction of a new sponsor, Paul Henderson Scott also noted that the *Scotsman* had 'offered to sponsor the Saltire Award for the Scottish Book of the Year from the current year onwards' and wished to sponsor a new award for 'the Scottish New Writer of the Year for the author of the best first published book', which would have a prize purse of £1,000.[1] Literary Award judge Isobel Murray swiftly replied to Scott's letter to say that 'a separate award for the Scottish New Writer is a splendid development' and assured Scott she would keep this news confidential until its public announcement.[2] The nomination and judging process for the new award would be similar to that of the Book of the Year Award, with eligibility for the First Book of the Year Award determined by whether an author was Scottish-born, living in Scotland, of Scottish descent or that their book dealt 'with the work or life of a Scot or with a Scottish problem, event or situation'. Nominations would be invited from the literary editors of newspapers, literary magazines and journals, and judged by the Literary Awards panel, which in 1988 included Angus Calder, Ian Campbell, Douglas Gifford, Isobel Murray, Alan Taylor and Derick Thomson. Scott remained as chair of the panel. While the suggestion of the creation of an award for 'the best first published book' was enthusiastically welcomed by the judging panel, it is unclear as to exactly where the idea came from. There was mention of the founding of an award for 'first novels' noted in the Society's 1937 annual report, but this suggestion was swiftly dismissed and seemingly forgotten by the Society over the subsequent fifty years. However, Scott's correspondence with the judging panel indicated that the idea for a first book award came from the *Scotsman*, and the then literary editor of the *Scotsman*, Catherine Lockerbie (who would be literary editor until becoming director of the Edinburgh International Book Festival in 2001), would reiterate this ten years later in 1999, stating that the First Book of the Year Award was 'inaugurated' by the *Scotsman*.[3] It is therefore reasonable to surmise that the newspaper was responsible for bringing the award to fruition in the late 1980s.

By April 1988, information about this new award was widely circulated and a press release announcing the 'Scottish First Book by a New Author Award' was sent to the editor of a newly founded weekly Edinburgh newspaper the *Citizen*[4] and the newly appointed information officer of the Scottish Arts Council, Barbara Thomson.[5] A month later, Lorraine Fannin, the director of the Scottish Book Marketing Group,[6] confirmed with Scott that the Society could announce the winner of its 'New Author and Scottish Book of the Year Awards' during Scottish Book Fortnight which took place between 22 October and 6 November 1988.[7] The announcement of the winner of the inaugural 'Best First Book of the Year', therefore, was made alongside the announcement of the winner of the 1988 Book of the Year Award on Tuesday, 1 November. The winner, Raymond Vettese for his book *The Richt Noise and Ither Poems* (1988), received £1,000.[8]

Although the progress made from Scott's first letter to the Literary Award judges about a new literary award for first books to the conferral of the award seemed swift and uncomplicated, Vettese's win was not without complication. According to a short biography about Vettese written in 1995, he won the Society's inaugural First Book of the Year Award 'despite having failed to appear on the official shortlist' (this article also noted that the Society published Vettese's second poetry collection, *A Keen New Air*, in 1995).[9] Indeed, the Society's records indicate that Vettese was not included in the original list of nominations for the award,[10] as illustrated in Table 3.

While Vettese was not included in this internal list of nominations, he was included in the official announcement of the shortlist in the *Scotsman* on Monday, 17 October 1988. Vettese was one of six authors shortlisted for the award, alongside Ian Abbot, Robbie Kydd and Candia McWilliam. As well as two other authors who were not, in fact, included on the original list of nominations (Table 3) – John J. Graham for his debut novel *Shadowed Valley* (1987), and John Burnside for his first poetry collection *The Hoop* (1988).[11] This half-page article announcing the inaugural First Book of the Year Award shortlist (which, it is important to note, was published by the sponsor and originator of the award, the *Scotsman*) offered short biographical descriptions of

Table 3 Nominations for the inaugural First Book of the Year Award, 1988

Author	Title	Publisher/year	Nominator
Candia McWilliam	*A Case of Knives*	London: Bloomsbury, 1988	Unknown
Robbie Kydd	*Auld Zimmery*	Glasgow: Mariscat Press, 1987	*Scotsman*
Matthew Yorke	*The March Fence*	London: Viking, 1988	Unknown
John Burns	*A Celebration of the Light*	Edinburgh: Canongate, 1988	Unknown
Peter Whitebrook	*Staging Steinbeck*	London: Cassell, 1988	*Scotland on Sunday*
George Marshall	*In a Distant Isle*	Edinburgh: Scottish Academic Press, 1987	Unknown
Ian Abbot	*Avoiding the Gods*	Blackford: Chapman, 1988	*Inter-Arts* (Angus Calder)
Jim C. Wilson	*The Loutra Hotel*	Puttenham: Making Waves, 1988	*Chapman*

the authors shortlisted for the award, who were said to represent 'a very wide range of backgrounds, age groups and literary concerns'.[12]

In a seemingly candid article about the 1988 Literary Awards, award judge Angus Calder revealed that the decision to award Vettese the inaugural First Book of the Year Award was unanimous:

> This year we knew that our task might be more difficult than usual because a new award was to go to the best first book. But in practice our decision was almost instantaneous, despite several strong challengers. Raymond Vettese's book of poems, *The Richt Noise*, uses Scots with extraordinary power throughout, for polemical, lyrical and descriptive purposes.[13]

Although this account offers an insight into Vettese's win, there is actually very little further discussion of the First Book of the Year Award in this article. Calder dedicates just two short paragraphs to the First Book of the Year Award, even though this was the award's inaugural year. Far from being celebrated as a significant addition to the Society's series of literary awards, in Calder's article the information about the award for 'best first book' is dwarfed by a much lengthier discussion of the two books that shared the 1988 Book of the Year Award (Neal Ascherson's *Games with Shadows*, and Tom Nairn's *The Enchanted Glass*). This may seem innocuous but, as the history of the Society's First Book of the Year Award indicates, the award has often been considered as 'minor' in comparison to the slightly older, and historically more affluent, Book of the Year Award.

The Minor Award?: The 1990s

Even though the founding of the First Book of the Year Award was swift and largely uncomplicated – conditions made possible by the immediate guarantee of sponsorship for the award – the optimistic start to the award did not last for long. Correspondence between the judges during the months of adjudication for the 1989 Literary Awards indicates that there were some misgivings about the number, and quality, of books eligible for the First Book of the Year Award. In October 1989, the journalist and Literary Award judge Alan Taylor wrote to Scott suggesting that there was an 'embarrassing lack of choice as regards to first books'.[14] Taylor continued, stating:

> As far as I'm aware we have only two books that can legitimately be considered: James Meek's *MacFarlene* [sic] *Boils the Sea* and *The Quincunx* by Charles Palliser. Meek's is palpably a 'first' book [...] To award it a prize would be daft [...] *The Quincunx* is of a different order and if it's eligible then I would be of a mind to give Charles Palliser the booty straight away.[15]

Taylor also referred to Scott's own 'reservations' about the eligibility of *The Quincunx* since the novel's author, Charles Palliser, was American-born but working as a lecturer in literature at Strathclyde University in Glasgow. With regard to the final decision about Palliser's eligibility, Taylor conceded that he would be 'guided' by Scott's decision. Taylor also noted that if *The Quincunx* was deemed eligible, it should 'take the "First Book" categorie [sic] and also be *considered* for the "Book of the Year"' (emphasis in original).[16] Taylor here inferring that the Society's Literary Award judges were open to a 'first' book being shortlisted for the Book of the Year Award if it was deemed 'good enough'.[17]

The way in which Taylor discusses Meek's *MacFarlane Boils the Sea* and Palliser's *The Quincunx* sets the two novels in opposition to each other in terms of their literary quality. In stating that Meek's debut novel is 'palpably a "first" book', while simultaneously suggesting that Palliser's novel could not only win the First Book of the Year Award but should also be pitted against non-debut titles by established writers for the Book of the Year Award, Taylor implies that Meek is bested by Palliser because *MacFarlane Boils the Sea* is obviously a first book. The implication being that Meek's novel is not as accomplished as Palliser's and that Meek's inexperience is evident in the text. Similarly, Isobel Murray wrote to Scott to state some 'preliminary opinions' about the books they had been reading for the 1989 awards.[18] Three months before the award would be announced, Murray, like Taylor, commented on the 'few nominations' for the award, noting that there were only five at that point.[19] Murray continued, asking if, since there were only five books apparently in contention for the award, it would be possible to have a shortlist of five, which might give the panel 'more time for the much harder task of starting to trim the main entries'.[20] In the remainder of her letter to Scott, Murray discusses the books and authors nominated for the Book of the Year Award, returning to the First Book of the Year Award in the final paragraph of her letter to maintain that she views *The Quincunx* as 'a likely contender for the first book prize' and that she would 'rather see it considered for that prize than the big one'.[21] Murray's letter illustrates the comparison the judges often made between the First Book of the Year Award and the Book of the Year Award, insinuating that the former was subordinate to its longstanding counterpart. Murray does this twice in her letter to Scott: at the beginning, she refers to the Book of the Year Award as the 'main one' and, before signing off, 'the big one'.

Despite such favourable discussions about Palliser's *The Quincunx*, the second First Book of the Year Award was actually awarded to Sian Hayton for her novel *Cells of Knowledge* (1989). Informing Hayton of her award in January 1990, Scott noted that the award would be announced during a lunchtime ceremony at the University of Edinburgh on Wednesday, 31 January.[22] Scott continued, explaining that the editor of the *Scotsman*, Magnus Linklater, would present Hayton with a cheque for £1,000 at the ceremony.[23] Responding to Scott's invitation, Hayton wrote to the Society's administrator Kathleen Munro in order to accept the invitation and ask if her editor and friend, Dr Robyn Marsack, could also attend the ceremony as Hayton's guest.[24] Such correspondence demonstrates the extent to which many people involved with the Society's Literary Awards in the past, either directly or indirectly, have remained engaged with the Society and its Literary Awards for many years. Magnus Linklater became president of the Society in 2011, and Robyn Marsack, who was the director of the Scottish Poetry Library between 2000 and 2016, was one of the judges of the Society's Poetry Book of the Year Award when it was founded in 2014.

Following the conferral of the 1989 First Book of the Year Award in early 1990, the award benefitted from the introduction of STV as a sponsor of the Society's Literary Awards. The introduction of this new sponsor, who would share sponsorship of the Book of the Year and First Book of the Year Awards with the *Scotsman*, led to an increase in prize money for the awards, with the First Book of the Year Award prize increasing to £1,500. The announcement of this joint sponsorship deal was made in September 1990, three months before the announcement of the 1990 Literary Award shortlists. Similarly to the 1989 First Book of the Year Award shortlist, only three books were shortlisted for the award in 1990: Janice Galloway's *The Trick Is to Keep Breathing* (1989),

Gordon Legge's *The Shoe* (1989), and Harry Tait's *The Ballad of Sawney Bain* (1990). Every book shortlisted was published by the independent Edinburgh publisher Polygon. This domination of the shortlist by Polygon coincided with the company's exponential growth and increasingly more important profile within Scottish literature. As Bell, Brown and McDougall note, Polygon was particularly influential in its support of new Scottish literature during this period:

> Polygon Press, initially begun as a student-run organisation affiliated to Edinburgh University in the 1970s, then managed between 1988 and 1990 by Peter Kravitz, played an important role in nurturing new Scottish talent. Under the editorial direction of Marion Sinclair between 1990 and 1997, it proved particularly fleet-footed in spotting and publishing significant works by James Kelman, Janice Galloway, Liz Lochhead, Louise Welsh and Alexander McCall Smith, among others.[25]

Polygon's success in 'nurturing new Scottish talent' between 1990 and 1997 is exemplified by the fact that during these years, eight first-time authors published by Polygon were shortlisted for the Society's First Book of the Year Award.

Of the three Polygon books shortlisted for the award in 1990, it was Harry Tait's novel *The Ballad of Sawney Bain* which was awarded the third First Book of the Year Award. The press release announcing Tait's win, which was distributed to newspapers on 31 January 1991, echoed Calder's description of the judges' selection of the inaugural winner, Raymond Vettesse, stating that the decision to award Tait the £1,500 prize was a 'unanimous' one.[26] The reason why *The Ballad of Sawney Bain* – a kind of historiographic metafiction retelling of the tale of Sawney Bean, a sixteenth-century Scottish clan leader who allegedly murdered and cannibalised several hundred people[27] – was chosen, the press release states, was 'in recognition of its bold treatment of an original and frequently horrifying historical subject on a large and vigorous scale'.[28] It seems, however, that such acclaim did not translate into ongoing financial success for Tait. A short news item published in the *Times* in February 1992, just over a year after Tait's win, claimed:

> Harry Tait, the Glaswegian writer who won the Saltire Society's first book award last year, has been forced to take out a classified advertisement in *The Scotsman* newspaper so that he continues to write. Tait, who wrote *The Ballad of Sawney Bain*, says he will have to move to Spain, Czechoslovakia or Canada to teach if he cannot find a way to live in Britain.[29]

This example of an author not being able to make a living from their writing is not only demonstrative of how association with the Society's Literary Awards did not necessarily impact or translate into financial success (in terms of an increase in book sales post-award win, for example), but it is also indicative of the kind of financial precarity writers can find themselves experiencing (both of these issues are discussed in more detail in the final chapter of this book).

As in 1990, Polygon were prominent on the 1991 shortlist, with two of the four shortlisted books coming from the Scottish publisher, and for the second year in a row, a Polygon author won the award. A. L. Kennedy received the award for her debut collection of short stories, *Night Geometry and the Garscadden Trains* (1990). While Kennedy was the definitive winner in 1991, correspondence between the judges from the period reveals that David S. Mackenzie's *The Truth of Stone* (1991) was the judge's second choice.[30] Unless making a specific commendation, the Society does not ordinarily comment on titles which were considered second place; and in an unprecedented move at the time, the press release for the 1991 Literary Award comments on Mackenzie's position as 'runner up', alongside the 'runner up' of the Book of the Year Award, Robin Jenkins's *Poverty Castle* (1991).[31]

The 1991 First Book of the Year Award was distinctive in another, much more problematic way. The ceremony for the 1991 awards revealed tensions between the sponsors of the Society's Literary Awards. Following the 1991 awards, Simon Forrest, then controller of corporate affairs for STV, wrote to Paul Henderson Scott to complain about a number of issues relating to the awards ceremony held on Monday, 20 January 1992. Forrest notes how he was unhappy 'to learn that instead of [STV newsreader] Viv Lumsden presenting the major prize [it was] decided that she would give the second prize'.[32] Continuing, Forrest suggested that he 'should have been consulted about this since it undermines [STV's] involvement for every year to be seen to be playing the junior role'.[33] This is a surprising, but telling, reaction from a sponsor on the perceived status of the First Book of the Year Award as the 'minor' or 'second place' award, and the Book of the Year Award as the 'major' award. For a sponsor to have such a strong reaction to an association with the First Book of the Year Award and to misguidedly refer to it as a 'second prize' illustrates the extent to which the identity of the First Book of the Year Award was unclear, and how this perhaps made sponsors wary of its cultural, social or journalistic capital. Or, in other words, how much they could, and would, get out of an association with the award.

A year later, the 1992 First Book of the Year Award was split between two books for the first time. Two collections of poetry were awarded – Jackie Kay's *Adoption Papers* (1991), and Christopher Whyte's *Uirsgeul/Myth* (1991). This was the first year in which the award was split between two shortlistees, with each author receiving £750. Kay was the first writer of colour to receive a Saltire Society Literary Award and would be the only writer of colour to win until 2016 when Chitra Ramaswamy received the First Book of the Year for her memoir about pregnancy, *Expecting* (2016), in 2016. The Aberdeen-based Sudanese writer Leila Aboulela, whose first book, *The Translator*, was shortlisted for the First Book of the Year Award, became the third author of colour to win a Saltire Society Literary Award in 2018, when she received the Literary Book of the Year Award for her novel *Elsewhere, Home* (2018). The fact that Kay, the only author of colour to receive a Saltire Society Literary Award, shared the award with a white male author prefigured the controversial splitting of the 2019 Booker Prize between Bernadine Evaristo – the first black woman to win the award – and Margaret Atwood. The decision to split the award (which goes against the Booker Prize's own rules) was criticised by the writer and Jhalak Prize co-founder Sunny Singh, who argued in an article titled 'As the first black woman to win the Booker Prize, Bernardine Evaristo deserved to win alone':

> The Booker's history and processes mean that it has never been the prize for great books but rather for those that receive the most backing. This is just one of the many reasons that no black woman writer has ever won the prize till Evaristo. Given the extraordinary output by eligible black women writers like Jackie Kay, Laura Fish and Aminatta Forna in the past half century, it's a travesty that only four have ever made the shortlist.[34]

The fact that Singh includes Kay in her list of Black women writers who have been routinely ignored by the Booker Prize could indicate that the Society's Literary Awards and judging panel were perhaps more inclusive in their shortlisting and selection of winners. However, the fact that Kay shared her win with a white, male author, and that she is one of only three writers of colour to ever win the Society's First Book of the Year Award (out of the 37 authors who won the award between 1988 and 2019), further exemplifies the disparity in the celebration and rewarding of writers of colour in literary award culture more broadly.[35]

To return to the 1992 First Book of the Year Award, following the awards ceremony, held on Friday, 23 January 1993, Ian Campbell wrote to the Society's administrator, Kathleen Munro, to inform her of how the ceremony unfolded. Campbell described how he had spoken to the *Scotsman*'s editor, Magnus Linklater, and the managing director of STV, Gus MacDonald, about how the awards and the ceremony may be developed in the future. One suggestion being, Campbell states, that 'there might be a place for a practising critic of the younger generation [...] to join the panel at some point', with former First Book of the Year Award winner A. L. Kennedy named as a potential candidate.[36] This idea was raised again, this time by Linklater, who wrote to Paul Henderson Scott later in the year stating that he had 'no quarrel with the format' of the awards, but that perhaps the 'composition' of the judging panels should be reconsidered: 'I wondered whether we shouldn't be considering incorporating one or two of the younger Scottish writers, but perhaps that can be a matter for discussion next year.'[37] Such comments alluded, once again, to concerns relating to the static nature of the Society's Literary Awards judging panel which, in 1993, had remained more or less unchanged since the founding of the First Book of the Year Award in 1988. The panel, which also judged for the Book of the Year Award, had consisted of Angus Calder, Ian Campbell, Douglas Gifford, Isobel Murray, Paul Henderson Scott, Alan Taylor and Derick Thomson since 1984 (except in 1989 and 1990, when Thomson was not a member of the panel). What is significant about Campbell's specific reference to A. L. Kennedy, and Linklater's emphasis on the inclusion of *younger* Scottish writers, is the fact that both suggestions seem focused on the Society's Literary Awards engaging with new and emerging writers. Such issues are inherently interconnected with the Society's First Book of the Year Award which was established for the very purpose of supporting emerging Scottish writers. Campbell and Linklater's comments suggest that the sponsors of the Society's Literary Awards were not convinced that the panel of judges was truly representative of the kinds of books and authors they were judging for the Society's Literary Awards, particularly with regard to the First Book of the Year Award.

It seems that such calls for the introduction of a new panel member were heeded because in 1994 the journalist and theatre critic Joyce McMillan joined the panel in place of the journalist and writer Alan Taylor. However, admittedly, this change was somewhat of a like-for-like exchange as both Taylor and McMillan were arts critics for the *Scotsman* at the time. Such changes coincided with STV ending their joint financial sponsorship of the Society's Literary Awards (although they would continue to broadcast the awards ceremony until 1997). While the *Scotsman* remained as sponsor of the Book of the Year Award (and would continue to do so until 1999), the First Book of the Year, as previously noted, received one year of sponsorship in 1995 from the Gaelic literary journal *Gairm*. When this one-year sponsorship deal came to an end, the Society's director, Ian Scott, wrote to a multitude of companies in April and May 1996, including Waterstone's, HarperCollins, Johnston Press and James Thin Books, in targeted attempts to secure financial support for the First Book of the Year Award. For example, in his letter to Eddie Bell, the chief executive of HarperCollins, Scott noted:

These Saltire Awards are widely acknowledged across the literary spectrum in Scotland and attract a good deal of media attention. Scottish fiction [...] is currently enjoying a period of special popularity and last year's winner of the first book, Ali Smith's 'Free Love', was acclaimed as the start of a potentially brilliant writing career.[38]

Writing in response to Scott on Wednesday, 19 June 1996, Bell declined to sponsor the First Book of the Year Award, suggesting that 'a book award sponsored by an individual publisher usually has little or no credibility', and continued to note that sponsoring the award would 'preclude us from ever submitting any HarperCollins books, as it would be seen as a conflict of interest'.[39] This was a fair assessment on Bell's part, since publisher sponsored awards are exceedingly rare.

Equally negative responses were received from Waterstone's and James Thin. Writing on Tuesday, 23 April 1996, Honor Wilson-Fletcher, the PR and publicity manager of Waterstones's, noted that, despite 'sympathis[ing] with the issues which concern [the Society]', the 'lion's share' of Waterstone's budget was 'fully spent'.[40] Similarly, the owner of the Edinburgh bookshop James Thin Books, D. Ainslie Thin, wrote a revealing letter explaining the negative impact the termination of the Net Book Agreement[41] had on the company's finances, which made any sponsorship impossible:

> I am sorry we cannot help you. As you know the Net Book Agreement disappeared on us on 1st October 1995 and since then our margin has been very severely dented. In the period between 1st October and end December, we lost margin which went straight through to a reduction in our profit to the amount of £253,000. So we are busy trying to mend our fences by making new arrangements with publishers, but meanwhile our profitability has been severely affected and we have been cutting back on every possible expense in order to ensure our future. We will have things in place in the course of the next year or so, I am sure, but meanwhile I am afraid we cannot possibl[y] provide the support you require for your prize[42]

However, in the midst of this series of rebuffs, the secretary of the Scottish Post Office Board wrote to the Society to enquire about the possibility of the Post Office (a subsidiary of the Royal Mail) becoming a sponsor. Kathleen Munro was encouraging in her response to Cummins, explaining that the Society would 'take on board [...] suggestions and requests' for prizes from potential sponsors, 'within reason'.[43] Munro signed off by thanking Cummins for 'showing such an interest' in the awards and assuring him that she would be 'in touch very soon with some figures' which would detail the potential expenditures and levels of financial support, that the sponsorship of the First Book of the Year Award would entail.[44] Writing to Cummins a month later, Munro informed him that the *Scotsman* had confirmed that 'their budget will not allow them to sponsor the Scottish First Book of the Year: £1500 (a published work by a new author)' and that the Society's 'search [for a sponsor] starts again'.[45] Munro asked Cummins if 'the Scottish Postal Board might be interested and allow its name to be associated with this award', stating that 'although the publicity material for our award has been issued, the ceremony provides an opportunity to announce the sponsors and to display P.R. material'.[46] Such details give an interesting insight into the management of a new sponsor late in the prize process, since Munro's reassurance to Cummins – that while a key marketing opportunity has already passed, there will be more to come – evidences the recognition of the importance of sponsors receiving marketing opportunities through awards sponsorship.

On Tuesday, 22 October 1996, Cummins responded to Munro confirming that the Post Office would 'support (rather than sponsor) the Saltire First Literary Award at this year's ceremony on 27 November for the **inclusive** sum of £1,500' (emphasis in original), which was the prize amount at the time.[47] Following this statement of support, Cummins listed a substantial series of conditions the Post Office wished for in return for their support. These included:

- The Post Office's support will be fully acknowledged in [the] televised introduction of the Award;
- Kenneth Graham, or other nominated Post Office representative, will be able to present the Award and speak (your good offices to be used to secure as much air time as possible) to camera for subsequent television broadcast;
- The Post Office will be able to display its logo (and associated slogan if possible) in any televised backdrop agreed with STV;
- After consultation about suitable wording, The Post Office will be mentioned in all media and promotional material issued by the Saltire Society in connection with the aforementioned Awards; [...]
- A set of books for consideration by the judges for the Saltire First Award will be made available to The Post Office at no extra cost;
- The Post Office will be offered first option to support the Saltire First Award for the next two years.[48]

Following consultation with Ian Campbell, who was chair of the Society's Literary Awards judging panel in 1996, Munro confirmed that the panel was happy to accept these conditions and wrote to Cummins to confirm that the

Society was 'delighted that The Post Office has agreed to support new writers this year' and that she could not 'at the moment, see any reason why we could not comply with [the conditions]'.[49] Such 'conditions' illustrate that the Post Office was seeking credited, and attributable, recognition for their association with the award.

A press release celebrating the new support asserted that the Post Office's backing had 'saved the Saltire Society's new writer's award for 1996'.[50] The press release, portions of which were published in an article announcing the 1996 shortlists in the *Scotsman* newspaper on Saturday, 26 October 1996,[51] also reported that the Society had 'almost given up hope of finding a supporter for this year's Saltire award for the best Scottish First Book' which was 'designed to recognise and encourage new writing talent'.[52] Keen to demonstrate the Post Office's literary credentials, Kenneth Graham, the chairman of the Scottish Post Office Board, was quoted as saying:

> Looking, as we do, after some 10 million letters every working day in Scotland, we felt it very reasonable to extend our own literary endeavours and help the Saltire Society's excellent award for Scottish 'letters' to continue. I'm sure the great novelist Anthony Trollope who worked for The Post Office for many years would approve.[53]

Graham's determination to illustrate the Post Office's apparent claims to literary history (via tenuous links to Trollope) is perhaps an attempt to illustrate their authority as a sponsor for the arts, and literature in particular. Indeed, the Post Office had developed somewhat of a reputation as a sponsor of the arts in Scotland during this period, and sponsorship of the Society's First Book of the Year Award was just one of a number of investments made by the Post Office in the late 1980s and early 1990s. An article in the *Glasgow Herald* in 1987 details the kind of philanthropic investment the Post Office would be making in that year alone: 'This year the Edinburgh Festival will receive £25,000, the Scottish Chamber Orchestra £20,000, the St Magnus Festival in Orkney £15,000, the National Galleries of Scotland £12,500.' The Post Office would also bequeath 'smaller sponsorships such as a £250 annual award for the Royal Scottish Academy and £1600 for the Commonwealth Writers' Conference'. Such investments were, according to this article, instigated by Ian Barr, the chairman of the Scottish Post Office Board (1984–88) and the 'man who made the Post Office patron of the Arts'. Accordingly, by the time the Post Office became sponsor of the Society's First Book of the Year Award, it had already established itself as a significant supporter and financier of arts and culture in Scotland.[54]

From the beginning of their sponsorship, the Post Office became actively involved in the marketing and administration of the First Book of the Year Award. Cummins was present, for example, at the final judging panel meeting for 1996 held on Monday, 4 November 1996.[55] According to the minutes of this meeting, Cummins discussed 'the pattern of this year's support and the future [of the award], and the award ceremony' before leaving so the judges could 'discuss and vote on the winners' of the 1996 awards.[56] A letter from Campbell to Munro sent after this meeting reveals that the Post Office had agreed to 'help in distributing information about [the] award to weekly newspapers'.[57] Furthermore, Campbell informed Munro that a copy of Kate Clanchy's *Slattern* (1995) – winner of the 1996 First Book of the Year Award – was 'going to [the] Post Office so that Kenneth Graham can read before the presentation ceremony'.[58]

Following the withdrawal of STV as a sponsor of the Society's Literary Awards in 1994, in 1997 STV also decided to end broadcasting of the Society's Literary Awards ceremony. This withdrawal of support in July 1997 triggered a series of changes to the promotion and marketing of the awards, which would affect them for a number of years to come. In a letter to Douglas Gifford, who was chair of the Literary Awards judging panel in 1997, Munro explained that she had 'spoken to Kathryn Ross of Book Trust Scotland [and] [i]t seems we are all going our own separate ways as Scottish Television has pulled out'.[59] Munro here making reference to the fact that the three Scottish major literary awards at the time – the McVitie's Prize for Scottish Writer of the Year, the Scottish Arts Council Book Award and the Saltire Society Literary Awards – were part of a televised ceremony broadcast by STV. Munro also informed Gifford that the hotel chain Stakis had replaced McVitie's as the sponsor of the Scottish Book of the Year Award, and that Stakis's 'PR people have been speaking to the PR people in the BBC but no-one seems to know what the result is'.[60] This abrupt end of the camaraderie between the leading literary awards in Scotland was unfortunate and would have a long-lasting impact. It seemed that the prizes found a kind of power in numbers in the early to mid-1990s, which was lost following the cessation of the televised joint ceremonies. What is more, the amity between the awards would soon give way to a near-direct competition, in terms of the accrual of cultural and social capital, with the prizes often going to the same authors (such as James Robertson winning both the Society's Book of the Year Award and SMITs in 2004 for *Joseph Knight* (2003), and James Kelman winning both awards in 2009 for *Kieron Smith, Boy* (2008)).

The news concerning the developments in the McVitie's/Stakis Scottish Writer of the Year Award would eventually have an influential impact upon the Society's own preparations. Writing to Gifford again a month later, Munro commented that 'as we are once again "going it alone", the proposed timing of the ceremony, the availability of accommodation and the announcement of the Stakis Prize shortleet are all affecting our arrangements'.[61] The announcement of the shortlist for the 1997 Stakis Prize for the Scottish Writer of the Year was scheduled to take place on Wednesday, 29 October, at the Grosvenor Hotel in Edinburgh, the same day the Society's Literary Awards judging panel had arranged to meet to decide and announce the shortlists for the 1997 Book of the Year and First Book of the Year Awards. The winner of the Society's 1997 First Book of the Year Award, Robin Robertson's *A Painted Field* (1996), was announced a month later at an awards ceremony held at the Traverse Theatre, Edinburgh, on Monday, 17 November 1997.

Moving On: 2000s–2010s

With the withdrawal of the *Scotsman*'s financial support to the Book of the Year Award in early 2000, Munro wrote to Cummins in March 2000 to offer the Post Office 'first refusal' on extending their sponsorship of the awards to include the Book of the Year Award.[62] Cummins responded three weeks later stating that the Royal Mail had 'considered this carefully' but were unable to 'extend [...] support beyond the First Book Award'.[63] Still, Cummins confirmed that the Royal Mail would be 'delighted to support' the First Book of the Year Award for 2000, and the award was presented to Douglas Galbraith's historical fiction novel, *The Rising Sun* (2000), at a ceremony held at the National Library of Scotland on Thursday, 30 November 2000. Galbraith's win was described as being particularly significant, since he was reported to have received a £100,000 advance[64] for his debut novel from Picador, reportedly 'the largest advance in Scottish publishing for a first novel'.[65]

Following Royal Mail's attempted rebranding of their company in 2001, which included changing the name of the Post Office to 'Consignia',[66] the First Book of the Year Award would be renamed the 'Consignia/Saltire Society First Book of the Year Award', which was awarded to Meaghan Delahunt for her novel *In the Blue House* (2001).[67] It was well known that Consignia – with its name being reverted to Post Office only fifteen months after the change and a major rebranding – was going through financial and logistical problems, which soon became a matter of concern to the Society's administrator.[68] Writing to Ian Campbell, the chair for the 2002 Literary Awards panel, on Tuesday, 8 January 2002, Munro stated that she had 'a feeling Consignia may not wish to commit itself [to further sponsorship] at this stage'.[69] However, email correspondence between Munro and Literary Award judge Isobel Murray from February 2002 reveals that Consignia had 'indicated (verbally) that it will sponsor for a further year'.[70]

Similarly to the 1992 and 1998 awards, the 2002 First Book of the Year Award was shared between two authors – Louise Welsh for her novel *The Cutting Room* (2002), and Liam McIlvanney for his Robert Burns biography *Burns the Radical* (2002). In 2003, a selection of bilingual short stories, Martin McIntyre's *Ath-Aithne/Re-Acquaintance* (2003), was the first book written predominantly in Gaelic (14 of McIntyre's stories are written in Gaelic, 4 in English) to become the sole recipient of the First Book of the Year Award. When accepting the award at a ceremony held at the National Library of Scotland on Friday, 28 November 2003, McIntyre stated that winning the award was a 'great personal boost' and that he hoped it would 'inspire more Gaelic writers to put pen to paper'.[71] However, it is possible that this selection was a controversial one since, in 2003, none of the members of the judging panel were Gaelic speakers, and they presumably sought counsel on the quality of McIntyre's book from Gaelic readers. Indeed, this may have influenced the Society's decision to invite Ian MacDonald, who was the director of the Gaelic Books Council at the time, to join the panel as a 'Gaelic advisor' in 2004. MacDonald was asked to read and proffer judgment on any Gaelic-language texts nominated for the Society's Literary Awards, becoming a 'full' member of the panel (which entailed reading every book nominated for the Society's Literary Awards) in 2006 until 2014. Further, in 2005, Marion Sinclair, a Gaelic speaker and former editorial director at Polygon, and Dr Ann Matheson, keeper of printed books at the National Library of Scotland and co-author of the *Scottish Gaelic Union Catalogue: A List of Books Printed in Scottish Gaelic from 1567 to 1973* (1984), also became 'full' members of the Society's Literary Awards panel.

After supporting the First Book of the Year Award for 14 years, in 2011 the Royal Mail withdrew their financial support – which, in 2010, totalled £2,000, with £1,500 for the prize and £500 towards administration expenses and the arrangement of the awards ceremony – of the First Book of the Year Award.[72] Following this withdrawal of support, the Society self-funded the award until 2014, when Tamdhu Speyside Single Malt Whisky sponsored the 26th First Book of the Year Award, conferred to Niall Campbell's debut poetry collection *Moontide* (2014). Also, in 2014, the prize fund for the First Book of the Year Award was raised – for the first time since 1990 – from £1,500 to £2,000: this was due to the change in the presentation of all of the Society's Literary Awards, as discussed in the previous chapter. With this change, from 2014, the winner of the award receives £2,000 and, for the first time in the history of the Society's First Book of the Year Award, the winner of the award now receives the same amount of money as the winner of the Book of the Year Award (now the Fiction and Non-Fiction Book of the Year Awards).

The late to mid-2010s also brought significant changes to the make-up of the Society's Literary Awards judging panels, after several decades of this being a regular cause for concern. In 2018, the Society released a 'call for judges' stating that they were looking for

> individuals who have a passion for literature and experience as authors, editors, readers, librarians, critics, booksellers, or other members of the literary community to join our panels of independent and impartial judges for our First Book, Non-Fiction and Fiction Awards.[73]

The call set out the criteria of the judging role as such:

- to read all the books designated to them in the Award category they are judging, recognising that some Award categories may receive more nominations than others; therefore, requiring a larger commitment of time.
- to commit to being impartial in their judging.
- attend up to five judging meetings at Saltire Headquarters with their fellow judges.
- where appropriate/possible take part in/ join us at the events announcing the Award shortlist and recipients.[74]

This call did bring new panel members, with the 2018 First Book of the Year Award judging panel including Alan Bett, literature officer at Creative Scotland; publisher, writer and cultural public programme manager at Perth & Kinross Council, Anna Day; the writer, journalist and publisher Laura Waddell; and the author and previous First Book of the Year Award winner Louise Welsh.

The 2018 First Book of the Year Award shortlist generated controversy when the journalist and former Saltire Society Literary Award judge Hannah McGill questioned the rationale for the omission of *Poverty Safari* (2017), the first book by Scottish writer and musician Darren McGarvey (also known as Loki). Writing in the *Herald*, McGill questioned why McGarvey's book – which was 'first published by Edinburgh's Luath Press, then picked up by Picador, then won the hugely prestigious Orwell Prize for political journalism' and examines the impact of systemic poverty in the United

Kingdom – was not shortlisted by the Saltire Society, 'even though there are only four books on a Best First Book shortlist that has room for six, and even though Luath has been nominated in [the Society's] Best Publisher Awards in part for its achievement in publishing it'.[75] While emphasising that 'prize juries make their own choices', McGill nonetheless bemoans McGarvey's exclusion, not only from the Society's First Book of the Year shortlist but also from the annual 'Hot 100' list published by the Scottish arts and culture magazine *List*.[76] McGill's fear, it seems, is that McGarvey's exclusion from such Scottish cultural honours was related more to his reputation (McGill herself notes that McGarvey had 'got many backs up in the past' due to his comments about domestic abuse in 2016) as opposed to the quality of his writing, arguing that

> it makes you wonder about tall poppy syndrome, when a work so honoured elsewhere gets junked in its homeland. And it calls to mind the current fad for 'no platforming' individuals whose viewpoint affronts particular sensibilities. [...] Finally, and unfortunately, it reinforces an impression held by many: that our cultural gatekeepers don't wish to hear from the wrong side of the tracks.[77]

McGill acknowledged that she did not 'endorse the latter idea', noting that the Saltire Society's Literary Awards in particular had 'certainly honoured writers from various backgrounds in the past', but continued to suggest that

> this snub should function as a reminder to keep an eye on the gradient of the playing field. [...] We who have influence in culture must be vigilant that we're not restricting where others feel they belong – and that personal animosities don't pollute processes that are, after all, conducted on behalf of all of Scotland.[78]

McGarvey had also expressed his surprise and disappointment at not being shortlisted (in now deleted tweets) but became apologetic for his initial response to the news that he was not shortlisted for the First Book of the Year Award, tweeting that

> personally, it does not bother me that much. Who am I to presume I should be shortlisted for anything? I didn't even know about these awards until people started messaging me about, saying how surprised they were I wasn't nominated. [...] Books are about personal taste and experience and judging panels are subjective.[79]

Both McGarvey's and McGill's responses highlight key issues about the Society's Literary Awards and book awards more generally. First, McGarvey's comment that he 'didn't even know about these awards' until people were surprised by the exclusion of his book is emblematic of the Society's almost paradoxical status of, on the one hand, being the only remaining series of awards dedicated to celebrating Scottish literature and, on the other hand, being unknown to many (including award-winning Scottish writers). Second, and relatedly, McGill's criticism brings to the fore concerns surrounding the elitist practices of prize culture, exemplifying Driscoll's reading of literary awards as examples of the new literary middlebrow which are 'reverent towards elite culture and reliant on cultural intermediaries'.[80] As a result, the debate caused by the omission of *Poverty Safari* from the 2018 First Book of the Year Award shortlist is a reminder of the precarious nature of the Society's cultural and social capital, and how the pursuit of, or reliance upon, these forms of capital has the potential to undermine the conferral of such capital on others. The Society's complex and contradictory status as a consecrator of Scottish literary culture is examined in more detail in the chapters in Part II of this book.

As this history of the Society's First Book of the Year Award has shown, the award has often struggled in attaining a strong individual identity away from the Society's Book of the Year Award which has had an almost overbearing presence within the Society's family of Literary Awards. Indeed, this notion of the First Book of the Year Award being secondary, or the younger sibling of the Book of the Year Award, would not only impact how judges spoke about the award but also influenced how sponsors understood the award and the cultural, social and journalistic capital they could acquire from an association with the award. Although, to look at this differently, given the smaller prize purse for the First Book of the Year Award (£1,500 between 1990 and 2013, compared to the Book of the Year Awards' prize purse of £5,000 during the same period), it was perhaps viewed as a more enticing and economical sponsorship opportunity. This history of the Society's First Book of the Year Award also begins to offer a broad, but by no means complete, illustration of how debut authors fared in Scotland more widely during the 1990s and 2000s. The significance of the prize, as well as the Book of the Year Award, in the shaping of the reputation of certain writers during this period will be discussed in more detail in Chapter 5.

The purpose of this history of the Saltire Society's First Book of the Year Award, and the history of the Book of the Year Award examined in the previous chapter, is to not only provide an insight into the largely unknown history and context from which the Society's Literary Awards developed and prospered in the late twentieth and early twenty-first centuries, but it also provides the foundation from which further critical examination of the awards and their role and influence – or lack thereof – in Scottish literary culture more broadly can be completed. Accordingly, building upon this groundwork knowledge, Part II of this book will examine the Society's Literary Awards in more detail and use them as a case study from which to scrutinise a broader understanding of literary awards culture.

Part II

Chapter 4

'WHAT'S THIS GOT TO DO WITH SCOTLAND?'

QUALIFYING SCOTTISHNESS THROUGH TERMS OF ELIGIBILITY

In 1947, Alison Sheppard, the Saltire Society's then honorary secretary, argued that 'Scottishness' alone was not enough for the Society, continuing to argue that 'far too much inferior work was acclaimed, simply because it was Scottish'.[1] Despite this proclamation (made over a decade after the founding of the Society in 1936) suggesting that there was a risk of the organisation's attentions being distracted by 'inferior work' because of a preoccupation with Scottish work, it was, and remains, impossible to detach the Society's founding principles from Scotland and 'Scottishness'. The organisation's status as a cultural charity, located in Scotland's capital city and dedicated to supporting and promoting Scottish cultural life, means engagement with notions of Scottish national identity and nationhood – and how this should be defined and supported – is intrinsic to the Society's activities. This, inevitably, feeds into how the Society facilitates their series of Literary Awards and how the award judges and shortlisted/winning authors and their publishers understand the awards. As previously noted, to be eligible for a Saltire Society Literary Award, an author must have a genetic or geographical connection to Scotland, or their work must have a clear contextual relation to Scotland through subject matter, setting or character. Such terms not only have a practical purpose, acting as a form of sifting process by which it is decided whether a book should or should not be considered for the Literary Awards, but they also have an ideological purpose. They are a means by which the Society can articulate what it considers to be representative of 'Scottishness' and Scottish cultural identity.

Debates regarding what exactly Scottish cultural identity is have emerged, and re-emerged, for centuries. Indeed, such arguments are historical and political in origin, relating to Scotland's contentious relationship with England from the Acts of Union 1707, which saw the political unification of Scotland

and England, to the more recent 2014 Scottish Independence Referendum, which saw Scotland unsuccessfully seek political and economic independence from the United Kingdom. As already described in Part I, this historical context is important when considering the Saltire Society, its literary awards and their contribution to Scottish cultural and literary life, since the Society was founded between, and inspired by, two so-called cultural renaissances in Scottish politics and culture. These nationalistic cultural revivals, during which Scotland's cultural stalwarts were fighting against a perceived suppression of their arts and traditions, corresponded with an increased interest in Scotland's autonomy and political identity, thus epitomising Neil Davidson's assertion that 'culture may in certain circumstances be as central to a nationalist movement as political activity'.[2] Examinations of Scotland's political identity are, therefore, entwined with discourses relating to Scotland's wider literary and cultural identity. From T. S. Eliot questioning 'Was there a Scottish Literature?' in 1919,[3] to Edwin Muir's proclamation that 'a Scottish writer who wishes to achieve some approximation to completeness has no choice except to absorb the English tradition' in 1936,[4] the debate as to exactly how Scottish literature could, and should, be identified thrived in the years preceding the founding of the Saltire Society and its earliest literary awards and commendations.

More recent arguments have continued to question the legitimacy of a cohesive understanding of 'Scottishness' and how Scottish literature (re)presents this. Despite Alan Bold claiming that 'Scottishness is a recognised state of mind', when discussing modern Scottish literature in 1983, the turn of the century brought with it new approaches to defining Scottish literature and Scottishness.[5] In 2003, Liam Connell argued that Scottish literature is a construct and not an innate element of Scotland's national heritage: 'Scottish literary criticism has been far too willing to accept the immanence of "Scottish literature" without conceding it[s] constructedness or charting the processes and motivations behind such construction.'[6] This notion of 'Scottish' literature as a construction was furthered by Alex Thomson in 2007:

> Once we accept that a nation is not so much a thing we can touch, as a story in which we believe, the historiography of Scottish literature itself becomes an act of determination, part of the continual re-imagination of the nation's forms of life.[7]

The Saltire Society Literary Awards invariably feed into this understanding of national identity as a constantly developing character. The Society can be identified as an organisation working within the parameters of what

Hutchison describes as 'cultural nationalism', a 'movement of moral regeneration, which seeks to re-unite the different aspects of the nation'.[8] It is for this reason, Hutchison continues, that

> [the] proponents [of cultural nationalism] are not politicians or legislators but are above all historical scholars and artists who form cultural and academic societies, designed to recover this creative force in all its dimensions with verisimilitude and project it to the members of the nation.[9]

While this approach can be problematised, as it is framed as a top-down understanding of culture which relies on a select few navigating and 'recovering' culture for the nation, the concept of cultural nationalism nonetheless effectively articulates how the Society's ambitions and motivations are explicitly placed within the wider context of preserving and promoting Scottish national identity and culture. The Society's influence and success in achieving such aims has arguably been legitimised by the fact that, as previously noted, the Scottish government assisted in financially supporting the Book of the Year Award and the creation of the Homecoming Award to celebrate Scotland's cultural influence internationally in 2008 and, in the 2010s, by Creative Scotland being a lead sponsor of the literary awards. Accordingly, in positioning itself as both an institution that is dedicated to preserving Scotland's culture, arts and traditions, *and* as an arbiter of Scottish literary culture and value through its Literary Awards, the Society is part of the 'continual re-imagination' of Scotland's culture and, in turn, its national identity.

Prizing Scottish Literature: Terms of Eligibility and Scottishness

The Saltire Society did not have a formal criterion of eligibility by which their earliest literary awards, conferred in the 1930s and 1950s, were assessed. Meeting minutes from 1954 indicate that 'a Book of the Year Award had been suggested' which would be 'made to the "person", publishers, authors, editor or journalist, who contributed most to Scottish Literature during the year'; however, it was never clearly explained exactly how this 'contribution' to Scottish literature would be quantified and who would be an eligible contender for the accolade.[10] There was little in the way of formal criteria of eligibility for the Society's Literary Awards until the founding of the Book of the Year Award in 1981. It was at this point that the Society outlined explicit terms by which a 'Scottish book' would be identified:

> The term, 'Scottish Book', would include any book by an author of Scottish descent or living in Scotland, or a book by anyone which deals with the work or life of a Scot or with a Scottish problem, event or situation [...] or a study of any Scottish issue.[11]

This definition has remained more or less unchanged since it was adopted 40 years ago: the criteria of eligibility for the 2018 Saltire Society Literary Awards (which was included in the awards' entry form sent to publishers and made available on the Society's website) is a condensed version of the original terms from 1981: 'Books must be written by authors of Scottish descent or living in Scotland, or dealing with the work or life of a Scot, a Scottish question, event or situation.'[12]

Ten years after Paul Henderson Scott settled on the terms of eligibility for the Book of the Year Award, Literary Award judge and co-chair Douglas Gifford claimed that, even though other literary awards for Scottish writers and books existed, the Society's broad terms of eligibility made the Society's awards unique. Writing in *Books in Scotland*, Gifford – who was also on the editorial board of *Books in Scotland*, as was his fellow Saltire Literary Awards judge and panel co-chair Ian Campbell – noted the 'glaring *unfairness*' (emphasis in original) in the lack of representation of Scottish authors in non-Scottish literary awards such as the Booker Prize.[13] Decrying the fact that the 'Booker rituals [...] seem so obviously centred on values and trends based on London and Oxbridge',[14] Gifford continues to explain why Scotland-specific literary awards are, in his opinion, necessary:

> Since Booker *et al* aren't going to go away, then we should join them [...] [The Society's Literary Awards], and McVittie's [*sic*], and Arts Council awards, [are] reinforcing a kind of positive discrimination for indigenous Scottish writing, centripetally moving all the books we consider around a hopefully ever-more-confident Scottish cultural consciousness which is manifesting itself in schools and exams doing much more to recognise native writing and language.[15]

He continues, noting that 'the [Society's Literary Awards] over the years *do* reflect range and national variety of voice [...] English, Scots and Gaelic have all appeared as the language of the winner'.[16] Gifford considers issues relating to the nature and apparent necessity for national awards here and hints at what has at times been considered prejudicial exclusion of Scottish writers in major (inter)national awards like the Booker. Such arguments reappeared, albeit more forcefully, decades later in 2012 when Scottish poet and activist Kevin Williamson decried what he called the Booker's '44 years of institutionalised anti-Scottish racism'.[17] In an article published on *Bella Caledonia*, an online magazine co-founded by Williamson focusing on Scottish cultural and political commentary, Williamson said he was surprised to see the 'dearth of Scottish writers [on the Booker longlist] in what has been a truly golden year for Scottish novels'.[18] The Booker, Williamson continues, 'has a huge institutionalised problem with Scottish authors which [...] lurches between Anglocentric elitism, barely disguised contempt, class hatred, and borderline racism'.[19] This indictment is a deliberate nod to James Kelman's 1994 Booker Prize acceptance speech (which Williamson references directly later in the article). When accepting his award, Kelman, the only Scottish author to have won the Booker in its 50-year history, stated that 'a fine line can exist between elitism and racism. On matters concerning language and culture, the distinction can sometimes cease to exist altogether.'[20] The day after Williamson's article was published, the author Alan Bissett shared similar concerns in the *Guardian*. Seemingly illustrating the 'unnoticed bias of the Booker prize', Bissett noted:

> Only 3.6% of all [Booker] shortlistees (4.4% if we include [William] Boyd and [Bernard] MacLaverty, 3.3% of the judges and a paltry 2.9% of the longlist have been Scottish [...] Such luminaries as Alasdair Gray, AL Kennedy, Alun Richards, Ron Berry, William McIlvanney, Janice Galloway, Niall Griffiths, Rachel Tresize and Iain Banks have never even made the longlist.[21]

While such figures appear convincing and demonstrative of Booker bias, some years earlier, Sharon Norris suggested that, far from being victim to conscious exclusion, Scottish books are actually 'marginally over-represented' in Booker shortlists.[22] Norris arrived at this conclusion through a statistical analysis of the number of Scottish authors shortlisted for the Booker relative to Scottish population figures in the United Kingdom:

> The UK 2001 census showed a total UK population of 59,553,800 of which England had 8.6%, Scotland 8.6%, and Wales 4.9%, with Northern Ireland at 2.9%. If one compares these figures with the relative percentage of Scottish and Welsh novels on the Bookers short-lists, it can be seen that, numerically, at least, Scotland is not under-represented.[23]

Considering, as Norris points out, that Scottish books represent 8.7 per cent of all novels shortlisted (between the founding of the Booker Prize in 1969 up to 2005 when Norris's article was published), the population figures certainly do suggest Scottish writers are 'over-represented' in Booker shortlists. However, as Norris notes, while this approach offers a novel means by which national representation in literary prize shortlists may be quantified, it is ultimately 'tokenistic nonsense', since 'it takes for granted a number of factors, not least of all that the percentage of those who write, or, more accurately, are published, is constant in each country'.[24]

To return to Gifford's discussion of the benefits of the 'positive discrimination' of Scottish literary awards, since the awards he mentioned – the Saltire Society Literary Awards, the McVitie's Prize and Scottish Arts Council (SAC) Book Awards – had very similar terms of eligibility based largely on genealogy or geographic links to Scotland, the ecology of Scotland's literary award culture remained interconnected. For example, to be eligible for a SAC Book Award in 1982, authors needed to be 'Scottish, resident in Scotland or writing books of Scottish interest'.[25] The only difference between these terms and those of the Society's being that the Society also includes an author's 'Scottish descent' as a valid criterion. Similarly, the terms for the McVitie's Prize for Scottish Writer of the Year concentrated on the national identity of the author or the 'Scottishness' of their work. The Frederick Niven Literary Award, administered by PEN Scotland, also requested submissions of the 'most outstanding contribution to the novel by a Scotsman or Scotswoman'.[26] As discussed in the Introduction of this book, in 1988, the terms of eligibility for the McVitie's Prize specified that the £5,000 prize would be presented to

> the best substantial Scottish work of an imaginative nature first published or performed between 1 September and 31 August (a novel, collection of short stories, poetry, autobiography, theatre, cinema, radio and television scripts etc). Writers born in Scotland, or who are or have been resident in Scotland or who take Scotland as their inspiration, are eligible. Submission accepted in Scots, English and Gaelic.[27]

As may be expected, the analogous nature of the terms of eligibility and the relatively small pool of authors who qualify for these awards meant that, on a number of occasions, the same authors were shortlisted for, or won, these awards. In 1990, Sorley Maclean won both the Society's Book of the Year Award and the McVitie's Award for his book *From Wood to Ridge/O choille gu bearradh* (1989). Likewise, in 1994, Kathleen Jamie's *Queen of Sheba* (1994), James Kelman's *How Late It Was How Late* (1994) and Candia McWilliam's *Debatable Land* (1994) were all shortlisted for both awards. The similarities in the criteria of eligibility for the various national literary awards in Scotland at the time suggest, therefore, that quantifying 'Scottishness' in terms of residence, genealogy or subject matter was considered the most effective – or seemingly legitimate – means by which to define a writer's eligibility for a Scottish literary award.

Judging Scottishness

What became evident when working with and observing the Society's Literary Awards judging panel was that, although the stipulations used by the Society to quantify the 'Scottishness' of an author or book help to manage the pragmatic issue of establishing eligibility, they are by no means clear-cut, and issues surrounding a book or author's 'Scottishness' linger. When observing judging panel meetings between 2012 and 2015, I noted numerous occasions on which the Society's Literary Awards judges would enquire as to the specific, and therefore qualifying, 'Scottish connection' of a book. One judge – who served as a judge for fifteen years – ruminated on this issue in interview, suggesting that 'sometimes you feel the author really has no real [connection to Scotland]' and questioned 'why should [this author] be considered when they are not really Scottish?'[28] The judge was reflecting on the fact that the Society's terms included 'books that are written in Scotland, with someone living for the moment in Scotland or writing in Scotland', conceding that this was perhaps an imperfect method of selection.[29] To illustrate this, the judge discussed a book which had been submitted for the 2013 Book of the Year Award:

> There's that very good book [...] it was a typically English novel, [...] and you wondered 'why are we actually reading this?' Although [the author] was originally Scottish [...] but she was living in England. There's sometimes things like that when maybe an English author [is] writing in Scotland, or a Scottish author [is] writing in England and [...] you feel it's not identifying with Scotland in the way that maybe we should be identifying.[30]

Although never explicitly stated, the judge is likely referring to Kate Atkinson's novel *Life after Life* (2013), which was shortlisted for the Society's Book of the Year Award in 2013. While the judge believed Atkinson's eligibility came from her having been born in Scotland, she was actually born in York and was eligible for the award because she was a resident of Edinburgh at the time of writing and/or publication of her nominated book. This judge is not the only person who has questioned how Atkinson's not-Scottish Scottishness has been quantified. Norris states how, in an email exchange, Ali Smith noted that 'nationality is also partially defined by how others see you'.[31] Smith, Norris writes, uses Atkinson as an example of this:

> [Smith] cites the example of her friend, the writer Kate Atkinson, who was born in Yorkshire, but has lived north of the border for twenty-five

years. Despite this, Atkinson, says Smith, is 'never considered as a Scot by all those short-list panels who award Scottish books, yet her fiction seems to me absolutely marked by Scottish metaphysic, experimentation and humour'.[32]

There is a sense of irony here since, while both Smith and the judge, a member of one of the 'shortlist panels' that Smith in fact refers to, are almost of the same opinion, the fact of the matter is that Atkinson has been shortlisted for the Society's Book of the Year Award four times (in 2003, 2004, 2013 and 2015) and won the award in 2005 for her 2004 novel *Case Histories*, a crime novel set in Cambridge, England.

However, the judge's comment about the 'typically English' book that the panel had read and discussed for the 2013 Book of the Year Award is suggestive. It not only assumes that there is a ubiquitous understanding of what a 'typically English' novel is, but in describing it as such, the judge highlights the way in which such forms of nationalistic classifications can influence the way they, and perhaps some of the Society's other Literary Awards judges, quantify the eligibility of the books they are reading: 'you feel it's not identifying with Scotland in the way that maybe *we* should be identifying' (emphasis added).[33] Furthermore, although indefinite, such comments nonetheless imply that there are clearly identifiable characteristics to 'Scottish' and 'English' literature and that the Society's judges should be able to recognise these. The judge's comments – and the use of national identity, geographical location or subject matter as a means of qualifying or disqualifying an author for a Saltire Society Literary Award – almost suggest that Englishness and Scottishness are juxtaposing signifiers that do not, or cannot, coexist. Comparatively, this goes against Gillian Roberts's arguments concerning the perceived 'Canadianness' of Sri Lankan-born Michael Ondaatje, who upon winning the Booker Prize in 1992 was considered 'a perfect model of modern Canada' by the media.[34] As there was no mention of Ondaatje's Canadian citizenship (he became a citizen in 1965, having moved to the country in 1962) in the media coverage, Roberts argues that the commentary 'naturaliz[es] Ondaatje's Canadianness as a personal development, rather than a legal question'.[35] Ondaatje's Canadianness is also undoubtedly tied to the politics of multiculturalism in the country, with the introduction of the Canadian Multiculturalism Act of 1988 coming after decades of the Canadian government actively promoting ideologies of multiculturalism.

The aforementioned judge continued to discuss the 'Scottishness' of books shortlisted for the Society's Literary Awards, commenting on the novels *Ramshackle* by Elizabeth Reeder, published by the Scottish publisher Freight Books in 2012, and *Tony Hogan Bought Me an Ice Cream Float Before He Stole My Ma* by Kerry Hudson, published by the Penguin Random House imprint Chatto & Windus in 2012. Both books were shortlisted for the Society's First Book of the Year Award in 2012 and, similarly to their deliberation on Atkinson's eligibility for the awards, the judge meditated on the 'Scottishness' of Reeder's and Hudson's novels:

> Kerry Hudson's novel was not entirely Scottish in a sense, although she was born in Aberdeen and a lot of the action does happen in Scotland, but I think she in many ways is [...] really English [...] and [Elizabeth Reeder] was American I think [and the book] was set in rural America. It was a very good book, it was a good book there's no question of that but again you kind of wondered 'well that ain't much to do with Scotland'. [...] She must be living and working here, but what's this got to do with Scotland, you know? Maybe that's too narrow a view.[36]

Although the judge cautiously hedges their concerns surrounding the 'Scottishness' of previous shortlistees with an admission that they may be expressing a 'narrow' point of view, their observations demonstrate the potential problems the judges can face when an author's national identity or a book's content and themes are used as a means of establishing eligibility for an award. In other words, if an author is born in Scotland, like Hudson, it does not make their writing inherently 'Scottish', and a non-Scottish author living in Scotland, like Reeder, can be nominated for writing that 'ain't much to do with Scotland'.

This judge is not alone in their expression of the possible issues of using 'Scottishness' as a prerequisite to determining an author's or book's eligibility for a Saltire Society Literary Award. Another judge, who was a member of the Society's Literary Awards judging panel for six years, also expressed how the criteria of eligibility used by the Society had the potential to be problematic. Specifically, this judge recalled a minor controversy regarding the eligibility of Alistair MacLeod's novel, *No Great Mischief* (2000). Although MacLeod was a Canadian author, his ancestry traced back to Scotland, and his novel dealt with the history of Scottish clan migration and settlement in Canada in the eighteenth century.[37] MacLeod's novel is also multilingual, including Scottish Gaelic alongside English. When discussing the book, the judge described how the panel decided that MacLeod's novel was not eligible for an award:

> The one book that there was some controversy about, and it was whether it was eligible, was Alistair MacLeod's *No Great Mischief*, which was obviously Canadian, but it's also very Scottish and the publisher had sent it, and there was a debate about whether it was eligible or not. [...] I think in the end we decided it wasn't, but [...] that was an interesting debate

> because it was about how you define a Scottish book [...] Because the definition is already fairly broad [...] There's a variety of ways in which you can be eligible, so it was interesting to have a conversation about the ways in which you couldn't be eligible![38]

Significantly, the judge misremembered this particular incident: Alistair MacLeod's novel *was* shortlisted for the Society's Book of the Year Award in 2000. However, this does not detract from the significance of the judge's memory of this incident, since it suggests that the discussion the judges had about MacLeod's book centred on whether his Canadian nationality undercut the Scottish content and themes of the book or his apparent Scottish ancestry. This contrasts with the more recent examples previously mentioned regarding the eligibility of Reeder who was shortlisted for the Society's First Book of the Year Award because she resided in Scotland, despite being American-born and her shortlisted novel, *Ramshackle*, being set in Chicago.

Quantifying Terms of Eligibility

While such examples, and the broad nature of the Society's criteria of eligibility for Scottish literature, may suggest that the kinds of books and authors shortlisted for, and winning, the Society's Literary Awards are diverse (in terms of whether a book is eligible because of its subject matter or author's nationality and geographic location), an analysis of shortlistees and winners of the Society's literary awards indicates that authors born and living in Scotland remain much more likely to be shortlisted for, and win, the Society's Book of the Year and First Book of the Year Awards. Using the Society's own criteria of eligibility (author is Scottish-born, live(s/d) in Scotland, of Scottish descent or book has Scottish themes and content), the below analysis categorises previous shortlists and winners of the Society's Book of the Year and First Book of the Year Awards to ascertain how many authors shortlisted for the awards were either Scottish-born, lived in Scotland or wrote about Scotland. For the purposes of this analysis, the 'Scottish content' of the books in question is identified in terms of the geographical setting of the action of the novel, or the subject matter (which is particularly relevant if it is a non-fiction title). Where the setting of a novel is uncertain or undisclosed, the Scottishness of the book's content is associated with the nationality or birthplace of the protagonist. A related issue to consider here is the fact that the Society has never explicitly explained what constitutes a 'Scottish theme', making this one of the more ambiguous elements of the criteria of eligibility. This count also includes memoirs or biographies about Scottish-born authors and historical figures, such as Jenni Calder's biography of the Scottish author Naomi Mitchison,

Table 4 Number of books shortlisted for the Book of the Year Award, 1982–2019, categorised by Saltire Society's terms of eligibility

Scottish-born only	117	41%
Scottish descent only	1	0.4%
Scottish content only	14	5%
Live(s/d) in Scotland only	25	9%
Scottish-born and Scottish content	119	42%
Scottish descent & Scottish content	3	1%
Scottish content and live(s/d) in Scotland	5	2%
Total	284	100%

The Nine Lives of Naomi Mitchison (1997); John Burnside's memoir *A Lie about My Father* (2006); and Nicholas Phillipson's biography *Adam Smith: An Enlightened Life* (2010). Indeed, the imperfections of this methodology arguably exemplify the issues noted by the judges: attempting to statistically quantify books in terms of their 'Scottishness' highlights the difficulty of such a task when the national identity of geographic status of an author is unknown, and raises questions as to how one should account for 'Scottish' content.

As illustrated in Table 4, the books shortlisted (284 total) for the Book of the Year Award between 1982 and 2019[39] fall into two categories: those that are eligible for the award because they adhere to only one criterion of eligibility, and those that traverse two or more criteria. For example, 41 per cent (117) of authors shortlisted for the Book of the Year Award were eligible for the award solely because they were born in Scotland. The next most common single term of eligibility, at 9 per cent (25), is authors who live in Scotland, or lived at the time of being shortlisted. Only 14 books (5 per cent) were shortlisted purely for their Scottish content, and one book (0.4 per cent), David Gilmour's *Curzon* (1994), was shortlisted because of the author's Scottish descent.[40] Such figures indicate that national identity and proximity to Scotland are the most common means by which an author is eligible for the Book of the Year Award. The books and authors that intersect two criteria of eligibility further back this up. There are even more authors shortlisted for the award who are Scottish-born *and* write Scottish content (42 per cent, 119).[41] This is followed by books by authors who live in Scotland and write Scottish content (2 per cent, 5), and finally books by authors of Scottish descent and who write Scottish content (1 per cent, 3). This final figure illustrates how such counts can be affected by the fact that it is very common for authors to be shortlisted for Saltire Society Literary Awards more than once: two of the three books shortlisted for the Book of the Year Award by authors of Scottish descent and who write Scottish content are by Emma Tennant, a London-born and -based author with Scottish parents.[42]

Table 5 Number of books shortlisted for the First Book of the Year Award, 1988–2019, categorised by Saltire Society's terms of eligibility

Scottish born only	54	35%
Scottish content only	14	9%
Live(s/d) in Scotland only	19	12%
Scottish born & Scottish content	58	37%
Scottish content & live(s/d) in Scotland	10	6%
Total	155	100%

There also appears to be a similar weight towards books by Scottish-born authors being more likely to be shortlisted for the First Book of the Year Award. As Table 4 shows, of the 155 books shortlisted for the First Book of the Year Award between 1982 and 2019, 35 per cent (54) were eligible because of the author's Scottish identity alone. This is followed by whether the author lives in Scotland at 12 per cent (19), and the Scottish content of the shortlisted book at 9 per cent (14). Similar to the Book of the Year Award, when it comes to intersections of criteria of eligibility, the most common criteria books shortlisted for the First Book of the Year fall under relate to national identity, geographical proximity and Scottish content. Books by Scottish authors with Scottish content make up 37 per cent (58) of all books shortlisted for the First Book of the Year Award. The remaining 10 books (6 per cent) are by authors living in Scotland and writing Scottish content, such as Leila Aboulela's 1999 novel, *The Translator*, about a Muslim Sudanese widow living in Aberdeen, and Alison Irvine's *This Road Is Red* (2011) about a once-vibrant Glasgow flats being prepared for demolition.[43] None of the authors of the books shortlisted for the First Book of the Year Award are identified as being eligible through Scottish descent.

While there are nearly twice as many books included in the Book of the Year Award shortlists data, there is an evident parallel between the two awards, which indicates a propensity by the Society's Literary Awards panel to shortlist Scottish-born authors writing Scottish content.

This trend follows through to the selection of winners for the awards. Of the 45 winners of the Book of the Year Award since 1982 (including winners of the Fiction/Non-Fiction Book of the Year Award, 2015–19), nearly half – 47 per cent (21) – were Scottish-born only and 11 per cent (5) lived in, or were living in, Scotland only. The remaining winners were Scottish-born authors writing Scottish content (40 per cent, 18) and an author who was living in Scotland and writing Scottish content (2 per cent, 1). This winner was the Irish writer Bernard MacLaverty whose Man Booker Prize-shortlisted novel *Grace Notes* (1997) won the Society's Book of the Year Award in 1997.

Table 6 Number of Book of the Year Award winners, 1982–2019, categorised by the Saltire Society Literary Awards' terms of eligibility

Scottish born only	21	47%
Live(s/d) in Scotland only	5	11%
Scottish born & Scottish content	18	40%
Live(s/d) in Scotland & Scottish content	1	2%
Total	45	100%

Table 7 Number of First Book of the Year Award winners, 1988–2019, categorised by the Saltire Society Literary Awards' terms of eligibility

Scottish born	16	42%
Scottish content	4	11%
Live(s/d) in Scotland	4	11%
Scottish born & Scottish content	12	32%
Scottish content & live(s/d) in Scotland	2	5%
Total	38	100%

Similarly, of the 38 winners of the First Book of the Year Award since 1988, 42 per cent (16) were Scottish-born only, 11 per cent (4) were by authors living in Scotland only, and 11 per cent (4) had Scottish content only (as shown in Table 7). The remainder of the winners are books containing Scottish content by Scottish-born authors (32 per cent, 12) and books with Scottish content by authors living in Scotland at the time of writing (5 per cent, 2).

These figures suggest that the dominance of authors who are Scottish-born, live in Scotland or write about Scotland is evident in the award shortlists and continues through to the winner, reiterating the fact that, despite the Society's fairly broad terms of eligibility, there appears to be a preference towards an author's biological, rather than purely geographical, connection to Scotland. Yet, this biological or inherited connection to Scotland is significantly more likely to come from the author's own nationhood than that of their ancestry: only one author has ever been shortlisted for the Society's Book of the Year Award or First Book of the Year Award because of 'Scottish descent' alone, and no one eligible for the awards because of their Scottish ancestry has ever won.

Who Publishes Scottish Books?

Such data not only gives some insight into how the Society's Literary Awards judges are 'judging' Scottishness, indicating a preference for books about

Table 8 Location of publishers of books shortlisted for the Book of the Year Award, 1982–2019, categorised by city (England)

England		
London	173	88%
Manchester	8	4%
Newcastle-upon-Tyne	7	4%
Basingstoke	2	1%
Oxford	2	1%
Bath	1	1%
Cambridge	1	1%
Huntingdon	1	1%
Norwich	1	1%
Total	196	100%

Scotland by Scottish authors, but it also reveals what kinds of books and authors publishers submit for the awards. Looking at the shortlisted and winning books from this angle, is it possible to ascertain who is *publishing* award-winning Scottish books?

Nearly all of the 284 books shortlisted for the Book of the Year Award were published in the United Kingdom; only two were published outside of the United Kingdom, – in Canada (Toronto) and the United States (Colombia, South Carolina). Of the 281 books published in the United Kingdom, 69 per cent (196) were published in England, 30 per cent (85) in Scotland and 0.4 per cent (1) in Northern Ireland. However, breaking these figures down further still reveals a regional imbalance of the publishers of the shortlisted books. Of the 196 books published in England, 88 per cent (173) were published in London, with Manchester (8) and Newcastle (7) following with 4 per cent, respectively. There is a similar leaning towards publishers in Scotland's capital city: 69 per cent (59) of the 85 books published in Scotland came from Edinburgh-based publishers, followed by Glasgow at 11 per cent (9) and Inverness at 9 per cent (8). Interestingly, despite the fact that more titles were published in England overall, there is a broader geographical spread of publishers in Scotland. As Table 8 shows, the majority of the publishers based in England, including Basingstoke, Oxford, Bath, Cambridge and Huntingdon, are located in the south of the country. Publishers were based in only two cities in the north of England – Manchester and Newcastle-upon-Tyne – but these publishers were shortlisted more frequently than their southern counterparts. Only one Manchester-based publisher, Carcanet, accounts for all eight shortlistings, and only two

Table 9 Location of publishers of books shortlisted for the First Book of the Year Award, 1982–2019, categorised by city (England)

London	57	81%
Newcastle	5	7%
Manchester	4	6%
Cambridge	1	1%
North Cadbury	1	1%
Richmond	1	1%
Cromer	1	1%
Total	70	100%

Newcastle-Upon-Tyne-based publishers account for the seven shortlistings, with six going to Bloodaxe Books and one to Galloping Dog Press (a now defunct poetry publisher). To put this into perspective, 56 London-based publishers and imprints published the 173 books shortlisted for the Book of the Year Award; however, this reduces to 21 when imprints are accumulated under their parent companies. Six publishers – Hachette; Harper Collins; Little, Brown; Orion; Pan Macmillan; and Penguin Random House – make up 71 per cent (122) of the total number of books shortlisted for the Book of the Year Award, with independent publishers making up the other 29 per cent (51). This prominence of major conglomerate publishers is perhaps unsurprising, given their hegemony within the literary marketplace in the United Kingdom, but this market domination is particularly problematic in relation to literary awards because, as has been demonstrated with regard to the Booker Prize, it not only leads to the dominance of prize shortlists and winners roll calls, but also, in the case of the Booker, increases the number of books a publisher is eligible to submit each year.[44]

This is noteworthy since, as Table 10 shows, there are not only more cities and towns represented by the range of publishers based in Scotland, but they are also much more geographically dispersed. The cities range from several central belt locations, including Edinburgh, Glasgow, Kirkcaldy, Dalkeith; to Inverness, Nairn and Ullapool in the north; Aberdeen in the north-east; Stornoway on the Isle of Lewis; and Lerwick on Shetland.[45]

There is a slight difference in the representation of publisher locations for the First Book of the Year shortlists. Of the 155 books shortlisted for the award, 45 per cent (70) were published in England and 53 per cent (82) in Scotland. The remaining three shortlisted titles were published in Belfast, Northern Ireland (1) and the United States (one each in Texas and South Carolina). The geographic spread of publishers is similar to that of the Book of the Year Award shortlists.

Table 10 Location of publishers of books shortlisted for the Book of the Year Award, 1982–2019, categorised by city (Scotland)

City	Count	Percent
Edinburgh	59	69%
Glasgow	9	11%
Inverness	8	9%
Stornoway	3	4%
Aberdeen	1	1%
Dalkeith	1	1%
Kirkcaldy	1	1%
Lerwick	1	1%
Nairn	1	1%
Ullapool	1	1%
Total	85	100%

Table 11 Location of publishers of books shortlisted for the First Book of the Year Award, 1982–2019, categorised by city (Scotland)

City	Count	Percent
Edinburgh	56	68%
Glasgow	11	13%
Inverness	7	9%
Ullapool	2	2%
East Linton	2	2%
Lerwick	1	1%
Lewis	1	1%
Glendaruel	1	1%
Newtyle	1	1%
Total	82	100%

As Table 9 shows, much like the Book of the Year shortlists, the majority of the books shortlisted for the First Book of the Year Award and published in England came from publishers based in the south of the country (London, Cambridge, North Cadbury, Richmond, Cromer), with four of the publishers, in Newcastle and Manchester, being based in the north of England. Significantly, this includes the once-Glasgow-based independent Scottish publisher Saraband who relocated to Manchester in 2017.[46] Accordingly, depending on the year of the shortlisting, Saraband has been counted as both a Glasgow- and Manchester-based publisher. Once again, the five books published in Newcastle came from one publisher – Bloodaxe Books.

When it comes to the books from Scottish publishers shortlisted for the First Book of the Year Award, there is a similar geographic spread covering the central belt, the north-east and islands off the coast of Scotland (see Table 11).

Although there are many similarities between the publisher breakdowns for the Book of the Year and First Book of the Year Awards, the one key difference – that more of the titles shortlisted for the First Book of the Year Award came from Scottish, not English, publishers – backs up common arguments regarding the apparent migration of well-known, established authors to major publishers, commonly based in London and south of England. What is more, 65 per cent of the publishers shortlisted for the First Book of the Year Award are independent, compared to 52 per cent of the publishers shortlisted for the Book of the Year Award, offering some sustenance to the claim that many authors, Scottish or otherwise, acquire their initial support and success with smaller, independent presses before moving on to much larger, London-based presses. Examples of this in the Scottish context include James Kelman, whose first three books – *Not Not While the Giro* (1983), *The Busconductor Hines* (1984) and *A Chancer* (1985) – were all published by the independent Edinburgh-based publisher Polygon Press. His fourth novel, however, was published by Secker & Warburg, an imprint of the London-based conglomerate publishers the Heinemann Group. Kelman remained with Secker & Warburg until October 2015 when he moved to the Edinburgh-based Canongate Books. Much was made of Kelman's return to Scotland, with he himself saying 'this is the first original publication I shall have had in Scotland in thirty years […] I must say it feels good to be back'.[47] Similarly, the Scottish author Janice Galloway also published her debut novel, *The Trick Is to Keep Breathing* (1989), with Polygon Press, but published her second novel, *Foreign Parts* (1994), with the London-based Random House imprint Jonathan Cape. Galloway returned to a Scottish publisher with the publication of her seventh book, *Jellyfish*, published by the Glasgow-based Freight Books in 2015 (following Freight Books going into administration in 2017, *Jellyfish* was republished with additional content by the London-based independent publisher Granta in 2019). Such examples indicate that there are instances of traceable migrations of Scottish authors from Scottish to English, or London-based, publishers in the mid- to late 1980s and 1990s. Whether this is a trend that has continued into the 2000s still needs to be determined through a further analysis of authors' publication histories. What has been confirmed in recent years is that the print run for fiction titles by new authors in Scotland is small, averaging at around 500, according to Squires and Kovač.[48] And, while the location of a book's publisher does not have any impact upon its eligibility for the Society's awards, it is nonetheless important to consider the location of the publishers of books shortlisted for, or winning, the Saltire Society Literary Awards since, as this chapter illustrates, an understanding of the 'Scottishness' of Scottish literature is closely connected to how Scottish literary identity is formed and quantified through geography, national boundaries and belonging.

The Politics of Publishing and Promoting Scottish Literature

The above analysis offers some credence to the apparent trend of established Scottish authors being published outside of Scotland. Such figures also offer some substance to claims that London publishers are less likely to publish work that is considered to be 'overtly' Scottish, particularly from a new author. This specific claim was made by Paul, the former publishing director of an independent Glasgow-based publisher (which has subsequently closed).[49] Paul suggested that the establishment of a literary magazine for 'new Scottish writing'[50] in 2009 'created a focal point for the new writing community' working in Scotland. The magazine – which continues to publish a biannual magazine of new writing as an 'independent cooperative' despite the demise of the publisher – provided a means by which a 'new writing community' could be published in Scotland, Paul argued. He suggested that 'a queue formed straight away of people saying either: "my London publisher's cut me loose post [the 2008 economic] crash" or "I've written a novel about Scotland and my London publisher doesn't want it because it's about Scotland"'.[51] When asked if he felt there was a tension between Scottish authors and London publishers, Paul said:

> I have absolutely, unequivocal evidence [of this], writers come to us and say [they have] 'written this book it's overtly Scottish [and] my London publisher doesn't want it'. On the other hand, our sales guys are saying to us 'take out the word "Scottish" from advance information sheets. Do not mention Scotland. Call it British not Scottish.' Etc. etc. [...] It's not London publisher's fault, it is a macro- economic fact that 45 million people in England are not interested in reading about Scotland, the content has to transcend the location. They have no particular interest in reading about Scotland, in a way that they kind of do have a bit of an interest in reading about America.[52]

When pressed on the fact that some Scottish authors have had success on a national scale and have been published by London-based publishers, such as Alan Warner, A. L. Kennedy, Jackie Kay and Janice Galloway, Paul suggested that this was because their work 'transcends [their] Scottishness'.[53] This idea of an author 'transcend[ing] national boundaries with their success' was repeated by Carol, the owner of another Scottish independent publisher once based in Glasgow.[54] However, the apparent Scotland/London divide is not, Carol argues, necessarily down to culture, content or genre differences, but down to the investment available to writers: 'It's not because [...] people think that they're better because they're published in London, it's because that's where the money is.'⁵⁵

Such issues have always been interconnected with the Society's Literary Awards. Writing in 1997, one of the years in which both the Book of the Year and First Book of the Year Awards were won by books published in London, the journalist and former Saltire Society Literary Awards judge, Alan Taylor, wrote that it was a 'tragedy [...] that neither [book] is published by a Scottish publisher'.⁵⁶ Taylor continued, arguing that 'if this was an isolated incident it could be dismissed as an aberration', but he noted that

> all of the books shortlisted for the premier award were published in England, including a first novel by Ali Smith, whose career was launched on the back of winning the Macallan/Scotland on Sunday short story competition, a sterling biography of Naomi Mitchison by Jenni Calder, Mr Banks's latest eruption, Edwin Morgan's *Collected Translations* and short fictions by AL Kennedy entitled *Original Bliss*.⁵⁷

Although Taylor was incorrect to suggest that all of the books shortlisted for the Society's Book of the Year Award in 1997 were published in London (Edwin Morgan's *Collected Translations* was published by the Manchester-based publisher Carcanet), he was acknowledging the apparent tensions between the publishing locales of Scottish writers and the impact this had on the Society's Literary Awards. Taylor also recognised the parallel between Scottish publishers and the First Book of the Year Award. After listing the 'big guns of Scottish literature' who were published in London, which includes William McIlvanney, James Kelman, Liz Lochhead and Alan Warner – all of whom had won, or been shortlisted for, a Saltire Society Literary Award by 1997 – Taylor continued to say that

> these are not the exceptions. Very few writers who expect to make a living from their art bother with Scottish publishers. They may, as the evidence of the shortlist for the best first book of the year [*sic*] shows, make their debut in Scotland, but they scarper southwards soon after. This is not disloyalty or a lack of patriotism. It is purely pragmatic.⁵⁸

Like Paul 17 years later, who stated that this pattern was not 'London publisher's fault', Taylor's conclusion foreshadowed that of Carol, since he suggests that the real reason why Scottish authors are attracted to London publishers is because, in Scotland, there is 'precious little hope of their needs being met'.⁵⁹

Such regional nit-picking may at first appear superfluous to definitions or explications of Scottish national identity and literature. Yet, the fact that the statistics included here appear to substantiate claims of regional biases – both in terms of 'established' Scottish authors migrating to London publishers and in terms of the Society's predilection to award Scottish-born authors – suggests that not only is there a complex negotiation of national identity in Scottish publishing, but also that, by their very nature as awards for *Scottish* literature and authors, the Society's Literary Awards are intrinsically involved with the ongoing negotiation and circulation of this literary national identity, confirming Pascale Casanova's assertion that 'literary heritage is a matter of foremost national interest'.[60]

As previously noted, Roberts has considered such intricacies between national identity and literary award culture with regard to Canadian literary and prize culture. Roberts has illustrated the significance of the intersection of national identity and literary award culture and how it relates to cultural and economic capital:

> Literary prizes do particular kinds of work; they promote and perpetuate competing forms of valuing [...] and, in the context of national cultural celebration, they contribute to defining the parameters of the nation and its culture [...] Cultural and economic capitals overlap in the workings of the literary prize, but prizes dedicated to national literature also reveal a national capital at work. The ideological implications that underpin national cultural celebrations in a Canadian context are essential to understanding the work that national prizes attempt, with varying degrees of success, and the borders of Canadianness that they draw.[61]

Even though Roberts uses Canada as an example here, her argument is applicable to Scotland and the Society's Literary Awards, particularly if Alan Bold's suggestion that Scottishness is a 'state of mind accepted by Scots and acknowledged by observers' is taken into account alongside Roberts' work.[62] Indeed, the parallels between Scotland and Canada's national and literary identities are, some have argued, historically based. Katie Trumpener has noted that 'Canada's English-language writers closely followed Scottish literary prototypes' and that 'writers of Scottish heritage, moreover, played a preeminent role in the literary life of Anglophone Canada'.[63] However, by the 1960s and 1970s, Trumpener argues, authors such as Alice Munro and Margaret Atwood 'wrote to correct long-standing Scottish views of Canada itself'.[64] Such 'rewritings' arguably parallel those that were happening during the same period in Scotland during its 'second renaissance'.

To stay with this analysis of how Scotland's and Canada's national and literary award cultures are comparable, Danielle Fuller and DeNel Rehberg Sedo have also explored how the elements of literary award culture in Canada intertwine with national identity. In an analysis of the national reading campaign 'Canada Reads', Fuller and Rehberg Sedo argue that such campaigns and related literary awards are a means by which the organisers of said campaigns '[imagine] "Canada" and Canadian literary culture'.[65] In their analysis, Fuller and Rehberg Sedo cite Benedict Anderson's definition of the nation as 'an imagined political community', which is to be 'distinguished, not by their falsity/genuineness, but by the style in which they are imagined', and this is yet another conceptualisation of national identity and nationhood that reflects that of Scotland and the Saltire Society.[66]

Related to this is the fact that Canada and Scotland both share borders with culturally and politically dominant neighbours. Casanova illustrates how the inequity and 'rivalry' between nations, which in the case of Scotland is national as well as international, impacts literary ecologies:

> The original dependence of literature on the nation is at the heart of the inequality that structures the literary world. Rivalry among nations arises from the fact that their political, economic, military, diplomatic, and geographical histories are not only different but also unequal. Literary resources, which are always stamped with the seal of the nation, are therefore unequal as well, and unequally distributed among nations.[67]

At a Saltire Society conference in 1947, it was explicitly stated that there 'was to be no feeling of inferiority' and that 'comparisons with Scotland's southern neighbour were abandoned'.[68] Furthermore, it was stated that 'international contacts were to be made direct with other countries, and members of the Society were to behave as representatives of a small, but important European country'.[69] Accordingly, the Society's own history as a (seemingly) apolitical Scottish-focused cultural charity is demonstrative of how the mix of political, economic and geographic inequities Pascale highlights, can impact understandings and reimaginings of national (literary) culture. Moreover, the above analysis of the Society's Literary Awards illustrates how such inequities or 'rivalries' can play out specifically in relation to publishing and literary award culture, with the apparent pull of established Scottish writers to London illustrating domestic literary 'rivalries' between Scotland and England.

Driscoll has also written about what she calls the 'crisis of national identity' in relation to Australian literary culture developing 'in the shadow of the United Kingdom'.[70] Australia's status as a British colony, Driscoll argues, puts Australian literary culture in a 'subordinated position' with not only the United Kingdom but also the 'commercially powerful United States', as a result: 'Australian intellectuals have long wrestled with "cultural cringe", a sense of inferiority that has driven advocacy for a national literature and for its support and protection by government.'[71] This notion of 'cultural cringe' that Driscoll refers to, coined by the Australian writer A. A. Phillips in 1950, echoes the sentiments shared in the years leading up to and during the founding of the Saltire Society in 1936. As discussed in Chapter 1, a number of Scottish writers and politicians, including Andrew Dewar Gibb, Edwin Muir, George Malcom Thomson and Hugh MacDiarmid, wrote about Scotland's apparent cultural depreciation, with Thomson going as far to say that there was 'no literature in Scotland'.[72] To continue with this analogous example, Driscoll also discusses how Australian literary prizes have contributed to 'nation-building' in Australian culture. Specifically, Driscoll notes how 'Australia's oldest literary prize' – the Miles Franklin Literary Award which was established in 1957 – is 'part of the legacy of an earlier nation-building moment in Australian Literary Culture'.[73] The Society's earliest Literary Awards and commendations certainly aimed to contribute to such '[cultural] nation-building' in Scotland, however, while the Miles Franklin Literary Award 'accumulated prestige' due to its status as Australia's oldest literary prize; the same could not necessarily be said about Saltire Society Literary Awards since, as the final chapters of this book demonstrate, the Society can struggle to uphold their status as signifiers and conferrers of literary prestige.

Such definitions and analytical frameworks are appropriate for an assessment of how the Society positions itself in relation to Scotland's national and literary cultures through its literary awards. Both the quantitative analyses and cultural theories discussed and analysed here demonstrate how the Society engages in the 'imagining' – to borrow Anderson, Fuller and Rehberg Sedo's terminology – of Scottish literary and cultural, and in turn national, identity in terms of what the Society identifies as being 'properly' Scottish. In establishing terms of eligibility based upon an author's national identity, or a book's 'Scottishness', the Society engages in what Roberts calls 'defining the parameters of the nation and its culture'.[74] As discussed in this book's introduction, as a cultural nationalist organisation, the Society is embedded within the celebration of 'national cultural uniqueness', and the Literary Awards are one means by which such celebration manifests.[75] As an award dedicated to rewarding books from and about Scotland, or by Scottish-born authors – a triad of factors that, as this chapter shows, are privileged by the Society's judges when selecting shortlists and winners – the Society's Literary Awards in turn influence how the books and authors receiving the awards are defined in terms of Scottish national identity. This influence is likely heightened by the fact that, since 2013, the Society's Literary Awards are the only series of 'Scottish' literary awards for adult fiction currently operating in Scotland.[76] And while definitions and understanding of national identity are ever changing, the Society's Literary Awards play a role in influencing current understandings of what a 'Scottish' book really is.

Chapter 5

NOTICING TALENT

MICHEL FABER, JAMES KELMAN, A. L. KENNEDY, ALI SMITH AND THE SALTIRE SOCIETY LITERARY AWARDS

In 2019 the literary critic and writer Lesley McDowell resigned from her role as a judge on the Saltire Society Fiction Book of the Year Award panel because, she argued, 'no-one on the panel had read all the books in their entirety' and 'Lucy Ellmann's Ducks, Newburyport – a book written by a woman about a woman – was being overlooked in favour of a book written by a man about a woman'.[1] A newspaper article discussing this controversy considered it in relation to the wider gender disparities of the Society's Literary Awards[2] and, indeed, in literary prizes in general, citing the work of Nicola Griffith who showed that 'books most likely to win awards [are] those written by men about men'.[3] However, one of the most striking aspects of the article was how the Society's programme director, Sarah Mason, had framed the Society's response to the incident:

> The Saltire Society literary awards have a strong track record in supporting Scottish writers. They enable books, authors and publishers that may not ordinarily receive attention in an incredibly competitive and saturated literary marketplace to be brought to the fore and commended for their achievements. [...] The roll call of previous winners is remarkable. Authors like Alasdair Gray, James Kelman, William McIlvanney, Tom Leonard, Muriel Spark, Norman MacCaig, Iain Crichton Smith, Alan Warner, Ali Smith, Liz Lochhead, Janice Galloway, James Robertson, Jackie Kay, Kate Atkinson, AL Kennedy, Sue Black and Michel Faber have all received Saltire Society Literary Awards over the past 37 years. [...] What's more, Kennedy, Kay, Faber and Smith all received the Society's First Book of the Year Award for their debut works before going on to have illustrious careers. Such trends indicate that the Society's Literary Award judging panels have, over the years, had an eye for recognising Scotland's best writing talent.[4]

Indeed, the Society's roster of literary award winners is somewhat of a who's who of contemporary Scottish literature. Many of the authors listed are those who, as discussed in the previous chapter, have seemingly transcended their 'Scottishness' and become nationally, if not internationally, renowned writers, going on to be shortlisted for, and winning, major prizes and have their work adapted for film, television and theatre. In reiterating the calibre of the previous winners the Society's Literary Award judges have selected in the past, Mason is not only attempting to reassert the credibility of the Society's selection processes – which had been brought under scrutiny following McDowell's resignation – but she is also borrowing from the social and cultural capital of the writers she names to affirm the Society's, and their Literary Awards', social and cultural capital, too. As is discussed in Chapter 6, much is made of the 'prestige' of the Society's Literary Awards, despite this being incredibly difficult to quantify. This chapter will examine how part of this prestige, as evidenced by Mason's response, is dependent on a kind of narrative of success that the Society can signal towards via their roll call of winners and shortlistees. However, as this examination of the impact of literary and cultural awards on four major Scottish writers – Michel Faber, James Kelman, A. L. Kennedy and Ali Smith – illustrates, the Society's ability to build this narrative of success depends upon intraconversions of cultural, social and economic capital that are unpredictable and insecure. While the Society frequently uses its list of previous winners as an illustration of its ability to recognise literary talent,[5] the precarious nature of the Society's status of prestige outside of Scotland means that, as authors acquire more recognition from other, more well-known and recognised institutions, the acknowledgement of their Saltire Society Literary Award win is often overtaken in author biographies and paratextual features of books published following the awards. As a result, the history of the Society's recognition of Scottish writers is in a constant state of erasure and replacement.

   This chapter will begin with a brief history of Faber, Kelman, Kennedy and Smith's careers through the awards and honours they have received. Following this, the chapter will illustrate how, as these writers have gone on to win other major literary awards, their 'award-winner' status has evolved, leading to a foregrounding of some prizes over others in their author biographies and the paratextual features of their books. Finally, informed by new interview material with Kennedy and Faber, this chapter considers the kinds of non-commercial impact the Saltire Society Literary Awards, and literary awards in general, can have on the careers and confidences of authors.

From First Book to Booker: Scottish Writers and Literary Awards

The Society's First Book of the Year Award has been awarded annually since 1988. It has, over the years, shortlisted and awarded the debut titles of a number of writers who have since become nationally and internationally renowned, including John Burnside (shortlisted 1988), A. L. Kennedy (winner 1991), Jackie Kay (joint-winner 1992), Irvine Welsh (shortlisted 1993), Ali Smith (winner 1995), Alan Warner (shortlisted 1995) and Michel Faber (winner 1999). This list, although a fair representation of contemporary Scottish writing, has two, perhaps conspicuous, omissions: Alasdair Gray and James Kelman. Since the First Book of the Year Award was not founded until the late 1980s, this was too late for Gray's debut novel *Lanark* (1981) and Kelman's debut collection of short stories *An Old Pub Near the Angel* (1973). However, since Gray received the inaugural Book of the Year Award in 1982 for *Lanark*, he, along with Kelman, has been either shortlisted or selected as winner of the Society's Literary Awards on numerous occasions. Despite never winning the Society's First Book of the Year Award, Kelman is included in this analysis because he is the only Scottish author to have won the Booker, has been shortlisted for the Society's Book of the Year Award ten times and won the award twice. His presence within the Society's, and wider literary award, culture has therefore been constant and warrants examination. Therefore, Kelman, along with Faber, Kennedy and Smith, who all won the Society's First Book of the Year Award and then the Book of the Year Award later in their career, will be the focus of this chapter.

Michel Faber

Faber is the only author of the four discussed in this chapter who is not Scottish: he was born in Holland and grew up in Australia, moving to Scotland in 1992. His location in Scotland has assured his eligibility for a number of Scottish literary awards, including the £6,000 Macallan/*Scotland on Sunday* Short Story Competition for his story 'Fish' in 1996,[6] and the Neil Gunn writing competition organised by the Highland Council in partnership with the Neil Gunn Memorial Trust in 1997.[7] He received the £2,000 Ian St James award (founded by James to 'encourage aspiring writers') a year later for his story 'Some Rain Must Fall'.[8] Faber's First Book of the Year Award win, then, was one in a long line of accolades early in his career. His debut collection of stories, *Some Rain Must Fall and Other Stories* (1998), won the £1,500 First Book of the Year Award in 1999 and a £1,000 Scottish Arts Council (SAC) Award in the same year. It was reported that 'an inventive definition of Scottishness was coined' by the SAC judging panel (chaired by another Saltire favourite, John Burnside) for Faber. Although he was eligible as a resident of Scotland, the panel described Faber as 'being of Scots "formation"', which 'hint[ed] at a certain Scottish cultural predilection in his work'.[9] This debut collection has since been formally 'canonised' by Faber's publisher Canongate, as part of their Canongate Canons series of books, alongside James Joyce, Charles Bukowski, Anne Donovan and A. S. Byatt.[10]

Faber continued to receive accolades for his subsequent books. *Under the Skin* (2000) was shortlisted for the Whitbread First Novel Award in 2000, losing out to Zadie Smith's *White Teeth* (2000). Faber's fellow Canongate author, Laura Hird, was also shortlisted for this award, a success described as a 'remarkable coup'[11] for the publisher and 'all the more remarkable when you consider how rarely Scottish publishers figure when it comes to the major prizes'.[12] *Under the Skin* was subsequently adapted into a film in 2013. Faber's fourth novel, *The Crimson Petal and the White* (2002), was the next to receive significant acclaim and recognition. It was shortlisted for a SAC award and became a commercial success, reportedly 'selling furiously all over the world' and was subsequently adapted into a television mini-series in 2011.[13] Faber's next book, a collection of short stories titled *The Fahrenheit Twins* (2005), was shortlisted for the Society's Book of the Year Award in 2005. A story from this collection, 'The Safehouse', was also shortlisted for the £15,000 National Short Story Prize, which was launched at the *Edinburgh International Book Festival* in 2005 and intended to 'do for the short story what the Booker does for the novel'.[14]

It was Faber's sixth novel, *The Book of Strange New Things*, which would cement his relationship with the Society's Literary Awards. Published in 2014, *The Book of Strange New Things* was shortlisted for the newly formed Fiction Book of the Year Award and went on to win the Society's 'overall' Book of the Year Award. Together, the two awards amounted to a £10,000 prize purse (£2,000 for the category win and a further £8,000 for the Book of the Year). Following the announcement, Faber said:

> When I emigrated from Australia to a remote part of Scotland in 1993, I never expected that it would be the beginning rather than the end of my literary career. I'm so moved and grateful that this honour has been bestowed on my work. You've made an alien feel very welcome.[15]

The novel, which was also shortlisted for the Arthur C. Clarke Award, the 'UK's top science fiction prize',[16] has been reported to be Faber's last. The writing, publication and ultimate success of *The Book of Strange Things* were enveloped in the passing of Faber's wife, which he discussed during his acceptance speech at the Society's Literary Awards in 2015. This context of

Faber's Fiction Book of the Year Award win will be discussed in more detail shortly.

James Kelman

Glasgow-born Kelman attended an evening creative writing class in 1971 where he met Alasdair Gray and Tom Leonard, both of whom he would go on to write with.[17] In 1976, Kelman joined Leonard and Alex Hamilton for the publication of *Three Glasgow Writers*, which showcased the authors' work. In 1985, Kelman, along with Gray and Agnes Owens, published a collection of stories, *Lean Tales*, which was shortlisted for the Saltire Society Book of the Year Award that year. A contemporaneous review of *Lean Tales* described it as 'a book of anger' containing stories by 'three struggling Scottish writers not overwhelmed by praise in Scotland, and largely ignored in England'.[18] *Lean Tales* was not, however, Kelman's first foray with the Society's Literary Awards. His fourth collection of short stories, *Not Not While the Giro* (1983), was shortlisted for the Book of the Year Award in 1983. His sixth collection of short stories, *Greyhound for Breakfast* (1987), was also shortlisted for the Book of the Year Award in 1987 and went on to win the £500 Cheltenham Prize and a SAC Books Award in the same year.

Kelmans's first novel, *The Busconductor Hines*, was submitted for the Booker Prize in 1984, but the chair of judges that year, historian Professor Richard Cobb, suggested it was 'one of the two worst books he had read that year', publicly bemoaning the novel at the 1984 award ceremony saying: 'There is even a novel written entirely in Glaswegian. Lacking a dictionary I soon gave up.'[19] However, Kelman's third novel, *A Disaffection* (1989), was shortlisted for the Booker Prize in 1989. It was considered alongside Margaret Atwood and Kazuo Ishiguro, with Ishiguro ultimately announced the winner for his novel *The Remains of the Day*.[20] Kelman, along with Atwood, was believed to be a 'joint outside[r] at 8-1'.[21] The 1989 Booker Prize shortlist was considered one of the more unusual in the prize's history. Sales of the six shortlisted books did not, it seems, see the usual increase a Booker shortlisting can generate. Ishiguro, who had been shortlisted for the prize three years earlier in 1986, was the only writer to be in the top 10 in the UK book charts in the month following the shortlist announcement, with one commentator suggesting this was 'owing to superb reviews [of *The Remains of the Day*] and little to Booker publicity'.[22] Despite his shortlisting, Kelman did not attend the 1989 Booker Prize ceremony, opting instead to 'spen[d] the day tutoring in Glasgow'.[23] Ishiguro was reportedly sympathetic to 'any author who doesn't turn up to face the huge hype'.[24] Notwithstanding the 1989 Booker 'drama' surrounding *A Disaffection*, the novel was shortlisted for the Society's Book of the Year Award and won the £1,500 James Tait Black Memorial Prize.

The next literary award for Kelman was his now infamous Booker Prize win in 1994 for his fourth novel, *How Late It Was, How Late*. In the weeks leading up to the 1994 Booker ceremony, Kelman was the joint-favourite for the prize, along with Alan Hollinghurst's *The Folding Star* (published in 1995, Hollinghurst's novel was considered a controversial choice for its graphic descriptions of gay sex[25]). As a result, Kelman's win did not, it seems, come as a shock, with one reporter noting at the time, 'There was little suspense at the ceremony, because Kelman had been the favourite and many people in the audience already knew who had won.'[26] This did not prevent Kelman's win from being marred by controversy in the days following the announcement. It soon became clear that the decision to award Kelman the £20,000 prize had split the judging panel, so much so that one judge, Rabbi Julia Neuberger, publicly stated her misgivings about selecting *How Late* as the winning book:

> Rabbi Julia Neuberger, the only woman on the judging panel, said she was made extremely cross by the decision. 'It's just a drunken Scotsman railing against bureaucracy,' she said. 'My eyes are stretched in disbelief. The voting system is completely mad. Kelman was the least favourite of the three front runners. If it had been a short story it would have been fine.'[27]

Neuberger also maintained that Kelman's novel was 'crap', 'deeply inaccessible' and stated that giving him the award was 'a disgrace'.[28]

How Late also won the Writers' Guild of Great Britain for Fiction in 1994 and was shortlisted for the Saltire Society Book of the Year Award, losing out to George Mackay Brown's *Beside the Ocean of Time* (which had also been shortlisted for the 1994 Booker Prize).[29] Kelman's next significant shortlisting would be for *The Good Times* (1998), a short story collection shortlisted for the Society's Book of the Year Award in 1998. *The Good Times* was a joint winner of the Stakis prize for the Scottish Writer of the Year. Kelman shared the prize with Edwin Morgan (who won for his poetry collection *Virtual and Other Realities* (1997)), with both authors receiving £5,500. Kelman's next book, the novel *Translated Accounts* (2001), was longlisted for the Booker Prize in 2001 (the first time the prize published a longlist) alongside Ali Smith's second novel *Hotel World* (2001). In 2004, Kelman was again shortlisted for the Society's Book of the Year Award, for his sixth novel, *You Have to Be Careful in the Land of the Free* (2004). It was also shortlisted for a SAC Award, for which each shortlistee received £2,000.

Kelman's next two novels, *Kieron Smith, Boy* (2008) and *Mo Said She Was Quirky* (2012), would receive the Society's Book of the Year Award in 2008 and 2012, respectively. *Kieron Smith* also won the SMIT Award in 2009, with the SMIT judges describing the book as Kelman's 'masterpiece'.[30] It was during this period, also, that Kelman was twice shortlisted for the Man Booker International Prize, a so-called 'sister award to the yearly Booker, recognising a writer's overall body of work': Kelman was shortlisted for the prize in 2009 (the only British writer shortlisted that year) and 2011.[31] In an incident which echoed the controversy that had followed Kelman throughout his literary award career, during the Saltire Society Literary Awards ceremony at which he received his award for *Mo Said She Was Quirky* in 2012, Kelman gave an impassioned speech about how, despite his awards and critical acclaim, he had struggled to make a living as a full-time writer. This event and Kelman's comments will be discussed in more detail in the final section of this chapter.

A. L. Kennedy

A. L. Kennedy won the Society's £1,500 First Book of the Year Award and the £5,000 *Mail on Sunday*/Llewellyn Rhys ('considered the most important for Britain's young writers') for her debut collection of short stories, *Night Geometry and the Garscadden Trains*, in 1991 and 1992, respectively.[32] Her first novel, *Looking for the Possible Dance* (1993), received a £1,000 SAC Award in 1993 and won the Somerset Maugham Award in 1994. She was also selected by the independent publisher Granta as one of the 'Best British writers under 40' (she was 28 at the time) in 1993.[33] Her second novel, *So I Am Glad* (1995), was shortlisted for the Society's Book of the Year Award in 1995 and won the £7,500 Encore Award (for second novels) in 1996.[34] Kennedy's third novel, *Original Bliss* (1997), was shortlisted for the Society's Book of the Year Award, the Stakis prize for the Scottish Writer of the Year and the SAC Autumn book awards in 1997.[35] *Everything You Need* (2000), Kennedy's fourth novel, was longlisted for the Orange (now Women's) Prize for Fiction in 2000, and her fifth novel, *Paradise* (2004), was shortlisted for the Society's Book of the Year Award in 2004, but was considered 'strangely absent' from the Booker longlist.[36] Amidst these long- and shortlistings, Kennedy was again selected as one of Granta's 'Best of Young British Novelists' in 2003.[37]

Kennedy's sixth novel, *Day* (2007), received a number of major literary awards, establishing her as somewhat of a stalwart of the literary prize scene. *Day* won the Society's £5,000 Book of the Year Award in 2007, the only novel shortlisted for the award that year. On accepting the award, Kennedy said:

> If we are going to ensure there will be further generations of Scottish writers, there is a need to ensure that everyone has [access to books] It's not an ivory tower thing. If you ensure that people can become writers if they wish to, you ensure that your population is able to express itself.[38]

In addition, when discussing the non-fiction book heavy shortlist and Kennedy's win, Literary Awards judge Joyce McMillan noted:

> I think we're going through a vintage period for history by Scottish writers. History can be a powerful literary form and some of these books were among the finest written in Scotland this year. It's unusual for us just to have one novel, although I think Day is the best thing she [Kennedy] has written for ages.[39]

Day also won the £5,000 Best Novel category at the Costa Book Awards, going on to be selected as the overall Costa Book of the Year winner and receiving £25,000. *Day* was reportedly 'hailed by the judges as "a masterpiece"' by the Costa Book Award judges.[40] However, like the omission of *Paradise* on the Booker Prize longlist, some believed it was unusual that *Day* was not shortlisted for the Orange Prize in 2007.[41]

On top of these well-known UK-based awards, Kennedy won a number of international accolades in 2007 and 2008. She received the $150,000 Lannan Foundation (a philanthropic cultural organisation based in New Mexico[42]) award for fiction and the Austrian State Prize for European Literature, awarded to European writers by the Federal Chancellery for Arts, Culture and Media. Kennedy is one of only 11 women to have won the Austrian State Prize in its 54-year history and was described as 'one of the most important and original voices of contemporary literature' during the awards' announcement at *Frankfurt Book Festival*.[43] She also received the inaugural Internationaler Eifel-Literatur-Preis, worth €15,000, for her 'fearless storytelling'.[44]

Kennedy's fifth and sixth collections of short stories, *What Becomes* (2009) and *All the Rage* (2014), were shortlisted for the Society's Book of the Year Award in 2009 and 2014, respectively. *All the Rage* was also shortlisted for the Frank O'Connor International Short Story Award in 2014 (the award was discontinued in 2015). Her ninth novel, *Serious Sweet* (2016), was longlisted for the Booker Prize in 2016 alongside fellow Scot Graeme Macrae Burnet, whose novel *His Bloody Project* (2015) from Contraband, the crime imprint of Saraband, went on to be shortlisted for the prize.[45] Kennedy was also awarded the Heinrich Heine Prize, 'one of the most important literary and personality awards in Germany', in 2016.[46] On receiving the accolade, Kennedy stated that she was 'immensely proud to have received such a prestigious and ethical award for my work', with the prize's jury commenting that

> the author is well known for her idiosyncratic literary work, which plumbs the limits of the human soul. Her views on political and social conditions sharpen social discussions about the Iraq war and

the proposed referendum on the United Kingdom's membership of the European Union [...] AL Kennedy is a great literary figure and a fractious European.[47]

Indeed, Kennedy began her award-winning novel *Day* while 'completely hemmed in writing anti-war stuff before the whole Iraq thing blew up', illustrating how her critical commentary and literary writing coalesced in the novel.[48]

Beyond winning awards, Kennedy has also been a judge for several major literary awards, including for the Booker Prize (1996), the Orange Prize for Fiction (2002) and the Guardian First Book Prize (2001).

Ali Smith

Like Faber and Kennedy, the Saltire Society's recognition of Ali Smith's work began at the beginning of her career. Her debut collection of short fiction, *Free Love and Other Stories* (1995), was shortlisted for, and won, the Society' First Book of the Year Award in 1995. She also received the £5,000 *Scotland on Sunday*/Macallan Short Story Prize a year later in 1996.[49] Her next book and first novel, *Like* (1997), was shortlisted for the Saltire Society's Book of the Year Award in 1997, as was her second novel *Hotel World* in 2001. *Hotel World* (2001) was awarded the Encore Award and the SAC Book of the Year Award in 2001; each prize came with a £10,000 prize purse. On receiving the SAC Book of the Year Award, Smith noted that she had not anticipated the novel to do well: 'It's an experimental book by a gay person from Scotland – it's unlikely to come to the top. It was pretty unlikely to get on the shortlist.'[50] The novel was also shortlisted for the Orange Prize for Fiction and the Booker Prize for Fiction in 2001. Smith's next book was another collection of short stories, *The Whole Story and Other Stories* (2003), which, although shortlisted for the Society's Book of the Year Award in 2003, did not receive the kind of award recognition her preceding and successive novels would.

Smith's subsequent novel, *The Accidental* (2005), was again shortlisted for the Booker Prize and Orange Prize, as well as the James Tait Black Memorial Prize in 2005.[51] The novel won the £5,000 Whitbread Novel of the Year Award. Her next novel, *Girl Meets Boy* (2007), was shortlisted for the Society's Book of the Year Award, won the £5,000 SAC Fiction Book of the Year Award[52] and was selected book of the year by *Diva* magazine's readers in 2008. Smith's next novel, *There But for The* (2011), was shortlisted for the Society's Book of the Year Award in 2011 and longlisted for the Orange Prize for Fiction in 2012. However, despite receiving significant critical acclaim from reviewers, the speculation from one commentator that *There But for The* was 'likely to scoop even more awards for Smith's virtual trophy cabinet' did not come to fruition.[53] Smith's first non-fiction title, *Artful* (2012), was shortlisted for the inaugural Goldsmiths Prize, founded to 'champion fiction that shares [...] exuberant inventiveness and restlessness', in 2013.[54] This was a fitting precursor to Smith's next novel, *How To Be Both* (2014), which would not only go on to win the second Goldsmiths Prize in 2014 (£10,000) but also win the 2015 Bailey's (formerly Orange) Women's Prize for Fiction (£30,000), the Costa Novel Award (£5,000) and the Society's Book of the Year Award (£2,000). It was also shortlisted for the Booker Prize and the Folio Prize.

Between 2016 and 2020, Smith published a series of related novels, *Autumn* (2016), *Winter* (2017), *Spring* (2019) and *Summer* (2020). *Autumn*, described as 'the first post-Brexit novel', was shortlisted for the Booker Prize in 2017.[55] Smith's Baileys Women's Prize for Fiction win for *How To Be Both* was illustrated on the back cover of the first paperback edition of *Autumn* by a small image of the novel's cover and 'WINNER OF THE 2016 BAILEYS WOMEN'S PRIZE FOR FICTION'. However, this was a misprint, as Smith won the award in 2015, not 2016. While rare, such misprints indicate how even paratextual features of the books of award-winning authors can provide the incorrect prize information.[56] The second novel of the quartet, *Winter*, was shortlisted for the British Book Awards' Fiction Book of the Year Award (2018)[57] and the Orwell Prize for political writing.[58] Smith's novel was the only fiction title of the six up for the Orwell Prize; if she had won, it would have been 'the first work of fiction to win the [prize] in more than a decade'.[59] The third book of the quartet, *Spring*, was also longlisted for the 2020 Orwell Prize.[60]

Like Kennedy, Smith has received a number of additional honours and accolades. She was elected a fellow of the Royal Society of Literature in 2007,[61] received the appointment of Commander of the Order of the British Empire (CBE) for services to literature in the Queen's 2015 New Year's honours list[62] and has a number of honorary doctorates, including from Anglia Ruskin University (2008),[63] the University of East Anglia (2016)[64] and Newcastle University (2019).[65]

Bumped for the Booker? Literary Awards as Marketing Tools

As the above overview of the literary award careers of Faber, Kelman, Kennedy and Smith illustrates, their Saltire Society Literary Awards success and recognition interweaves with a large number of other literary awards and cultural and professional accolades. As discussed in the introduction of this book, Claire Squires has explained how a prize 'strapline' can become 'part of a wider marketing mix set to build on the book's [and, I would add, author's] achievements'.[66] Squires uses the Booker Prize as the exemplar of this marketing tactic, and the Booker Prize is an obvious example since the print runs of Booker-winning books, and books by Booker-winning authors, will certainly include this information on the front or back cover of new editions. While this is a usual and recognisable feature of the marketing of award-winning books and authors, it remains important to consider how this employment of award wins is actually used. When examining the publications by multi-award-winning authors discussed above, it becomes clear that certain awards or accolades are favoured over others when they are being used as part of the 'marketing mix' of a book or author. While this may seem like an obvious point – of course it makes good marketing sense for a publisher to highlight a Booker Prize win over a lesser-known prize – there are two key reasons why it warrants further examination. First, in favouring certain awards over others in their marketing of award-winning authors and books, publishers are contributing to how the negotiation and intraconversion of cultural and social capital of awards is enacted in the literary marketplace. This, in turn, adds to the wider perception of the status of literary awards. Second, and relatedly, such favouring of certain awards over others is further evidence of the hierarchy of literary awards that is constantly at play in literary award culture. The use of certain awards over others on book cover straplines or author biographies acts to strengthen an effective ranking of literary awards. This can be in quite literal terms when a 'major' award shortlisting is favoured in an author's biography over earlier, or subsequent, 'smaller' award wins – even if the award is for the very book in which the information is included (the hierarchy of literary awards is examined in more detail in the final chapter of this book). Analysing different editions of books by Faber, Kelman, Kennedy and Smith from throughout their career demonstrates how awards like the Saltire Society Literary Awards might be 'bumped' from book covers and author biographies in favour of other prizes.

A paperback version of Michel Faber's Saltire Society Book of the Year Award–shortlisted *The Fahrenheit Twins*, published in 2006 (a year after the original hardback release), includes the following information about the author:

> Michael Faber has written five previous books, including the international bestseller *The Crimson Petal and the White*, and the Whitbread-shortlisted novel, *Under the Skin*, both of which have been published all over the world. He has also won several short-story awards, including the Neil Gunn, Ian St James and Macallan. *Some Rain Much Fall*, his debut collection, won the Saltire First Book of the Year Award in 1999.[67]

Here it is the best-seller status of *The Crimson Petal and the White*, followed by the Whitbront shortlisting of *Under the Skin*, that is positioned at the forefront of Faber's career highlights up until this point, indicating that best-sellerdom or a shortlisting for a 'major' award is more notable (at least in terms of what is most marketable to readers) than 'smaller' award wins.

Changes in author information in a paperback edition of *Under the Skin*, released in 2014, coincide with the film's release (the novel was originally published in 2000). This author bio, provided on the inside of the back cover, reads:

> Michel Faber has written eight books. In addition to the Whitbread-shortlisted *Under the Skin*, he is the author of the highly acclaimed *The Crimson Petal and the White*, *The Fire Gospel* and *The Fahrenheit Twins*. He has also written two novellas, *The Hundred and Ninety-Nine Steps* and *The Courage Consort*, and has won several short-story awards, including the Neil Gunn, Ian St James and Macallan.[68]

Initial focus has been drawn to *Under the Skin*'s shortlisting for a Whitbread Award, which makes sense given that this is a new edition of the book. The best-seller and award-winning status of *The Crimson Petal* and *The Fahrenheit Twins* has been amalgamated under the descriptor 'highly acclaimed', yet the references to specific short story awards has remained. This edition of *Under the Skin* also notes that '*The Book of Strange New Things*, Faber's new novel is coming in Autumn 2014'.[69] The author information on the inside back cover of the 2015 paperback edition of *The Book of Strange New Things* is very similar to that of the 2014 edition of *Under the Skin* bar two differences: the number of books Faber has written is updated to nine, and there are two puff quotes from reviews of *The Crimson Petal*. The publisher's (the Scottish independent publisher Canongate) website does not observe *The Book of Strange New Things*'s winning of the Saltire Society Book of the Year Award, but does state that it was adapted for the television and film streaming service Amazon Prime in 2017.[70] The highlighting of this over any literary achievements of the book suggests that film or television adaptations of award-winning books may well overtake literary award wins in the marketing mix of an author's work. Indeed, the fact that a Scottish publisher who has been shortlisted for and won a number of Saltire Society awards but fails to foreground Faber's Literary Awards suggests that there is a lack of recognition of the import of these awards even within Scottish publishing. What is perhaps more likely, however, is the fact that the adaptation of books into new, mainstream media forms brings with it its own signifiers of prestige and negotiations of cultural value(s). As Colleen Kennedy-Karpat and Eric Sandberg argue when applying James F. English's Bourdieusian readings of prize culture, 'intraconversion [of symbolic capital] can also occur between media through the processes of adaptation'.[71] Accordingly, in this instance, it may be the case that the publisher has favoured the prestige and cultural cache that comes with adaptation over Faber's literary award wins, to both attract new readers-cum-viewers and signpost this development to existing readers.

As the only winner of the Booker Prize out of the authors discussed – and, indeed, the only Scottish author to win – Kelman's post-Booker publications almost always highlight his win. For example, a 1994 hardback reprint of *How Late It Was, How Late* includes a 'Winner of the 1994 Booker Prize' banner printed along the top of the front cover.[72] Likewise, the author information in a 1999 paperback edition of *A Disaffection* (originally published in 1989) states:

> James Kelman['s] books include *Not not while the giro*, *The Busconductor Hines*, *A Chancer*, *Greyhound for Breakfast*, which won the 1987 Cheltenham Prize, and *A Disaffection*, which won the James Tait Black Memorial Prize and was shortlisted for the Booker Prize. His most recent novel, *How Late It Was, How Late* won the 1994 Booker Prize.[73]

This succinct summary of Kelman's work is similar to that of the 'About the Author' blurb included in a 2009 paperback edition of *Kieron Smith, Boy*, but it is updated to include additional prize wins:

> [Kelman] is the author of numerous novels and collections of short stories, including *Greyhound for Breakfast*, winner of the Cheltenham Prize for Literature; *A Disaffection*, awarded the James Tait Black Memorial Prize; *How Late It Was, How Late*, winner of the Booker Prize and Writers' Guild Best Fiction; *The Good Times*, winner of the Scottish Writer of the Year Award; and, most recently, *You Have to be Careful in the Land of the Free*.[74]

Unlike the author information provided in Faber's books, Kelman's publications and accolades are listed in chronological order, meaning the Booker Prize win is not foregrounded, as might be expected. This may be an aesthetic marketing choice by Kelman's publishers, reflecting the author's preference for a low-key profile (he has acquired a reputation for being a 'difficult recluse', although even the journalist who noted this says Kelman 'seems aeons away from [this] popular portrayal' of him[75]) and the negative impact the Booker Prize had. In a 2019 interview, Kelman 'used the word "suppression" to describe the publishing industry's response to his work'.[76] The article continued to note how booksellers were reluctant to stock *How Late It Was, How Late*: 'Dillons, then the second biggest booksellers in the UK, declared that it would no longer stock

Kelman's books. Another major bookstore in Glasgow displayed every Booker winner except for his.'[77] Even the Saltire Society, who had already displayed their advocacy of Kelman's work, even shortlisting *How Late It Was, How Late* for the Book of the Year Award in 1994, were reported as reacting negatively to Kelman's win, with the Society's administrator, Kathleen Munro, reportedly saying, 'It's an unfortunate portrayal of Scotland. I am afraid we are our own worst enemy sometimes'.[78] Munro's contradictory comments, which the Society apologised for in a letter to Kelman, likely only added to the author's sense that his writing was unwelcome in his home country. Accordingly, the apparent equalising of prizes in the bios included in Kelman's books may be influenced by the author's complex relationship with the Booker Prize.

However, the 2009 paperback edition of *Kieron Smith, Boy* makes noticeable reference to winning the Saltire Society Book of the Year Award. Not only is 'WINNER OF THE SALTIRE SOCIETY SCOTTISH BOOK OF THE YEAR 2008' printed in bold on the top half of the back cover of the book, but the book's first page also includes a quote from Douglas Gifford, who is listed as 'Saltire Society Literary Panel Convenor' (which is slightly anomalous since Gifford was not the panel chair the year *Kieron Smith, Boy* won the Book of the Year Award, but he was chair a year later when this paperback edition was published).[79] Gifford's quote – 'One of Scotland's greatest novels – and by far the greatest novel about a city boy's childhood' – is at the top in a list of seven; the six other quotes are identified only by the newspapers from which they come. Accordingly, Kelman's Saltire Society Book of the Year Award win and the praise from one of the award judges is given 'top-billing' in this edition of the book, indicating recognition of the accolade the book received. Indeed, this particular example of how awards are used in the marketing of Kelman's books suggests that the Society's award has not, in fact, been 'bumped' for the Booker, and it is not the only example of a puff quote from a Saltire Society Literary Awards judge appearing on a paperback edition of one of Kelman's books. Former Literary Awards judge Isobel Murray is quoted on the cover of a 2007 paperback edition of *The Busconductor Hines* (originally published in 1984). Murray's quote – 'The book enacts the physical life of the character brilliantly. I recommend reading it. And re-reading it' – is included on the back cover of the book, alongside a short quote from the *Observer* newspaper and a one-word quote – 'Masterly' – attributed to Alasdair Gray.[80] In addition to these quotes is a short biography of Kelman which makes reference to his Booker Prize win and the fact that he won the award 'amidst a storm of controversy'.

Recent editions of Kennedy's award-winning novels are less consistent in their recognition of her Saltire Society Literary Award wins. A 2004 paperback edition of *Night Geometry and the Garscadden Trains* (originally published in

1990) does not reference the fact that the book won the Society's Book of the Year Award, but the author biography on the book's front matter does include Kennedy's Book of the Year Award win:

> [Kennedy] has received many prizes for her work, including the Somerset Maugham Award, the Encore Award and the Saltire Scottish Book of the Year Award. She was chosen as one of *Granta*'s twenty Best of Young British Novelists in 1993 and 2003.[81]

Kennedy's subsequent publications or reprints have made reference to her most successful novel *Day*, either directly or indirectly, in terms of literary awards. Upon receiving the Costa Book of the Year Award in 2007, hardback editions of *Day* included the strapline 'Winner of the 2007 Costa Book of the Year' along the bottom of the front cover. The Costa Award, along with Kennedy's inclusion in the Granta Best Young Novelists list in 1993 and 2003, has subsequently become the leading accolade referenced in new publications. A 2017 paperback edition of Kennedy's novel *Serious Sweet* includes a 'Longlisted for the Man Booker Prize 2016' strapline on the front cover, but the 'About the Author' information in the book's front matter only references Kennedy's Granta selection, the Costa Book of the Year Award and her role as a lecturer in creative writing at Warwick University.[82]

However, the most interesting example of the use of Kennedy's Costa Award win in the promotion of her more recent publications is its use on the cover of her 2018 novel *The Little Snake*. The front cover of the paperback edition, released in 2019, includes the strapline 'Winner of the Costa Book of the Year'. Likewise, the publisher's (Canongate) website also references Kennedy's Costa Award win, describing the novel as 'a magical, charming and deeply moving fable about love, family, war and resilience from the Costa Prize-winning author of *Day*'.[83] What makes these references to Kennedy's past award noteworthy is how vague they are. The strapline 'Winner of the Costa Book of the Year' on the paperback edition of Kennedy's 2018 novel is ambiguous enough to suggest that *The Little Snake* is the novel that won Kennedy the award. The publisher's website description of the novel as coming 'from the Costa Prize-winning author of *Day*' is similarly ambiguous since, although *Day* is mentioned, the phrasing does not make it clear whether Kennedy won a Costa Award specifically for *Day*. Such a technique simultaneously relies on a prospective reader understanding the significance of winning a Costa Award, without necessarily knowing exactly which novel by Kennedy won the prize.

Similar practices are used in the marketing of Ali Smith's books which, of all the books discussed here, use award shortlistings and wins most persistently and discerningly. Smith's first book, *Free Love and Other Stories*, is an excellent example of this. As noted above, Smith received the Saltire Society First Book of the Year Award for *Free Love*, and a 2002 edition of the book (which was originally published in 1995) refers to this in the author biography at the start of the book:

> [Smith's] book of short stories, *Free Love* (Virago 1995), won the Saltire First Book of the Year Award and a Scottish Arts Council Book Award. Her first novel, *Like* (Virago 1997), was nominated for the Saltire Award. She is also the author of *Other Stories and Other Stories* (1999), *Hotel World* (2001).[84]

This edition of *Free Love* is one of the few books discussed here which foregrounds Scottish literary awards over others. However, the front cover of an updated 2015 edition of *Free Love* includes the header strapline: 'The first book by the author of *How to be Both*, winner of the Baileys Prize for Fiction'.[85]

As a multi-award-winning book, *How to Be Both* is also illustrative of the using, and updating, of literary awards on book covers. *How to Be Both* was released in August 2014, and as the Booker Prize longlist was announced in July, there was time for some copies of *How to Be Both* to be printed with the strapline 'Longlisted for the Man Booker Prize 2014' on the front cover. However, when the book was published in paperback just under a year later in April 2015, Smith had been shortlisted for the 2014 Booker and won the Costa Novel of the Year Award and the Bailey's Women's Prize for Fiction. Accordingly, these accolades were added to the book's front cover, with the Bailey's Prize represented with the prize's logo – a bottle of Bailey's – along with 'Women's Prize for Fiction 2015 Winner' in a golden flag. On the back cover of the paperback of *How To Be Both*, Smith's Goldsmiths Prize win, Saltire Society Literary Book of the Year Award win and Folio Prize shortlisting are listed.[86] While the Saltire Society Literary Book of the Year Award win is included in these prize listings, joining a host of well-known awards, the way in which the prizes are listed essentially hierarchises them. The placement of the Costa Year Award win and the Booker Prize shortlisting on the front cover suggests they are favoured as a signal of literary value and prestige over the Goldsmiths Prize, which Smith won; this is despite the fact that the Goldsmiths Prize's prize purse was £10,000, significantly more than the Costa's £5,000 and the Booker's £2,500 for shortlisted authors. However, 2014 was only the Goldsmiths' second year, so it is possible that the cultural capital of the Costa and Booker Prizes was considered more significant and commercially recognisable than the relatively new Goldsmiths.

What such analyses of the paratextual elements of books by literary award–winning authors indicate is that the referencing of literary awards and accolades in and on an author's book is not without biases which reflect, and reaffirm, the capacity for book awards to signify an author's or book's success. As the examples discussed here illustrate, there are clear tendencies to emphasise certain types of award wins or shortlistings over others, so much so that some award shortlistings – such as for the Booker – are perhaps considered more valuable in terms of cultural capital than actually winning a lesser-known or emerging award. Such industry ranking of awards through book marketing has contributed to the development of a hierarchy of literary awards, discussed in more detail in the final chapter of this book.

The Impact of Winning Awards

The following statement, which A. L. Kennedy published on her website, was quoted in a 2008 newspaper article announcing her Costa Book of the Year Award win:

> Prizes do not make sense. Keep away from them, do not consider them, they are none of your business, if you write, unless you happen to be judging one, in which case, try to arrange for the best book to win. If you win one, keep your head down and try to pretend it was because your book was good.[87]

Here Kennedy intimates that cultural prizes are somewhat of a lottery that writers should 'keep away from', since they can make little sense, even to those who are involved in their administration or adjudication. Kennedy suggests that even when one is judging for a prize, the best one can do is to '*arrange* for the best book to win' (emphasis added), and that if writers do win, they should 'pretend it was because your book was good'. Such comments hint at the fact that judging processes are rarely straightforward debates which end with a settlement on one single 'best' book, but are actually negotiations and compromises which might see one judge's favourite pipped to the post by a more generally favoured title. Such allusions to judging processes align with observations both myself (as researcher) and Claire Squires (as award judge) have made about the Society's Literary Awards. Squires described her experience of the Society's Literary Awards' judging panel process, which included a 'vote' for a shortlist that required judges to numerically rank entries, effectively giving books a score by which their popularity among the panel could be ascertained. Squires, however, would write that this process meant that there was no real discussion about how the books had been ranked, and about whether it meant that books which were consensus choices made it onto the shortlist by getting 5s and 6s, rather than a book which one person had ranked really highly, but others seemed to dislike. [...] It also meant that whichever book was sitting at the top of the rankings would then become the winner, without any further discussion. This also seemed odd, and didn't seem to work like any other prize I was aware of.[88]

Squires did alert the panel to the problems with this method, and when a number of judges agreed that more discussion could help, the voting process (in this instance, at least) was abandoned. However, for Squires, the point being made was that 'numbers weren't objective' and she was 'urging [the panel] to be more discursive in [their] decisions'.[89] While there is nothing to suggest that, in her comments, Kennedy is referring to the judging processes that attempt to numerically quantify the ranking of books in the running for awards, her comments nonetheless make reference to the prevalence of bargaining in prize adjudication, which Squires's experience also attests to.

Elsewhere, Kennedy has written specifically about how she felt following a prize win:

Last night I won a book prize and for ever after journalists have been asking me, 'How do you feel?' [...] Me, I don't know what I feel, and meanwhile I am being distracted by the other question they keep asking, which is: 'What're you going to do with the money, Al?' [...] And meanwhile why don't I feel anything? I just won a prize. If I can't be happy for myself, I can be happy for my words – they just won a prize.[90]

Back in London, when I won the prize, I didn't feel anything because I don't write for prizes. They are very nice. [...] Which is a good thing, because the only way – I hate to say this – to really do it is for love.[91]

Such observations indicate a certain level of ambivalence towards literary awards and the kind of media intrigue and invasion that an award win can invite. When I asked Kennedy about the specific experience of winning a Saltire Society Literary Award, she admitted that, when she was first informed by her publisher that she was nominated, she 'wasn't aware of them [...] and then looked up what they were' going on to say that 'at that time the reports really did seem to revolve around encouraging the flying of the Saltire'.[92] Kennedy said she was 'pleased' to have been selected, but acknowledged that, compared to other awards she had won, the tangible impact of winning a

Saltire Society Literary Award was minimal, largely due to their low profile outside of Scotland:

> The Saltire's don't have that much of a profile outside Scotland. The English literary establishment isn't that interested in Scottish prizes and other countries don't understand them. I got much more attention and increased sales from the Costa Prize and winning something like the Austrian State Prize for International Literature or the Heinrich Heine Preis […] If I compare German awareness of what is a 'regional' prize – the Heinrich Heine – it's much greater than UK awareness of the meaning of Saltire awards. […] In summaries made by national and international interlocutors – which are their choice of awards to mention – they don't usually choose to highlight the Saltires, which is a shame, I think. I would hope that Scotland's increasing national and artistic confidence would lead to an increase in attention for Saltire and understanding of its role. […] Sadly, the amount of money being awarded seems to be all that the press understands, especially in the UK and Saltire doesn't compare that well with […] Costa and so forth.[93]

Kennedy's observations align with the findings of this examination of the Saltire Society Literary Awards which illustrates how they have failed to garner much in the way of media attention and cement their status as a significant national award. Kennedy's comments also aptly reflect the findings discussed in this chapter, most notably the fact that there is a hierarchy of awards at play and that the media and publishing industry's interest in one prize is not necessarily reflected in others. If the impact of award wins can fluctuate from prize to prize, what, then, do authors 'get' out of winning a Saltire Society Literary Award?

With regard to her First Book of the Year Award, Kennedy noted that the 'amount of money made a massive difference and, of course, there is some kind [of] increase in confidence'.[94] Faber echoes this in his reflection on winning the First Book of the Year Award in 1999 for his first book, *Some Rain Must Fall*, stating that 'this was a big encouragement for me'.[95] Like Kennedy, Faber noted how he was in a 'precarious' financial situation as an early-career writer and recalled:

> Delicately negotiating with the Saltire people about whether I could afford to make the journey from the Highlands to Edinburgh, which would involve train tickets and an overnight stay in a hotel. We understood that the winners were supposed to be a secret revealed only on the day of the award, but we needed some sort of clue that we wouldn't be

making this long and expensive journey only to eat some hors-d'oeuvres and travel home again. I think the organisers said something about it being 'a very good idea' that we should come, so we took that as a hint.[96]

This notion of the First Book of the Year Award being a symbol of encouragement and support is, in fact, recognised by the Society's judges. One judge, who was a Saltire Society Literary Awards judging panel member for over ten years, has suggested that judging a first book is slightly different to judging a book by a more established writer:

When you're looking at first books I think you are conscious at the back of your mind that this is the first published book by a new writer, and therefore if a book has many other excellent qualities, but there's perhaps just something – let's say about the characterisation or perhaps the plot, or whatever – then I think you could overlook that if the sum of the parts is sufficiently good in a way that you wouldn't for a well-established writer.[97]

The judge here suggests that there is perhaps some latitude for the First Book of the Year Award since the award is generally given to authors in the early stages of their career, and therefore the awards provide encouragement as well as recognising a book's 'excellent qualities'. Considered together, Faber's and the judges' comments support the notion that early-career prize wins are important not only for an author's confidence but also, at times, for their financial security. Indeed, the fact that Faber wanted to delicately confirm if he had won the First Book of the Year Award before making the financial commitment to travel and stay in Edinburgh, where the Society's Literary Awards ceremonies take place, foregrounds some of the very practical issues that writers can come up against. Kelman has also spoken candidly about this in relation to a Saltire Society Literary Award. During his acceptance speech for the 2012 Book of the Year Award for *Mo Said She Was Quirky*, Kelman admitted that the £5,000 prize fund would be 'really useful' since he had only made £15,000 from his writing in 2011.[98] More recently still, when Anna Burns won the Booker Prize in 2018 for her third novel *Milkman* (2018), with a prize purse of £50,000, she stated that this meant she would no longer need to receive benefits from the Department of Work and Pensions, who she thanked in the acknowledgements of her book.[99] A 2018 survey of authors' earnings in the United Kingdom by the Authors' Licensing and Collecting Society (ALCS) further demonstrated how authors are not only earning less from their writing – authors' 'actual earnings solely from writing' went down from £12,330 in 2005 to £10,437 in 2017 – but that 'grants and bursaries

[...] prizes and fellowships' are viewed as 'additional income streams'.[100] Such examples and surveys reveal that, while lottery-like in their conferral, another key impact of prizes and their economic capital is their ability to provide an immediate boost to an author's income.

Following a recollection of his earliest encounters with the Saltire Society Literary Awards, Faber discussed his 2015 Book of the Year Award win for *The Book of Strange New Things* in detail. His recollection is significant, and so is quoted at length:

> My last encounter with the Saltires was in 2015. My wife Eva had died of cancer the year before and I was deep in grief. *The Book Of Strange New Things* was supposed to be my final novel – it had been planned as such before Eva was even diagnosed – but once she was ill, the story evolved to incorporate her decline, and its finality loomed large for both of us. She gave me lots of good editorial advice as always, and saw the book through to its completion, although she didn't live to see it published. I knew it was the most extraordinary thing I'd ever written and a fitting farewell to my career as a novelist for adults (I've since written a book for children and am working on non-fiction) but I was too lost in the isolation of my grief to have much conception of how the wider public perceived it.
>
> I almost didn't make it to the Saltire ceremony, as it was snowing lightly that day and Scotrail's trains predictably ground to a halt, stranding me first in Inverness and then again somewhere further down the line. Upon arrival in Edinburgh, I ran to the venue [...] I arrived flustered and haunted and exhausted, and got much comfort from the hugs of my friends at Canongate. As the evening went on, I became more and more aware of the love and appreciation that the Scottish literary community felt for me and my work. *The Book Of Strange New Things* won Fiction Book Of The Year, which was not just an honour in itself but an affirmation of how the Scots had taken this Dutch-Australian immigrant to their hearts. I gave a speech about how I'd always felt like a person without a nationality but that I was feeling very Scottish, and I meant it. I left the stage, intending to retreat to the back rows of the venue to watch the presentation of the next award, the overall Book Of The Year. One of the Saltire staff touched my arm as I tried to pass, and indicated that I should stay in range of the stage. Minutes later, to my astonishment, *The Book Of Strange New Things* was awarded that prize too. I have no idea what I said in response, as I had no speech prepared. It's no exaggeration to say that it was the high point of my literary career – far more

significant to me than *The Crimson Petal* having been in the *New York Times* bestseller list, which felt to me more like an abstract statistic whereas that evening at the Saltires felt like a perfect combination of critical respect and affectionate goodwill.[101]

Faber's eloquent recollection of the 2015 ceremony rings true. I was lucky enough to witness this prize-giving, and there was something particularly poignant and momentous about it. It was not only because of the trace of sadness with which Faber accepted the award and acknowledged the passing of his wife, but it was also his expression of his feelings of acceptance and appreciation that came from the Scottish literary community. As Faber notes and as illustrated in this chapter, *The Crimson Petal* is his most successful book in terms of sales and international recognition, but he suggests here that winning the Book of the Year Award was more significant. It was 'a perfect combination of critical respect and affectionate goodwill' encapsulated at the ceremony not only by monetary and cultural value but also a cordiality between Faber, his publisher, the award administrators and judges. This indicates that for the Saltire Society Literary Awards, while economic and journalistic capital may not be at the forefront, a clear acknowledgement of an author's accomplishments can be, as Faber suggests, of uniquely personal significance.

The purpose of this chapter was to investigate how the Saltire Society Literary Awards have fared, both in terms of reputation and impact, in effectually contributing to the celebration and support of four multi-award-winning authors throughout their careers. Through case studies of the literary prize careers of Michel Faber, James Kelman, A. L. Kennedy and Ali Smith, this chapter has revealed that, while consistent in their support and celebration of these authors, the Society has remained vulnerable to the structures of a literary prize hierarchy that can see similar or even ostensibly less impressive accolades (that is to say, longlistings and shortlistings versus wins) pitted against each other in the promotion and marketing of prizes. While this may at first seem an innocuous, and perhaps even normal, aspect of competition culture, it shows that there is significant variance in the cultural value placed on prizes, with a longlisting from one award being more highly regarded than a win of another. Moreover, as the case of Faber illustrates, there can be more to winning a prize than the cultural accolade and financial reward, which are generally used as markers by which we attest to a prize's impact. Faber remarked that the receipt of the 2015 Book of the Year Award 'was not just an honour in itself but an affirmation of how the Scots had taken this Dutch-Australian immigrant to their hearts', with the award being indicative of 'affectionate goodwill'. Such comments reveal how there can almost be a form of emotional capital involved in the process of prize-giving, especially when an institution has celebrated an author from early in their career. As a result of such findings and the ambiguity they cause, it is necessary to interrogate current understandings of literary award culture and consider how a more nuanced and inclusive model, through which the individualities of cultural awards can be explored, might be developed. The final chapter of this book begins these interrogations and proposes some new ways by which to understand literary awards.

Chapter 6

NOT YOUR TYPICAL BOOK AWARD

NEW WAYS OF THINKING ABOUT LITERARY AWARDS

Throughout this book I have made reference to key scholars and texts that have become central to academic scholarship about prize culture, and literary award culture in particular. These are discussed in detail in the introductory chapter, where I illustrate the fields use and development of the work of Pierre Bourdieu regarding the identification, negotiation and intraconversion of cultural, social, economic and journalistic capital. While scholars may agree on the transactions and intraconversions of capital within literary prize culture, this chapter will challenge current understandings of how literary award culture functions. As this history of the Saltire Society Literary Awards reveals, literary awards do not exist within a cultural vacuum, but are in fact shaped by the external sociocultural and political events and circumstances from which they are created and exist. What this examination of the Saltire Society Literary Awards also illustrates is how constructing such cultural histories of prizes not only enables for a better understanding of the sociocultural and political environment from which prizes emerge but also reveals more insight into how literary prizes function within the literary and publishing industry. Accordingly, in this chapter I will demonstrate that, in order to progress current understandings of literary prizes (and, indeed, cultural prizes more generally), it is important to consider new methodologies and conceptualisations for critical analyses of literary awards.

Current Understandings of Literary Awards Culture

As it stands, there are certain prizes which hold, and will hold forevermore, a pinnacle status within the hierarchy of literary awards (and cultural awards more generally). James F. English argues that there is a 'single-winner axiom' which underlies the 'entire prize economy'.[1] He applies this to the Nobel Prize for Literature, suggesting that the single-winner axiom underlying the entire prize economy assures that the dominance of the Nobel is in no way diminished (and may even be enhanced) by the increasing field of contenders, none of which can ever rise above a decidedly secondary position.[2]

English also employs this concept to the founding of the Booker Prize, maintaining that, although the Booker did have two of the United Kingdom's oldest pre-existing literary awards to contend with, it was still able to take advantage of the 'single-winner axiom' because

> the earliest surviving book prizes in Britain – the James Tait Black and the Hawthornden (both contemporary with the Pulitzer) – had neither sought nor attained the limelight [...] this meant that an upstart prize in Britain [i.e. the Booker Prize] had the rare chance to become *the* prize, to seize belatedly the virtually unassailable position of the *prize of prizes*: a position that is mandated by the single-winner axiom that underpins the entire prize economy, but which, in Britain, appeared to be unoccupied.[3]

While not framed in the exact terms, Pascale Casanova's estimation of the role of the Nobel Prize for Literature as a consecrator of literary value leans into this notion of the single-winner axiom, suggesting that the Nobel is

> the greatest proof of literary consecration, bordering on the definition of literary art itself [...] It is also indisputably the most prestigious prize beyond the border of the literary world. For more than one hundred years now, the Nobel has been the virtually unchallenged arbiter of literary excellence. No one (or almost no one) professes any longer to be surprised at the esteem in which this institution is everywhere held, nor does anyone doubt the validity of the worldwide reputation that it confers upon a single writer each year.[4]

Such an assertion seems almost hyperbolic in its absolutism, especially given that the actions and decisions of the Swedish Academy have received criticism and scrutiny in mainstream media since the publication of Casanova's work.[5] However, Pascale's views reveal the kind of opinions about literary awards that can exist, particularly in terms of oft-called 'major' prizes like the Nobel.

It is worth spending some time here to comment on some of the criticisms Casanova's work has received, since they relate to the problems inherent with the placement of such cultural authority. A key criticism of Casanova's *The World Republic of Letter* was her focus on Paris as a defining centre of cultural taste and values. As Bali Sahota noted, 'for Casanova, universality is best determined by Parisian taste'.[6] Similarly, Christopher Prendergast has argued that '[Casanova's] theoretical framework of reference creates the impression of an inescapably Eurocentric purview. Wherever she goes, Europe – and Paris in particular – seems not to be far behind.'[7] Highlighting this critical commentary of Casanova's work is important here for two reasons. First, it is important to bear this in mind when using her work in conversations concerning the negotiation and circulations of literary value(s), as it reveals the bias of the work. Second, and more importantly for this study, Casanova's proclivity to consider Paris as a cultural hub on which to base broader understandings of world literature(s) is, ironically, very similar to what has happened in literary prize discourse in terms of the favouring of acquiring understandings of literary prizes through an 'inescapably Eurocentric purview' which has favoured examinations of awards like the Booker Prize and Nobel over all others.[8]

Beth Driscoll has also considered potential rivalries existing among literary awards hierarchy – rivalries that English's placement of the Booker as a 'prize of prizes' in the United Kingdom, and Pascale's proclamation that the Nobel is the world leader of literary awards seemingly ratify – noting that 'the competition between prizes is relentless: the hierarchy of prizes is always in dispute and never finally settled'.[9] However, despite noting that there is constant fluctuation in the conditions of such a hierarchy, with a prize's position being changeable, Driscoll still finds the exceptionalism of English's 'single-winner axiom' useful and expands upon it to demonstrate that 'the competition between prizes produces middlebrow literary effects, as their extensive use of media both celebrates the mystique of high culture and stimulates trade'.[10] Nevertheless, this 'single-winner axiom' is not only continually destabilised and undermined by joint winners, cancelled prizes and refused and shared prize purses, but it also greatly limits how literary awards might be understood. This approach emphasises a top-down power dynamic of prize culture which implies a small number of awards maintain control over arbitrating literary and publishing culture, and this implication has led to an over-reliance on the examination of such awards to provide understandings of literary award culture. As a result, our current understandings of literary award culture are based largely on the proceedings of an exceptional few as opposed to being informed by the more ordinary singularities of literary awards (which this study of the Saltire Society Literary Awards provides). Indeed, the power that 'major' literary awards are imbued with is not – as will be stressed throughout this chapter – inherent to the prize, but is perpetuated, orchestrated and managed by prize organisers and industry and media commentary. However, what if there are prizes, like the Saltire Society Literary Awards, which do not attract regular or substantial media coverage? If, as Driscoll suggests, a 'fundamental stake in the competition between prizes is not prestige but visibility' and that the aim of prize administrators is to 'raise the visibility of their prize above that over other awards' – and this is how prizes like the Booker and Nobel have achieved their top-tier status in the hierarchy of literary awards – where does this leave prizes like the Saltire Society Literary Awards which, as this study has proven, have continually struggled to maintain media interest, or garner significant journalistic capital, for the awards?[11]

Such journalistic capital is commonly measured through a prize's ability to increase book sales. The quite reasonable assumption being that more coverage of authoritatively consecrated books leads to more interest in books and authors, and, therefore, more sales. However, if book sales are seen as a means by which to quantify a prize's journalistic capital and, in turn, cultural and economic capital, since investment in prize winners indicates a level of trust in the prize's decision-making process, what happens when a literary prize receives little media coverage and has a diminutive, or uncertain, impact on book sales?

The Saltire Society Literary Awards and Quantifying Prestige

As discussed in Chapter 2, the Saltire Society Book of the Year Award was formally reinstated in 1982 because there was no existing award specifically for Scottish literature. Therefore, at the time, it had its own specific set of motivations and own 'niche' to fill. Thus, it arguably had the opportunity to become the lead of the so-called single-winner axiom for literary awards for Scottish literature in Scotland. However – despite the Society founding the Book of the Year Award at a time at which there were no other national prizes for Scottish writing, a landscape which provided ample room for the Book of the Year Award to establish its reputation as the authoritative arbiter of Scottish literature – the Society and its series of Literary Awards were unable to establish and maintain a commanding reputation in the UK literary scene.

The reputation and prowess of the Society's Literary Awards, or lack thereof, has been scrutinised over the years. In 2001, the literary agent Giles Gordon, whose clients included Alasdair Gray, Sue Townsend and Fay Weldon, was quoted in a *Sunday Herald* article stating that it was 'depressing' that few people outside of Scotland had heard about the Saltire Society Literary Awards.[12] Gordon felt that 'one of the disadvantages of the Scottish literary awards is they don't have any kudos or impact outside of Scotland itself, which surely has to be depressing'. He added: 'The Booker Prize has been heard of in Scotland, have the Saltire awards been heard of in England? No.'[13] Continuing, Gordon suggested:

The main advantage of authors winning prizes, particularly the Booker, is not so much that the author gets a sizeable cheque in his or her pocket, but it does mean that with the author's next book the publishers will pay far more money, because there will be competition between publishers to take on that book. It will be translated into many more languages than ever before, it will probably be filmed.[14]

For Gordon, the Society had failed to garner significant publicity, which he referred to as 'kudos and impact' for their Literary Awards. This, as a result, limited the awards' potential to further the spoils for the victor (e.g. book sales, rights sales), as promised by other prizes like the Booker. This is despite the fact that, as the article notes, the Society's Literary Awards were at that point 'Scotland's foremost literary award since the demise of the Scottish Book Trust's awards' (see the Introduction for more on SBT Awards).[15] In response to Gordon's comments, then chair of the Society's Literary Awards panels, Douglas Gifford, argued:

> Publicity for us has never been the major factor. Paradoxically I think we've managed because we haven't courted publicity. Of course the Saltire wants the results to be known, but we've worked on the basis that if we worked at being credible, we would establish the award as something people accepted more and more as, let's not say authoritative, but people would tend to trust that judgment.[16]

Gifford's argument suggests that, far from being a negative, the Society's determination to avoid 'courting publicity' is indicative of the credibility of the Literary Awards. This idea relates to the wider, oft-repeated notion that integrity is favoured over renown when it comes to the Society's judges (literary or otherwise). On the announcement of the 2016 winners of the Saltire Society Literary Awards, then Executive Director, Jim Tough, stated that 'excellence is the common thread [of the award winners], built on the integrity and freely given commitment of our expert panels'.[17] This point was reiterated again in a report for the Society's trustees in March 2017, in which it was noted that 'our awards panels give our awards credibility and integrity'.[18] Similarly, a student who attended the 2013 Literary Awards ceremony wrote in a blog about the event that 'the awards are the oldest and among the most prestigious for authors based in Scotland. The society is well known for their integrity and commitment to excellence.'[19] While such comments may well be hyperbolic, they are nonetheless significant, since integrity is almost posited as being mutually exclusive to fame or publicity. In this way, the Society's Literary Awards are not wholly dissimilar to the Booker Prize. As Driscoll has noted:

> The Man Booker Prize has consistently eschewed celebrity and non-expert judges because judges, through their own symbolic capital and through their chosen winners, are significant determinants of a prize's reputation and influence on the field. English is perceptive on this point: 'it is the first axiom among prize administrators that the prestige of a prize is reciprocally dependent on the prestige of its judges' (2005, 122). Judges of the Booker Prize tend to be academics, authors, literary editors of major newspapers of the literary media (such as broadcasters or critics).[20]

However, Driscoll's and English's assertions reveal one of the many contradictions that exist within current understandings of literary award culture. If the 'prestige of a prize is reciprocally dependent on the prestige of its judges' – and the Booker Prize has acquired symbolic and cultural capital through its judges who, like the Saltire Society Literary Awards judges, 'tend to be academics, authors, literary editors of major newspapers etc.' – why is there such disparity, in terms of this particular kind of capital intraconversion, between the awards and their judges? This is not to suggest that, because the Society's Literary Awards share a similar approach to judges as the Booker Prize that they should be considered on par with one another, but such incongruity in the application of existing interpretations of prize culture highlights how current discourse on the subject is not necessarily transferable.

It is worth pausing, here, to explain how 'prestige' is being understood herewith. Colleen Kennedy-Karpat and Eric Sandberg have argued that, in its simplest terms, prestige 'denotes the admiration felt by a particular community for a particular person or thing, and is linked directly to the idea that its bearer possesses some sort of exceptional quality'.[21] However, notions of prestige – or cultural value to apply a more Bourdieusian terminology – are complicated by the fact that it is a 'largely constructed phenomenon that relies on various economic, social, and institutional forces that join together to "consecrate" selected works'.[22] As Kennedy-Karpat and Sandberg explain, 'there is little room here for any sense of the object itself acting as an authentic, rather than constructed, source of cultural prestige' and if 'prestige is "simply" an external recognition of this internal value', it is 'little more than a consensual validation of a communal hallucination'.[23] Accordingly, prestige is not a fixed attribute of cultural objects or art, but is a state of being applied by external forces. We recognise this in literary award culture as an awarding body selecting a particular book as 'the best' of any given year, but what if we apply this perception of prestige to literary awards themselves? What makes a literary award prestigious, enabling it to effectively 'pass on' this prestige to its associates (shortlisted authors and publishers, winners, judges, etc.)?

The Saltire Society has always persevered to present its literary awards as highly regarded and prestigious within Scottish literary culture. Press releases announcing that submissions for the awards are open have stated that the awards are 'widely recognised as Scotland's most prestigious book awards' and that the awards 'represent a long-standing commitment [...] to celebrate and support Scottish literary achievement'.[24] Newspaper reports often repeat this, leading with the Society's reputation. There are a multitude of examples of the Society's Literary Awards being referred to as 'prestigious' or Scotland's 'top' award (albeit often by the same journalists in the same publications).[25] Writing in 2006, Rosemary Goring, the literary editor for the *Herald*, stated that 'if there was a prize for the best book prize, the Saltire would walk it'.[26] Goring continued, arguing that the Society's Literary Awards are dependable in ways other awards have failed to be:

> The Saltire has proved itself a stalwart of the literary scene, mercifully unsullied by the whims of sponsors and determined to acknowledge the best rather than the most fashionable writers. [...] That decision reveals the Saltire to be an outstanding literary arbiter, willing to rectify what may be seen as wrongs or simply to bestow distinction on those who richly deserve it.[27]

Although at times erroneous (the histories of Literary Awards detailed in this book reveal instances in which the Society *has* been influenced by, or at the very least has responded to, the 'whims of sponsors'), Goring's commendations epitomise the kind of praise the Society's Literary Awards can receive. However, Goring has also been a critic of the choices made by the judges of the Society's Literary Awards, stating that the decision to award the Book of the Year Award in 2004 to Andrew Greig's *In Another Light* (2004) 'dimmed' the 'prize's reputation as a champion of literary excellence' because she disagreed with the selection of Greig over fellow shortlistees James Kelman and A. L. Kennedy.[28] Indeed, while Goring's apparent change of attitude towards the Society's Literary Awards between 2004 and 2006 may be explained merely by a change in perspective, this oscillation of opinions on the Society's prestige and impact has been echoed by a number of people. A previously shortlisted author said that the Society's Literary Awards 'added to the richness of Scottish cultural life' but had perhaps 'gotten tired, and a wee bit worn, like an old book itself'; but this author also intimated that the 'Saltire does have a significant brand affect'.[29] Carol, a Glasgow-based independent publisher, argued that, generally, the awards are 'seen as quite prestigious awards in Scotland' but are not 'very recognised outside Scotland', continuing to suggest that the prize winners 'impress booksellers and I'm not really sure about the general public, but [the Saltire Society] is a well-known body'.[30] Another Highlands-based publisher, Derek, said that they considered the Literary Awards a 'major cultural milestone in Scotland's year', but also said the Saltire Society needed to 'make the public more knowledgeable of [the Awards]' and make them 'more respected or respected to the degree that they are worth, that they should get. Many people in Scotland don't know about the Saltire Society prizes at all.'[31]

Such comments echo those from Gordon regarding the awards' 'kudos and impact' and imply that, if the Society's Literary Awards are not making some kind of tangible impression outside of Scottish literary culture, then they are not 'doing their job' as well as they should be. This idea that a prize's prestige is associated with the kind of impact it has on a book's reputation (demonstrated, in theory, through increased post-award sales) or an author's career (quantified by new opportunities such as new book contracts or rights sales) is perpetuated by media coverage. The Booker Prize has grown to become synonymous with 'best-seller' status: the Booker website even comments that 'to win is to become a best-seller' and refers to this upsurge in a book's sales as the 'Man Booker effect'.[32] Claire Squires has commented on how the conscious 'intention to increase book sales' was in fact 'central to the [Booker Prize's] mission from its inception'.[33] A 2012 analysis of Booker Prize shortlists and winners revealed the extent of the impact an association with the award could have on books' sales.[34] Books shortlisted for the 2011 Booker Prize, for example, saw an average increase of 51 per cent in the volume of sales the week following the shortlist announcement. Between 2001 and 2011 winners saw an average increase in sales of over 1000 per cent – with some books' sales increasing by as much as 1918 per cent – in the week following the announcement of the winner.[35] The Booker is not unique in its status as an award which stimulates sales for authors and books associated with it. The Scotiabank Giller Prize for Canadian literature, which offers a substantial $100,000 to its winner and $10,000 to each shortlistee, has also been credited with increasing book sales, with winners seeing an average 543 per cent rise in sales.[36] Likewise, the Prix Goncourt for French literature is said to have a nominal prize fund of €10 because 'the "prestige" of the Goncourt is generally explained in terms of the tremendous increase in book sales it effects: the Goncourt winner becomes an instant millionaire'.[37]

However, if such measures are used to determine the impact of winning or being shortlisted for a Saltire Society Literary Award, it becomes clear that, like the attainment of 'prestigious' judges, this cannot be used as a universal signifier of prestige within literary prize culture. Previous winners of shortlisted books and their publishers have acknowledged that an association with a Saltire Society Literary Award does not necessarily equate to a boost in book sales or exposure. One London-based independent publisher said that their book being shortlisted for the First Book of the Year Award made no difference to the number of books being ordered by bookshops: 'in sales terms, no store took [the book] into stock, including Waterstones, and the award seems to have generated three sales'.[38] Likewise, the founder of a Scottish-based publisher of pamphlets and books of poetry also observed that the impact the awards have on book sales is minimal. They had published a debut collection of poetry which was a co-winner of the Society's First Book of the Year Award in 2012. Following the win, the publisher felt that this led to a sale of 'about 25 copies' of the book, with most of these being 'ordered by Waterstones'.[39] Accordingly, the publisher felt that 'in terms of actual number[s] that I could say "those have definitely come from the fact that it won that award" [it would be] about 5 or 6 copies', which the publisher felt was 'a tiny, tiny impact'.[40]

An analysis of book sales pre- and post-announcements of Saltire Society Book of the Year Award shortlists and winners between 2013 and 2015 certainly indicates that the impact of the awards was erratic at best, and non-existent at worst.[41] In 2013, seven books were shortlisted for the Book of the Year Award:

- Kate Atkinson, *Life after Life* (Doubleday, 2013)
- John Burnside, *Something Like Happy* (Jonathan Cape, 2013)
- Julie Davidson, *Looking for Mrs Livingstone* (Saint Andrew Press, 2012)
- Gavin Francis, *Empire Antarctica* (Chatto and Windus, 2012)
- Donnchadh Macgilliosa, *Máiri Dhall agus Sgeulachdan* (Clár, 2013)
- James Robertson, *The Professor of Truth* (Hamish Hamilton, 2013)
- Ali Smith, *Artful* (Hamish Hamilton, 2012)

This shortlist was announced on Sunday, 6 October 2013, and the awards ceremony was held on Thursday, 14 November 2013. Books sales data[42] are available for all but one of the titles (Donnchadh Macgilliosa's book of short stories and poetry, *Máiri Dhall agus Sgeulachdan*). The data indicate that some titles saw an increase in sales following the shortlist and winner announcements. Sales for Francis's *Empire Antarctica* and James Robertson's *The Professor of Truth* increased in the month following the shortlist announcement (period ending 2 November 2013) by 58 and 86 per cent, respectively. Likewise, there was an increase in sales for most of the titles in the month preceding the awards ceremony, ranging from 32 per cent for both Davidson and Smith, to 263 per cent for Robertson and 245 per cent for Atkinson. There was, however, a small decrease in sales of Burnside's *Something Like Happy* – by 10 per cent – despite it winning the 2013 Book of the Year Award.

Similarly, some of the books shortlisted for the 2014 Literary Book of the Year Award shortlist saw a similar increase in sales in the weeks following the shortlist and winner announcements (on Saturday, 4 October, and Tuesday, 11 November, respectively).

- Anne Donovan, *Gone Are the Leaves* (Canongate, 2014)
- A. L. Kennedy, *All the Rage* (Jonathan Cape, 2014)
- Sally Magnusson, *Where Memories Go* (Two Roads, 2014)
- Martin MacIntyre, *Cala Bendita 'S a Bheannachdan* (Acair, 2014)
- Rona Munro, *The James Plays* (Nick Hern Books, 2014)
- Ali Smith, *How To Be Both* (Hamish Hamilton, 2014)

Donovan and Kennedy saw an increase of 28 and 68 per cent, respectively, in the month following the shortlist announcement. Donovan also saw an increase in sales by 76 per cent following the awards ceremony. That year's winner, Ali Smith's *How To Be Both*, actually saw a decrease in sales following the shortlist announcement, by 53 per cent , but an increase of 232 per cent following the awards ceremony. However, Smith's novel also won the 2014 Goldsmiths Prize which was announced a couple of days after the Saltire Society Literary Awards ceremony on 13 November. While it is difficult to ascertain which award had the most impact on Smith's sales, given the inconsistency of the sales of books shortlisted for and winning the Book of the Year Award, coupled with the evidence presented in Chapter 5 of the Society's struggles to compete with other awards when it comes to author biographies and book paratext, it is unlikely that the Book of the Year Award alone was responsible for this increase in sales, if at all.

Finally, in 2015 (at which point the Book of the Year Award had been split into the Fiction and Non-Fiction Book of the Year Awards), six titles were shortlisted for the Fiction Book of the Year Award:

- Kate Atkinson, *God in Ruins* (Transworld Publishers, 2015)
- Michel Faber, *The Book of Strange New Things* (Canongate, 2015)
- Janice Galloway, *Jellyfish* (Freight Books, 2015)
- Norma Nicleoid, *An Dosan* (Acair, 2015)
- Andrew O'Hagan, *The Illuminations* (Faber & Faber, 2015)
- Irvine Welsh, *A Decent Ride* (Jonathan Cape, 2015)

The 2015 shortlist announcement was held on Thursday, 22 October (slightly later than in previous years). This later announcement makes ascertaining any impact the shortlist may have had on book sales more difficult, as there was less time between the shortlist and winner announcements to see a change in sales. Despite this, there was an uptick in sales – by 63 per cent – for Atkinson's *God in Ruins* in the month following the shortlist announcement. Likewise, Welsh's novel, *A Decent Ride*, saw a slight sales increase by 16 per cent. The most dramatic increase in sales appears to be for Norma Nicleóid's novel, *An Dosan*, which saw an increase of 400 per cent – but this was an increase in sales from one to five copies. This is perhaps a noticeable difference for a Gaelic-language title (which will likely sell fewer copies anyway), and it may have been influenced by the announcement of the Fiction Book of the Year shortlist; but, nevertheless, the dataset remains too small to provide a definitive indication as to the level of influence the announcement had. Alternatively, some titles actually saw a reduction in sales following the shortlist announcement: Galloway and O'Hagan saw a drop in sales of 57 and 45 per cent, respectively, in the month following the shortlist announcement.

There were significant leaps in sales in the period following the winner announcement on Thursday, 26 November 2015, but this sales period ended on 2 January 2016, meaning this includes figures for the lead up to and post-Christmas.[43] The Literary Awards winner announcements being held at the end of November complicates determining an impact on sales due to an award win, since an uptick in sales is expected at the beginning of the Christmas shopping season. This – coupled with a number of peculiarities in the sales data (such as sales for Burnside's *Something Like Happy* going down in the month following his win in 2013, and Smith's Goldsmiths Prize overshadowing her 2014 Saltire Society Book of the Year Award win), and the fact that the books that see the largest sales increases in late November and early December are from well-known, bestselling authors (which we would expect to see anyway at that time of year) – suggests that the Society's Literary Awards may have little to no impact on the sales of shortlisted and winning books.

On the other hand, it is tempting to argue that, since the authors of the books shortlisted for the First Book of the Year Award are potentially unfamiliar to a wider readership, upsurges in sales of their books could reflect the publicity generated by their inclusion on the Society's First Book of the Year shortlist. In 2015, for instance, the sales for Helen McClory's *On the Edges of Vision* (2015) doubled in the month following the announcement of her winning of the First Book of the Year Award. Both McClory and her publisher began immediately promoting her award win with a blog post.[44] The day after the ceremony, the publisher posted a picture of McClory holding her winning book and trophy on Twitter.[45] Considering that monthly sales for McClory's debut collection of short stories had fallen to an average of five in the lead-up to the awards ceremony, but increased by 138 per cent between her award win and the start of January 2016, it is possible that receiving an award from the Society did increase the sales of her book. Similarly, sales for

Kellan MacInnes's *Caleb's List: Climbing the Scottish Mountains Visible from Arthur's Seat* (2013), which was shortlisted for the First Book of the Year Award in 2013, improved by 900 per cent in the month following the awards ceremony. However, such sales surges also corresponded with the Christmas shopping season. It is also worth noting that while these percentage increases may seem dramatic, they could, as already noted, signify an increase from single-figure to double-figure sales. MacInnes's *Caleb's List*, for example, sold six copies in the week before the 2013 awards ceremony, with this increasing to 60 copies in the weeks leading to Christmas.

What this brief analysis indicates is the problematic nature of using book sales data – particularly when the data sets are small – as a means of quantifying the impact, both economically and culturally (in terms of having a strong enough reputation as a consecrator of value that it can influence book sales), of the Society's Literary Awards. Other factors also problematize the accuracy of placing the impact of a book's sales on the Society's influence alone. For example, Gavin Francis's *Empire Antarctica* won the £30,000 SMIT Book of the Year Award in November 2013, weeks before the Society's awards ceremony.[46] The large cash fund of the SMIT Award made it 'the richest prize in Scottish literature', with this status garnering much in the way of media coverage for the prize.[47] It would be fair to suggest then that the upsurge in sales for *Empire Antarctica* in November 2013 was influenced by the SMIT Award win rather than it being included on the Society's Book of the Year Award shortlist. This example goes against English's hypothesis that it is 'nearly impossible' for a new prize to displace a pre-existing prize:

> But the reality is that [...] it nearly impossible for a newer prize to supersede an older one that has begun to be recognized as the 'Nobel' of its subfield. The ambition of the newer prize, rather, is to situate itself in a relationship of marked, and possibly antagonistic, complementarity to the dominant one, establishing its own apparent necessity by reference to some failing or lack in its more esteemed predecessor.[48]

As previously noted, the Society's status as the first series of awards established to celebrate Scottish fiction might lead us to expect that the Society's Literary Awards would, by default, be considered as the ' "Nobel" of [their] subfield' – the subfield here being Scottish literature; however, once again the fact that the Society's Literary Awards were over-shadowed by much younger awards arguably subverts our current understandings of how literary awards operate in the broader literary economy.

Consequently, it is clear that the Saltire Society Literary Awards do not function as existing academic scholarship and cultural commentary suggests.

They are highly regarded, with many arguing they are prestigious (albeit this is often mitigated with calls for the Society to better promote the awards both within and outwith Scotland), but the awards have no discernible or consistent impact on the sales of shortlisted or winning books. And, as the previous chapter demonstrated, their influence on an author or book's reputation can be easily erased or superseded by other prizes. They were the first, are the longest running and are currently the only (at the time of writing) awards dedicated to Scottish literature, and yet they have been unable to maintain the status of the 'single-winner axiom', frequently being overshadowed by awards with similar remits but more substantial prize purses. Accordingly, if we cannot use the methods or theorisations of economic, cultural and social value exchange(s) and prestige to quantify – or qualify – the status and impact of the Saltire Society Literary Awards, how might their position in the literary marketplace be conceptualised?

Not All Prizes Are Created Equal: Literary Award Hierarchies

Cultural prizes and awards for literature and other creative endeavours share commonalities in process (a set of competition rules, terms of eligibility, winners and runners up, etc.) and perhaps theme (awarding a specific aspect or type of work within a creative industry). Nevertheless, each prize has a unique origin story, which reveals the different motivations of the prize's founders and organisers. The Academy of Motion Picture Arts and Sciences (AMPAS), for example, first awarded Oscars for 'distinctive achievements' in film in 1929.[49] However, the AMPAS itself was founded in part because of studio fears of increasing unionisation among workers, and the awards were viewed as a means by which to collectively celebrate 'the honor and good repute of [moving pictures]'.[50] The Women's Prize for Fiction (formerly Orange Prize (1996–2012) and Bailey's Women's Prize for Fiction (2014–17)) was founded in response to an all-male Booker Prize shortlist in 1991.[51] The Mercury Prize for the best album by a British or Irish act[52] was first awarded in 1992 and is said to have been founded as an alternative to the more commercial and mainstream Brit Awards,[53] which claim to be 'the annual showcase for the UK music industry'.[54] Accordingly, while there are a multitude of prizes that celebrate the same kinds of creative endeavour, each award's motivations and position within the broader hierarchy of cultural prizes is very different, and such positions affect the levels of influence, impact and prestige an award might have.

What has become evident throughout this cultural history and examination of the Saltire Society Literary Awards is that a recognition of prestige is not enough to ensure a prize's position in the field. It may guarantee an award's status among those directly related to the award and its work – judges, shortlistees, winners, booksellers, journalists, invested readers – but it is in the interest of such parties to maintain this sense of prestige, as it ensures their own relative prestige. What has also become evident is that, while exchanges and intraconversions of cultural, economic, social and journalistic capital happen on a micro level for each individual prize, they also affect the status of prizes on a macro level. This means that an award's status within the hierarchy of literary awards is dictated not only by its own negotiations of capital but also by how it compares to other prizes within the hierarchy.

Bourdieu has written extensively on the mechanisms of hierarchies in the arts, and specifically in literature, discussing the hierarchies of value and literary 'legitimacy' with regard to genre and writers in *The Field of Cultural Production*. However, the following passage, which describes the monopolies of power at play within literary hierarchies in relation to writers, can be easily modified ('writer' has been here replaced with 'literary awards') to illustrate how a hierarchy of literary awards might function:

> The established definition of the [literary award] may be radically transformed by an enlargement of the set of people who have a legitimate voice in literary matters. It follows from this that every survey aimed at establishing the hierarchy of [literary awards] predetermines the hierarchy by determining the population deemed worthy of helping to establish it. In short, the fundamental stake in literary struggles is the monopoly of literary legitimacy, i.e., *inter alia*, the monopoly of the power to say with authority who are authorized to call themselves [literary awards]; or, to put it another way, it is the monopoly of the power to consecrate producers or products (we are dealing with a world of belief and the consecrated [literary award] is the one who has the power to consecrate and to win assent when [it] consecrates an author or a work – [...] a prize, etc.).[55]

When 'writer' is substituted for 'literary awards', Bourdieu's explanation of the 'struggles [in] the monopoly of literary legitimacy' becomes strikingly apt for an analysis of the hierarchy of literary awards. All of this is to say that there is no innate power or 'legitimate voice' to literary awards; such power is generated both through external factors – media hyperbole, publishers using awards as promotional signifiers on book covers and websites – and the interior processes of literary award culture itself. So, because the Booker has established itself as a significant arbiter, or 'consecrator', of literature, the annual consecration it goes through, which is spectacularised in a near-identical fashion each year, sustains its status as *the* significant consecrator of literature. As a result, there is an inevitable imbalance of power since – while other potential consecrators such as the Saltire Society Literary Awards are also 'taking part in a struggle to impose the legitimate definition of literary or artistic production' alongside the Booker Prize – their inability to 'win assent' beside or over the Booker only acts to further strengthen the cultural domination of the Booker (and apparent inferiority of the Saltire Society Literary Awards). As a result, the Booker's 'monopoly of literary legitimacy' overshadows the entire literary award culture.

David Savran has employed this logic of the hierarchies of cultural legitimacy to illustrate how the canonisation of creative work also contributes to the construction of cultural hierarchies and

> represents an itinerary of cultural legitimation that privileges and excludes certain kinds of tests as well as their makers and consumers; it constructs cultural hierarchies [...] and it establishes aesthetic, ideological, and moral values and standards that masquerade as disinterested and universal.[56]

Literary prizes, like all cultural prizes, are implicated in such acts of canonisation. Both in terms of the public-facing and publicised creation of a canon of prize winners and shortlistees, and in the formation of their roll call of winners which becomes part of the prize's own identity and narrative of success (as discussed in the previous chapter). What is also important about Savran's analysis of cultural hierarchies, and which encapsulates the arguments against applying homogenous interpretations of literary awards, is the fact that the development of cultural hierarchies leads to the 'masquerad[ing]' of understandings of cultural production as 'disinterested and universal'.[57] As illustrated throughout this chapter, the analysis of the Saltire Society Literary Awards proves that drawing universal understandings of award culture(s) from those prizes at the top of cultural hierarchies, which have been given the power to establish 'aesthetic, ideological, and moral values and standards', can be unhelpful when trying to identify the nuances that reveal what makes an award's contribution to its cultural landscape unique.

Furthermore, as Savran notes, canonisation 'more often than not functions as a tool of domination', acting as an agent in the symbolic violence of hierarchical culture supremacy.[58] This symbolic violence is

> the inevitable by-product of the operation of systems that classify through the operation of binary oppositions in which one terms (e.g., man, white, heterosexual) is privileged at the expense of its supposed contrary (e.g., woman, black, homosexual). All symbolic systems

function by grouping persons and properties into opposing classes and they engender meanings and values through a 'binary logic of inclusion and exclusion'.[59]

The 'binary logic of inclusion and exclusion' is a fundamental logic of prizes: there needs to be a loser, for there to be a winner. However, the arbitration of who such winners and losers are is continually proven to be problematic. This imbalance of power within literary prize culture and the implications of symbolic violence within it is explored in work by Dane, Huggan and Norris. As Dane explains:

> The inclusion and exclusion of different groups of authors, in the construction of shortlists and selection of the winner, is an act of symbolic violence that seeks to maintain traditional hierarchies of power in the literary field.[60]

The selection processes of prizes are, as Dane highlights, examples of such acts of 'symbolic violence', but the prize hierarchy – which empowers certain prizes, like the Booker Prize and the Nobel Prize for Literature, to ordain value and prestige within literary prize culture more broadly – is also an act of symbolic violence. Huggan indirectly evidences this in his examination of the Booker Prize and postcolonial writing, illustrating ways in which the Booker has influenced the 'postcolonial field of production'.[61] Huggan argues that 'the Booker Prize, even as it has expanded public awareness of the global dimensions of English-language literature, has paradoxically narrowed this awareness to a handful of internationally recognised postcolonial writers', and has commercialised what he refers to as the 'postcolonial exotic' which is 'integral, rather than peripheral, to the postcolonial field of cultural production'.[62] Likewise, Norris has argued that the Booker Prize is a particularly useful exemplifier of how symbolic violence operates in literary award culture:

> The issue of symbolic violence is highly pertinent to the Booker Prize, since those involved with this award, including judges, shortlisted authors, and members of the management committee, tend to be from a particular class. This at very least calls into question whether the 'best novel' is assessed on aesthetic grounds or in relation to social values (insofar as it is ever possible to separate the two).[63]

While such studies illustrate how the Booker Prize uses its power to impose regulatory standards of cultural and literary value, it has also come to do this in the literary prize hierarchy. Huggan hints at this, noting that the Booker is involved in a 'self-perpetuating process of recognition, much enhanced of course by the global media'.[64]

Emmett Stinson signals towards this problem, too, in relation to Australia's 'most significant literary awards' – the Miles Franklin Award.[65] In reference to English's argument regarding a literary award being recognised as the Nobel of its subfield, Stinson notes:

> Major prizes exert a disproportionate effect on the way that cultural products within a given field are valued. It is for this reason that the Miles Franklin Award [...] continues to be an important reflection of the way that the Australian field *values itself* [...] the provenance of the books that are longlist, shortlisted, and win the Mile Franklin, suggests that the prize's notion of literary value is disconnected from the realities of contemporary literary production.[66]

While not going so far as to frame the 'disproportionate effect' of 'major prizes' as a form of symbolic violence, Emmett indicates that the Miles Franklin Award's status as a major prize means it is almost entirely detached from the real workings of Australian literary culture, making it near unworkable in its efforts as a consecrator of literary value. Driscoll, on the other hand, has argued against considering the Booker Prize's cultural supremacy as symbolic violence, specifically refuting the suggestion that Booker Prize judges 'exert symbolic violence' because they 'have been unable to present a coherent idea of literary value'.[67] In this sense, Driscoll argues, 'the case of the Man Booker Prize is not unique; prizes in general are not effective at defining literary value. Prizes, in fact, unsettle literary value.'[68] While it would be fair to say that the Booker Prize is not unique in the sense that it is part of a wider network of literary value arbitration which does indeed include other prizes, as well as literary reviews, book blogs, scholarly writing and other discourse(s) concerning the qualities of literary value(s), the Booker Prize is unique in its status as a 'major' award, from which knowledge of literary prizes more generally has been deduced. It is for this reason that the power imbalance of prizes at the top of the hierarchy, such as the Booker Prize, extends beyond their own arbitration of literature and infiltrates the literary award economy as a whole.

Such imbalances of power, sustained, as Huggan identifies, through media commentary, have led to an almost obsessive observance of the work of some literary awards over others in critical literary award discourse. As this examination of the history and impact of the Saltire Society Book of the Year and First Book of the Year Awards has shown, the Society's Literary Awards – bar during the late 1980s and early 1990s when the awards had substantial corporate sponsorship – have continually struggled to garner much in the way of significant media coverage and, as a result, have never acquired the kind of mainstream, non-industry-focused prestige or cultural capital that is considered central to a literary award's identity and success. However, this book argues that this approach to understanding literary prizes and their wider impact has developed because major, internationally known literary prizes, like the Booker or the Nobel, are used as archetypes, as opposed to exceptions, of literary prize culture. As English has noted, prizes like the Nobel and Booker, and our understanding of their apparent prestige in the collective cultural consciousness, have led to them becoming examples by which other awards are compared:

> Each prize that achieves a premier position in a particular field, and that becomes, however contestably, the 'Nobel' of that field, produces a host of imitators with various legitimating claims of similitude and difference. Each successful act of differentiated imitation in turn gives rise to another order of imitators, and so on.[69]

Though it is true that this kind of hyperbolic paralleling is common within prize culture, such embellishment is perhaps less about imitation and more about trying to establish a prize in terms that are widely understood. For example, the Mercury Prize for music states that it is the 'music equivalent to the Booker Prize for literature and the Turner Prize for art'.[70] This is done to position the prize within the hierarchy and establish its credibility and reputation alongside other high-value, well-known prizes. This can work in opposition, too. The *Guardian* newspaper holds an annual 'Not the Booker' prize to 'find the year's best book, which may – or may not – tally with the assessment of the Booker prize judges'.[71] The prize involves the newspaper's readership, who nominate titles, submit reviews of their chosen books and vote for entries, which are then combined with votes from a panel of judges. This, of course, being a much more open and, seemingly, more democratic approach to the judging process than the Booker itself, and this is exactly how the 'Not the Booker' prize has carved its niche: 'Not the Booker' works because we know what the Booker *is*. We might call this what English refers to as 'differentiated imitation'. However, whereas English argues that this 'in turn gives rise to another order of imitators', I would suggest that what is happening is that yet more prizes solidify their status, or lack thereof, in comparison to those prizes at the top of the hierarchy and, in so doing, only further reaffirm the power of prizes at the top.

Literary prizes, therefore, engage in the 'symbolic violence' of power inequity not only in terms of the content and artists they celebrate (with an exclusion, or exoticisation, of the work of women writers and writers of colour, for instance) but also in terms of how they negotiate their status within the literary prize hierarchy. It is important, therefore, to consider how such a literary prize hierarchy has developed and what continues to sustain it.

False Equivalence and Literary Awards Culture

One of the key factors that enables such hierarchies to flourish and, in turn, influence how literary awards are discussed in both academic and media discourse is the assumption that because they share certain qualities – such as rules and terms of eligibility, submission processes, judging panels, winners, runners-up, award ceremonies – literary awards are inherently analogous: a prize is a prize is a prize. However, as this examination of the Saltire Society Book of the Year and First Book of the Year Awards suggests, this is not the case. The Society's Literary Awards share many of the characteristics of major prizes like the Booker and Nobel: longevity and a record of recognising major writers and their work; corporate sponsorship (albeit this has been extremely inconsistent in the case of the Society); considered 'prestigious' by the industry and those within it; expert judges; and, perhaps most importantly, being the 'first' to do what they do. But they are also very different, and quite deliberately so. Not just in terms of what they award but also in how the awards are administered and managed. From the beginning, the Booker Prize was active in its courting of the media in order to establish the prize within popular culture. This is a very different founding motivation to that of the Saltire Society whose impetus, it has always maintained, was to 'recognise' and 'celebrate' Scottish writers and their work. The Society, and likely many other prize institutions, perhaps assumed that an annual celebration of literature over several decades would inevitably lead to a building of status and momentum akin to the Booker, but this does not happen and, because of the literary prize hierarchy, cannot happen. All this is to say: using prizes like the Booker as the model for literary prize culture *en masse* does not work. Such a comparison assumes a level playing field which, this study proposes, does not exist.

Accordingly, using prizes like the Nobel and the Booker is a form of false equivalence, which assumes that similar phenomena can be treated and considered in the same terms. As Phillips and Bostian illustrate:

> Sometimes instead of treating similar things inconsistently, people will treat different things as if they are the same. This is a fallacy of false consistency, or false equivalence, treating things as the same when they really aren't the same.[72]

While this logical fallacy is most frequently applied to the falsity of the need for equal representation of opposing arguments to ensure balance, particularly in the media, it is a useful means by which to consider exactly how the literary prize hierarchy – and, indeed, the hierarchy of cultural prizes more broadly – has been sustained.[73] The penchant for comparisons, or a presumed aspirational envy, between the Booker and emerging or smaller, lesser-known awards, by the media, academic commentary and prize administrators themselves has come to dictate perceptions of prestige and value in prize culture and has infiltrated the parlance to such an extent that the notion of 'equivalence' is often quite literally emphasised. Journalists frequently highlight how the Booker Prize influenced the creation of prizes, with one arguing that 'the culture of prize-giving has gone mad' and that 'every arts bureaucrat, it seemed, wanted his or her own equivalent of the Booker, which led, in time, to the creation of the Turner Prize (1984), for the visual arts; the Mercury Prize (1992), for music; and the Stirling Prize (1996)'.[74] The Booker Prize is also used as a term of reference to illustrate a different literary award's level of status or prestige in its particular field. The UK-based Crime Writers' Association's Dagger Awards, for example, have been described as being the 'sine qua non of excellence in the crime fiction field – its Booker equivalent'.[75] Such comparisons are also employed for major literary prizes: a *New York Times* article noted that the 'National Book Awards [are] the equivalent of the Booker'.[76] This is a particularly interesting example, since the Booker Prize, a UK-based but internationally recognised prize, is being used to illustrate the status of a US prize in a US publication, suggesting that the Booker is as ubiquitous, if not more so, as the country's own major literary award. The Booker Prize is also used as a point of reference for a broad range of other cultural awards. The Turner Prize for visual artists born or based in Great Britain is often discussed[77] as being 'like'[78] the Booker or 'art's equivalent to the Booker Prize',[79] and the now defunct Glenfiddich Food and Drink were once described as 'food and drinks' equivalent of the Booker'.[80]

Prize administrators themselves will even use the Booker as a descriptor for their own award. In his history of the now defunct Portico/Constable Trophy for Northern Writers, Will Smith reveals how the prize's administrators were deliberate in their comparisons of their award to the Booker:

> In planning and in process, the aim of the Portico was to define itself against the Booker, often seeking to cast itself as the 'Northern Booker' or 'Booker of the North'. A 1992 press release was widely reprinted which cast this comparison firmly as an alternative name 'The Portico Prize (The Northern Booker) was founded […]', and later iterations of the prize repeat this naming. (Portico Press Release, 1992)[81]

This example, therefore, illustrates how the founders and administrators of the Portico/Constable Trophy simultaneously used the Booker as an exemplar of the field and a site of differentiation for their own prize.

Of course, it is not just the Booker Prize which is used as a signifier of prize greatness. Other prizes at the top of their own prize hierarchies are also used in such a way. It is common for the Nobel Prize for Literature, for example, to be used to illustrate the importance of a prize that may not be known outside of its home country, such as the Cervantes Prize, considered the 'Spanish-speaking world's equivalent of the Nobel Prize in literature'.[82] The Oscars are similarly used in such a manner to explain the influence of specific prizes both within film and the performing arts (including the César, 'France's equivalent of the Oscar';[83] the Golden Horse Awards, 'known as the Oscars-equivalent for Chinese-language films';[84] the Taurus World Stunt Awards, 'the industry's equivalent of the Academy Awards';[85] and the Olivier Awards, described as 'the theatre world's equivalent to the Oscars'[86]) and in entirely different areas such as the World Brain Expo and 16th Annual World Congress of Society for Brain Mapping and Therapeutics (SBMT), described by the chairman of the board for SBMT as an event 'considered as the equivalent of the Oscars for Neuroscience'.[87] There are even, perhaps tongue-in-cheek, references made to the Oscars in news articles about fairly obscure industry-specific awards, such as the Pearson Teaching Awards described as the 'Oscars for teachers'[88], and the Aviano Airbase community theatre's 'top honours in what is the European military's equivalent to the Academy Awards'.[89] Indeed, the fusing of such disparate cultural events and entities is yet further evidence of just how pervasive collective recognition of major cultural prizes is.

The above examples are a clear illustration of the proliferation of cultural prizes identified and discussed by English and also John Street, who argues:

> There are, it seems, prizes for almost every kind of cultural endeavour: for fiction, of course, and for poetry and non-fiction, and for music, architecture, are, film, sculpture, journalism, broadcasting, television, teaching and even academic research.[90]

But what unites such occurrences of prize proliferation is their recognition of what 'the best of the best' prizes are, and which prizes have become ubiquitous and synonymous with prestige and cultural value. Such allusions not only provide context and a point of reference for readers and audiences, but they also reify the status of these awards at the top of the prize hierarchy, effectively making them the archetypes of cultural prizes par excellence. However, this has made such prizes so exceptional as to be near useless for a nuanced examination of prize culture because they function and negotiate power, cultural value and legitimacy from a position of inequitable hegemony. It is no coincidence, also, that there is a Western, Anglo-American leaning to the cultural awards we know most about; this is merely further evidence of a recognised dominance of Anglo-American culture more broadly. The cultural control and influence over certain literary and cultural prizes of others should be considered the exception, not the rule. As this study demonstrates, the continued reliance on top-tier prizes as key reference points has the potential to impede acquiring a full understanding of how all kinds of literary prizes function within the literary marketplace. What may be more useful for the field moving forward is the reframing of our assessment of how prizes feature in contemporary culture, progressing beyond methodologies and concepts which rely upon a prize proving its worth or cultural value (through analyses of their negotiations of cultural and economic capital exchanges or intraconversions) in terms established by extraordinary prizes. As this study of the Saltire Society Literary Awards illustrates, there is more to the development of our regional, national and international cultural identities than the hegemonic forces we so frequently refer to in order to demonstrate how cultural value, legitimacy and agency evolves. Rather than exceptionalise some prizes over others, and see them as career-defining pinnacles, it would be more useful to consider the role of all prizes within the hierarchy and the different role they each play, both within the prize economy and also in the careers of the individuals. It is important, too, to bear in mind that no cultural prize has an innate power or ability to confer value; their power and influence is a construction established and moulded through a critical and cultural discourse about prizes. It is imperative that scholars of literary or cultural awards interrogate, as opposed to contribute to, the cultural dominance of a few institutions which determine our understanding of the field.

Accordingly, this book has attempted to illustrate not only the significant role the Saltire Society Literary Awards have played in Scottish cultural life over the years, but also how valuable such hitherto untold cultural histories of prizes that can influence our culture really are. Indeed, this book is not just a cultural history of a particular literary award: it is an incitement, calling for more nuance and specificity in our analyses of cultural awards and the work they do. This specific study focuses on one little-known literary award and argues that, without such histories and micro-analyses of such awards, we cannot fully understand the mechanisms of literary awards – which are one of the most influential and dominant forms of cultural award in contemporary society – more broadly.

CONCLUSION

In 2002 James F. English wrote:

> There is no form of cultural capital so ubiquitous, so powerful, so widely talked about, and yet so little explored by scholars as the cultural prize. Prizes and awards fairly dominate the cultural landscape these days, literally tens of thousands of them vying for our notice, lists of them appearing in every resume, every promotional blurb, every feature story or obituary of practically anyone connected with the production of art.[1]

Since making this statement, many scholars, including English himself, have taken significant strides to develop an interdisciplinary field of scholarship which scrutinises the intricacies of the cultural prize in popular culture and examines the negotiations and exchanges of value central to prizes and awards. The existing scholarship has provided instrumental valuations of prize culture, providing critical frameworks by which to begin to understand the prize-giving phenomenon. Often central to this is the work of Pierre Bourdieu and his sociological approach to cultural production and spectacle. It is the application of his understandings of economic, social and cultural capital exchange that has, in particular, provided the most significant contribution to the scholarly field; this process has consolidated a framework by which researchers can attempt to quantify, or interrogate, the impact and influence of prizes upon culture.

As a result of this, when I began my research into the Saltire Society Literary Awards in October 2012, I believed I had a good sense of how I would approach the project, what knowledge I would need and how I might be able to explore the impact of the Society's Literary Awards. I began thus armed with scholarship on the workings of literary award culture in the United Kingdom and existing writing on awards like the Booker Prize, the Women's Prize for Fiction and the Costa Book Award. However, the more I delved into the Society's history, and the history of its literary awards and commendations, the more I realised that this knowledge, while providing a helpful context, could not necessarily be applied directly to the Society's Literary Awards. This was not just because it was a different award, with different motivations and criterion, but also because – as this study of the Saltire Society Literary Awards evidences – there is no one size fits all when it comes to literary awards. While fundamentals may stay the same – all prizes require terms of eligibility, judges, shortlists, winners, losers – there are a significant amount of variable factors which determine and inform how a prize can negotiate its position within contemporary literary and publishing culture. Using the Saltire Society Literary Awards as a case study, this book shows that scholars of literary award culture, and contemporary literary and publishing culture(s), need to treat literary prizes not only as a homogenous form of book marketing and consecration, but also as their own field made up of singularly significant agents and institutions with different levels of impact, influence and value.

The Society's Literary Awards are an appropriate phenomenon through which to make this argument. Founded in 1936, a key interwar period during which Scotland was attempting to reassert its sociopolitical and cultural standing within the United Kingdom and Europe, the Society was deliberate in its approach to consecrating Scottish cultural production and created the first series of awards specifically for Scottish arts and culture. Part I of this book is therefore dedicated to examining the sociopolitical and cultural milieu in which the Society was formed. An understanding of this is key to the Literary Awards and commendations, in terms of not only the books and authors celebrated but also their criteria of eligibility, both of which are fundamentally tied to the Society's status as a Scottish cultural charity. This hitherto untold history of the Society thus fills a discernible gap in knowledge about Scotland's literary and cultural history in the mid-twentieth century, and also enables us to see the kind of role the Society has played, and continues to play, in the celebration of Scottish literature and culture. The Society has often been conspicuous in its omission from cultural or literary histories of Scotland, an absence made all the more surprising given its consistent, if at times uncertain, presence in Scotland's cultural and literary scene – a reflection, perhaps, of the often ghostly presence of the societies and bodies behind literary prizes. The narrative of the Society included in this book thereby provides essential information to further understand Scotland's cultural landscape from the 1930s to the present day. Of course, one inevitable limitation of this research, and of contemporary research more broadly, is the continuous emergence of new information and material. This is particularly the case with cultural awards which, more often than not, repeat the prize-giving process on an annual basis, providing new data and cases for analysis year-on-year and at a pace that academic publishing often struggles to match. Accordingly, while

Part I of this book has sought to be comprehensive in its critical description of the Book of the Year and First Book of the Year Awards, their histories continue to grow and so do the opportunities for a further examination of the awards, particularly with respect to the Society's expansion of the Literary Awards categories between 2014 and 2016. Therefore, Part I of this book is viewed as a comprehensive introduction, as opposed to a conclusory examination of the Society's Literary Awards.

Part I also provides a detailed history of the Society's Book of the Year and First Book of the Year Awards, which, as the Society's longest-running awards for literary writing (including poetry, novels, short stories and nonfiction), are arguably the most influential of the Society's awards. They are certainly the ones with the most valuable historical records and data by which to construct a narrative of the history of the awards and examine their role and influence(s) within Scottish literary culture in the late twentieth and early twenty-first centuries. One of the most notable aspects of the Book of the Year and First Book of the Year Awards during this period was the fluctuation in sponsorship, which caused issues relating to the financing and coverage of the Literary Awards. When the Society's Literary Awards sponsors were media organisations, such as the *Scotsman* newspaper and STV, the awards received significant media coverage. However, when such sponsors were lost, or replaced by non-media-based organisations, like the Royal Mail, the Society's Literary Awards would receive inconsistent levels of media coverage. These factors stymied the Society's ability to present itself effectively and consistently as Scotland's leading series of literary awards, even when it became the only series of awards for Scottish literature still presented. This lack of regular media attention and reporting – which is both emblematic of, and contributive to, the Society's Literary Awards being overlooked – is one of the factors at the crux of how the Society's Literary Awards should be understood differently, particularly in relation to other major literary awards both within and outside Scotland. If recognition is one of the key ways in which a prize can invoke and use its cultural and social capital, what happens to prizes, like the Saltire Society Literary Awards, that cannot garner and sustain interest to those outside of the already existing network of agents involved in the prize (judges, publishers, shortlisted and winning authors)? What kind of influence and role can prizes like the Society's Literary Awards have in contemporary literary and publishing culture?

Part II uses the history of the Society's Literary Awards as the groundwork by which to answer these questions, performing a more detailed examination of the awards in relation to national identity, exchanges of cultural, social and economic capital, and literary prize hierarchies. Chapter 4 considers how the Book of the Year and First Book of the Year Awards engage in the identification and negotiation of Scottishness and national identity through terms of eligibility and judging processes which aim to ascertain what makes a Scottish book 'Scottish'. Since the Society's Literary Awards' terms of eligibility require an author to be living in, born in or writing about Scotland, the awards are fundamentally engaged in discourses concerning Scottish national identity and literature. Like previous examinations of national and literary prize culture(s) by Driscoll and Roberts, Chapter 4 illustrates how 'national capital' is also at play and is in a constant state of (re)negotiation and debate among judges, particularly when it comes to the technicalities of prizes which aim to remain inclusive in their definitions of nationhood while still being a nation-specific prize. Such inclusivity is, perhaps, overstated with regard to the Society's Literary Awards. As the analysis in Chapter 4 of shortlisted and winning authors and books indicates, while there are a number of instances when non-Scottish writers have been shortlisted for, or won, the Society's Book of the Year or First Book of the Year Awards, there remains a propensity for the awards to go to Scottish-born writers whose books include Scottish content.

Such details afforded a useful foundation from which to consider the literary award successes of four authors who the Society has rewarded throughout their careers. The case studies of Michel Faber, James Kelman, A. L. Kennedy and Ali Smith in Chapter 5 reveal the Society's consistent support of these authors through award shortlistings and wins. The chapter also demonstrates that as some of these authors have accrued connections to (either by winning or being shortlisted for) more well-known and often richer prizes, such as the Booker Prize, the Whitbread/Costa Book of the Year Award or the Women's Prize for Fiction, seemingly 'smaller' awards, both monetarily and reputationally, begin to lose their place in the biographical narratives and paratextual details of the authors and their books. In other words, a shortlisting for a Booker Prize can supersede a Saltire Society Book of the Year Award win. This is significant since it adds to the continual underestimation of the Society's reputation as a consecrator of (Scottish) literary value and prestige and, in turn, can reinforce the sense of literary cultural inferiority as experienced by national literatures dominated by bordering countries or colonial legacy. The favouring of some prizes over others perpetuates the symbolic autocracy of a literary prize hierarchy, which pits cultural awards against each other and, in doing so, considers their value and impact according to the commendations, awards and prizes at the top of the hierarchy. This becomes a cycle of power struggles and reaffirmation, as prizes like the Saltire Society Literary Awards are couched in terms of major prizes, rather than existing within its own standards and sets of cultural value exchange.

As a result of this, Chapter 6 uses the Society's Literary Awards to cross-examine existing understandings of literary prize culture(s). It posits that, since many analyses of prize culture focus on the major, most well-known and richest prizes, prevailing interpretations of how literary awards (and, perhaps, cultural awards more broadly) function within contemporary literary and publishing culture take a top-down approach; what are in fact extraordinary examples (like the Booker Prize and the Nobel Prize for Literature, for example) are made to represent prize culture en masse. This is problematic because, as this examination of the Saltire Society Literary Awards has shown, the negotiations and intraconversions of capital that we may expect to exist within prize culture can happen on massively variable scales, or may not happen at all. Literary prizes are, therefore, not only involved in the business of hierarchising authors and books through the literal process of prizing literature, but are themselves subject to placement within a hierarchy of prizes. This hierarchy places awards like the Booker and the Nobel Prizes at the top in terms of influence and levels of cultural, social, economic and journalistic capital while simultaneously pitting them as both aspirational targets and competitors to 'smaller' prizes. Ultimately, this creates a kind of false equivalence that both academic and media commentaries preserve and perpetuate in their preoccupations with understanding prize culture predominantly through the workings of 'major' prizes.

It is hoped, then, that this study of the Saltire Society Literary Awards has illustrated how such micro-studies of prizes are beneficial in providing more nuance to current macro-understandings of prizes as fields of cultural production and promotion. As this study suggests, further examinations into the intricacies and oddities of prize culture may contradict, as opposed to reaffirm, current understandings of literary award culture and their negotiations of value and prestige. Indeed, there is room – and a need – for more analyses like this; for focus to be paid to 'smaller', seemingly niche or provincial awards, which may not receive international or even national attention, but will nonetheless play their own important role in the exchange of cultural, social and economic capital within literary and publishing networks.

APPENDIX

Saltire Society Book of the Year Award Shortlists and Winners, 1982–2019 (winners in bold)

Year	Sponsor/prize fund	Author	Title	Publisher	Judges
Book of the Year Award					
1982	Royal Bank of Scotland, £1,000	Dorothy Dunnett	*King Hereafter*	Michael Joseph, 1982	Anne Smith
		Alasdair Gray	***Lanark***	**Canongate, 1981**	David Daiches
		F. R. Hart & J. B. Pick	*Neil Gunn: A Highland Life*	John Murray, 1981	Edwin Morgan
		Robert McLellan	*Collected Plays Vol I*	John Calder, 1981	James Allan Ford
		Ian Crichton Smith	*Selected Poems 1955–80*	MacDonald Publishers, 1982	Paul H. Scott
					Tom Crawford
		David Toulman	*Hard Shining Corn*	Paul Harris, 1982	Angus Calder
		Cedric Watts & Laurence Davies	*Cunninghame Graham: A Critical Biography*	Cambridge University Press, 1979	
1983	Royal Bank of Scotland, £1,000	George Mackay Brown	*Andrina and Other Stories*	Chatto & Windus, 1983	Ian Campbell
		Alasdair Gray	*Unlikely Stories Mostly*	Canongate, 1983	James Allan Ford
		James Kelman	*Not Not While the Giro and Other Stories*	Polygon, 1983	Douglas Gifford
					Isobel Murray
		William McIlvanney	*The Papers of Tony Veitch*	Hodder & Stoughton, 1983	Paul H. Scott (chair)
		Edwin Morgan	***Poems of Thirty Years***	**Carcanet Press, 1982**	
		Christopher Rush	*Peace Comes Dropping Slow*	Ramsay Head, 1983	
		Ian Crichton Smith	*The Search*	Gollancz, 1983	
		Derick Thomson	***Creachadh Na Clàrsaich / Plundering the Harp***	**MacDonald, 1982**	
		David Watt, ed.	*The Christian Watt Papers*	Paul Harris, 1983	

Year		Author	Title	Publisher	Judges
1984	Royal Bank of Scotland, £1,000	George Mackay Brown	Time in a Red Coat	Chatto & Windus, 1984	Angus Calder
		David Daiches	**God and the Poets**	**Clarendon, 1984**	Ian C'mpbell
		Alasdair Gray	1982 Janine	Cape, 1984	Douglas Gifford
		Tom Leonard	**Intimate Voices**	**Galloping Dog Press, 1984**	Isobel Murray
		W. L. Lorimer	New Testament in Scots	W. L. Lorimer Memorial Trust Fund/Southside Publishers, 1984	Paul H. Scott (chair)
		Alistair MacLean	Night Falls in Ardnamurchan: The Twilight of a Crofting Family	Gollancz, 1984	
1985	Royal Bank of Scotland, £1,500	A. Gray, J. Kelman, A. Owens	Lean Tales	Cape, 1985	Ian Campbell
		Norman MacCaig	**Collected Poems**	**Chatto & Windus, 1985**	Angus Calder
		William McIlvanney	The Big Man	Hodder & Stoughton, 1985	Douglas Gifford
		Naomi Mitchison	Among You Taking Notes	Gollancz, 1985	Isobel Murray
		Christopher Rush	Twelve-Month and a Day	Canongate, 1985	P. H. Scott (chair), Derick Thomson
		Ian Crichton Smith	Tenement	Gollancz, 1985	
1986	Royal Bank of Scotland, £1,500	Iain Banks	The Bridge	Macmillan, 1986	Ian Campbell
		George Davie	The Crisis of the Democratic Intellect	Polygon, 1986	Angus Calder
		Stuart Hood	**A Storm from Paradise**	**Carcanet Press, 1985**	Douglas Gifford
		Robin Jenkins	The Awakening of George Darroch	Glasgow Herald, 1985	Isobel Murray
		Jessie Kesson	Where the Apple Ripens & Other Stories	Hogarth, 1985	P. H. Scott (chair)
		Ian Crichton Smith	A Life	Carcanet Press, 1986	Derick Thomson

(continued)

Year	Sponsor/prize fund	Author	Title	Publisher	Judges
1987	Royal Bank of Scotland, £1,500	Ron Butlin	Sound of My Voice	Canongate, 1987	Angus Calder
		Maoilios M. Caimbeul	Bailean	Gairm, 1987	Ian Campbell
		Ian Jack	Before the Oil Ran Out	Secker & Warburg, 1987	Douglas Gifford
		James Kelman	Greyhound for Breakfast	Secker & Warburg, 1987	Isobel Murray
		Allan Massie	Augustus	Bodley Head, 1986	P. H. Scott (chair)
		Naomi Mitchison	Early in Orcadia	Drew, 1987	Alan Taylor
		Ian Crichton Smith	In the Middle of the Wood	Gollancz, 1987	Derick Thomson
		Muriel Spark	**Collected Stories**	**Macmillan, 1985**	
1988	The Scotsman, £1,500	W. R. Aitken	Poems of William Soutar: A New Selection	Scottish Academic Press, 1988	Angus Calder
	Prize fund divided equally between two winners (£750 each)	**Neal Ascherson**	**Games with Shadows**	**Radius, 1988**	Ian Campbell
		Alan Bold	MacDiarmid: A Critical Biography	John Murray, 1988	Douglas Gifford
					Isobel Murray
		Douglas Dunn	Northlight	Faber & Faber, 1988	P. H. Scott (chair)
		John Graham	Shadowed Valley	Shetland, 1987	Alan Taylor
		Robin Jenkins	Just Duffy	Canongate, 1988	Derick Thomson
		Frederick Lindsay	A Charm against Drowning	Deutsch, 1988	
		Tom Nairn	**The Enchanted Glass**	**Radius, 1988**	
		Jane Rowlinson	Cargo	Deutsch, 1987	
		Duncan & Linda Williamson	A Thorn in the King's Foot: Folktales of the Scottish Travelling People	Penguin, 1987	
1989	The Scotsman, £1,500	James Kelman	A Disaffection	Secker & Warburg, 1989	Angus Calder
		Liz Lochhead	Mary Queen of Scots Got Her Head Chopped Off	Penguin, 1989	Ian Campbell
					Douglas Gifford
		Allan Massie	**A Question of Loyalties**	**Hutchinson, 1989**	Isobel Murray, P. H. Scott (chair), Alan Taylor
		William McIlvanney	Walking Wounded	Hodder & Stoughton, 1989	

Year	Award	Author	Title	Publisher	Judges
1990	*The Scotsman*/Scottish Television, £5,000	William Boyd	*Brazzaville Beach*	Sinclair-Stevenson, 1990	Angus Calder
		Denis Forman	*Son of Adam*	Deutsch, 1990	Ian Campbell
		Sorley MacLean	**From Wood to Ridge / O choille gu bearradh**	**Carcanet Press, 1989**	Douglas Gifford
					Isobel Murray
		Tom Pow	*The Moth Trap*	Canongate, 1990	P. H. Scott (chair)
		Muriel Spark	*Symposium*	Constable, 1990	Alan Taylor
		Emma Tennant	*Sisters and Strangers*	Grafton, 1990	
1991	*The Scotsman*/Scottish Television, £5,000	Janice Galloway	*Blood*	Minerva, 1991	Angus Calder
		Robin Jenkins	*Poverty Castle*	Balnain, 1991	Ian Campbell
		James Kelman	*Burn*	Secker & Warburg, 1991	Douglas Gifford
		Maurice Lindsay	*Collected Poems 1940–1990*	Aberdeen University Press, 1990	Isobel Murray
					P. H. Scott (chair)
		Michael Lynch	*Scotland: A New History*	Century, 1991	Alan Taylor, Derick Thomson
		Duncan McMillan	**Scottish Art**	**Mainstream, 1990**	
1992	*The Scotsman*, £5,000	David M. Black	*Collected Poems 1964–87*	Polygon, 1991	Angus Calder
		George MacKay Brown	*Vinland*	John Murray, 1992	Ian Campbell
		Robert Crawford	*Devolving English Literature*	Clarendon Press, 1992	Douglas Gifford
		Alasdair Gray	*Poor Things*	Bloomsbury, 1992	Isobel Murray
		John Purser	*Scotland's Music*	Mainstream, 1992	P. H. Scott (chair)
		Iain Crichton Smith	**Collected Poems**	**Carcanet Press, 1992**	Alan Taylor
		Muriel Spark	*Curriculum Vitae*	Constable, 1992	Derick Thomson
1993	*The Scotsman*, £5,000	William Boyd	*The Blue Afternoon*	Sinclair-Stevenson, 1993	Angus Calder
		Michael Fry	*The Dundas Despotism*	Edinburgh University Press, 1992	Ian Campbell
					Douglas Gifford
		Robin Jenkins	*Willie Hogg*	Polygon, 1993	Isobel Murray
		Joan Lingard	*After Colette*	Sinclair-Stevenson, 1993	P. H. Scott (chair)
		James Mackay	**A Biography of Robert Burns**	**Mainstream, 1992**	Alan Taylor
					Derick Thomson
		Dilys Rose	*Red Tides*	Secker & Warburg, 1993	
		Tom Scott	*The Collected Shorter Poems of Tom Scott*	Chapman, 1993	

(continued)

Year	Sponsor/ prize fund	Author	Title	Publisher	Judges
1994	*The Scotsman*, £5,000	**George Mackay Brown**	***Beside the Ocean of Time***	**John Murray, 1994**	Angus Calder
					Ian Campbell
		Douglas Dunn	*Dante's Drumkit*	Faber & Faber, 1993	Douglas Gifford
		W. N. Herbert	*Forked Tongue*	Bloodaxe Books, 1994	Joyce McMillan
		Kathleen Jamie	*The Queen of Sheba*	Bloodaxe Books, 1994	Isobel Murray
		James Kelman	*How Late It Was, How Late*	Secker & Warburg, 1994	P. H. Scott (chair)
		Bernard MacLaverty	*Walking the Dog*	Blackstaff Press, 1994	Derick Thomson
		Candia McWilliam	*Debatable Land*	Chivers, 1994	
1995	*The Scotsman*, £5,000	**Neal Ascherson**	***Black Sea***	**Cape, 1995**	Angus Calder
					Ian Campbell
		Iain Banks	*Whit*	Little, Brown, 1995	Douglas Gifford (chair)
		David Gilmour	*Curzon*	John Murray, 1994	Joyce McMillan
		Andrew Greig	*Western Swing*	Bloodaxe Books, 1994	Isobel Murray
		A. L. Kennedy	*So I Am Glad*	Jonathan Cape, 1995	Derick Thomson
		Frank Kuppner	*Something Very Like Murder*	Polygon, 1994	
		Alan Spence	*Stone Garden*	Phoenix House, 1995	
1996	*The Scotsman*, £5,000	Janice Galloway	*Where You Find It*	Jonathan Cape, 1996	Angus Calder
		Carl Macdougall	*The Casanova Papers*	Secker & Warburg, 1996	Ian Campbell (chair)
		John McGrath	*Six-Pack*	Polygon, 1996	Douglas Gifford
		William McIlvanney	***The Kiln***	**Sceptre, 1996**	Joyce McMillan
		Shena Mackay	*Orchard on Fire*	Heinemann, 1995	Isobel Murray
		Janey Paisley	*Paisley, Janet, Alien Crop*	Chapman, 1996	Derick Thomson
1997	*The Scotsman*, £5,000	Iain Banks	*A Song of Stone*	Abacus, 1997	Angus Calder
		Jenni Calder	*The Nine Lives of Naomi Mitchison*	Virago, 1997	Ian Campbell
					Douglas Gifford (chair)
		A. L. Kennedy	*Original Bliss*	Jonathan Cape, 1997	Joyce McMillan
		Bernard MacLaverty	***Grace Notes***	**Jonathan Cape, 1997**	Isobel Murray
		Edwin Morgan	*Collected Translations*	Carcanet, 1996	Derick Thomson
		Ali Smith	*Like*	Virago, 1997	

Year	Prize	Shortlist	Title	Publisher	Judges
1998	*The Scotsman*, £5,000	Jackie Kay	*Trumpet*	Picador, 1998	Allan Boyd
		James Kelman	*The Good Times*	Secker & Warburg, 1998	Ian Campbell (chair)
		Shena Mackay	*The Artist's Widow*	Jonathan Cape, 1998	Douglas Gifford
		Alan Spence	*Way to Go*	Phoenix House, 1998	Joyce McMillan
		Emma Tennant	*Strangers: A Family Romance*	Jonathan Cape, 1998	Isobel Murray
		Alan Warner	***The Sopranos***	**Jonathan Cape, 1998**	Iain Crichton Smith (Gaelic advisor)
1999	*The Scotsman*, £5,000	Priscilla J. Bawcutt	*The Poems of William Dunbar*	Association for Scottish Literary Studies, 1998	Allan Boyd
					Ian Campbell
		George Bruce	***Pursuits: Poems 1986–1998***	**Scottish Cultural Press, 1999**	Douglas Gifford (chair)
					Alison Lumsden
		William Darylmple	*The Age of Kali: Indian Travels & Encounters*	Flamingo, 1999	Joyce McMillan, Isobel Murray
		Andrew Greig	*When They Lay Bare*	Faber & Faber, 1999	
		Andrew O'Hagan	*Our Fathers*	Faber & Faber, 1999	
2000	Saltire Society, £5,000	Stewart Conn	*Stolen Light*	Bloodaxe, 1999	Allan Boyd
		Carol Ann Duffy	*The World's Wife*	Anvil Press, 1999	Ian Campbell (chair)
		Ronald Frame	***The Lantern Bearers***	**Duckbacks, 1999**	Douglas Gifford
		Hamish Henderson	*Collected Poems and Songs*	Curly Snake, 2000	Alison Lumsden
		Alistair MacLeod	*No Great Mischief*	McClelland & Stewart, 1999	Joyce McMillan
		Alan Massie	*Nero's Heirs*	Hodder & Stoughton, 1999	Isobel Murray
2001	Saltire Society, £5,000	John Burnside	*The Locust Room*	Jonathan Cape, 2001	Allan Boyd
		Robin Jenkins	*Childish Things*	Canongate, 2001	Ian Campbell
		Liz Lochhead	***Medea***	**Nick Hern, 2000**	Douglas Gifford (chair)
		Bernard MacLaverty	*The Anatomy School*	Jonathan Cape, 2001	Alison Lumsden
		Alan Massie	*The Evening of the World*	Weidenfeld & Nicolson, 2001	Joyce McMillan
					Isobel Murray
		Ali Smith	*Hotel World*	Hamish Hamilton, 2001	Ian MacDonald (Gaelic advisor)
		Muriel Spark	*Aiding and Abetting*	Viking, 2000	

(continued)

Year	Sponsor/ prize fund	Author	Title	Publisher	Judges
2002	Saltire Society, £5,000	Rosemary Ashton	*Thomas & Jane Carlyle: A Portrait of a Marriage*	Pimlico, 2002	Allan Boyd
		John Burnside	*The Light Trap*	Jonathan Cape, 2002	Ian Campbell (chair)
		Janice Galloway	***Clara***	**Jonathan Cape, 2002**	Douglas Gifford
		Arthur Herman	*The Scottish Enlightenment: The Scots' Invention of the Modern World*	Fourth Estate, 2002	Alison Lumsden
					Joyce McMillan
		Jackie Kay	*Why Don't You Stop Talking*	Picador, 2002	Isobel Murray
		Alan Warner	*The Man Who Walks*	Jonathan Cape, 2002	Ian MacDonald (Gaelic advisor)
		Irvine Welsh	*Porno*	Jonathan Cape, 2002	
2003	Saltire Society, £5,000	Kate Atkinson	*Not the End of the World*	Doubleday, 2002	Allan Boyd
		John Burnside	*Living Nowhere*	Jonathan Cape, 2003	Ian Campbell
		W. N. Herbert	*The Big Bumper Book of Troy*	Bloodaxe Books, 2002	Douglas Gifford (chair)
		Robin Jenkins	*Lady Magdalen*	Canongate, 2003	Alison Lumsden
		Liz Lochhead	*The Colour of Black and White*	Polygon, 2003	Joyce McMillan
		Edwin Morgan	*Cathures*	Carcanet, 2002	Isobel Murray
		James Robertson	***Joseph Knight***	**Fourth Estate, 2003**	
		Ali Smith	*The Whole Story and Other Stories*	Hamish Hamilton, 2003	

Year	Sponsor	Author	Title	Publisher	Judges
2004	Faculty of Advocates, £5,000	Alasdair Campbell	*Visiting the Bard*	Polygon, 2003	Allan Boyd
		Angus Peter Campbell	*An Oidhche Mus Do Sheol Sinn / The Night before We Sailed*	CLÀR, 2004	Ian Campbell (chair)
					Douglas Gifford
		Andrew Greig	***In Another Light***	**Weidenfield & Nicolson, 2004**	Alison Lumsden
					Joyce McMillan
		Roger Hutchinson	*The Soap Man: Lewis, Harris and Lord*	Birlinn, 2003	Isobel Murray
					Ian MacDonald (Gaelic advisor)
		James Kelman	*You Have To Be Careful in the Land of the Free*	Hamish Hamilton, 2004	
		A. L. Kennedy	*Paradise*	Jonathan Cape, 2004	
		Muriel Spark	*All the Poems*	Carcanet, 2004	
2005	Faculty of Advocates, £5,000	**Kate Atkinson**	***Case Histories***	**Doubleday, 2004**	Allan Boyd
		Michel Faber	*The Fahrenheit Twins*	Canongate, 2005	Ian Campbell
		Claire Harman	*Robert Louis Stevenson: A Biography*	HarperCollins, 2005	Douglas Gifford (chair)
					Joyce McMillan
		David Harrower	*Blackbird*	Faber & Faber, 2005	Isobel Murray
		Màrtainn Macan t-saoir	*Gymnippers Diciadain*	CLÀR, 2005	Marion Sinclair
		James Meek	*The People's Act of Love*	Canongate, 2005	
		Barry Menikoff	*Narrating Scotland: The Imagination of Robert Louis Stevenson*	University of South Carolina Press, 2005	
		Ali Smith	*The Accidental*	Hamish Hamilton, 2005	
2006	Faculty of Advocates, £5,000	**John Burnside**	***A Lie about My Father***	**Jonathan Cape, 2006**	Allan Boyd
		David Crane	*Scott of the Antarctic: A Life of Courage and Tragedy in the Extreme South*	HarperCollins, 2005	Ian Campbell (chair)
					Douglas Gifford
					Ian MacDonald
		Carol Ann Duffy	*Rapture*	Picador, 2005	Joyce McMillan
		Duncan Glen	*Collected Poems 1965–2005*	Akros, 2006	Ann Matheson
		W. N. Herbert	*Bad Shaman Blues*	Bloodaxe Books, 2006	Marion Sinclair
		Andrew O'Hagan	*Be Near Me*	Faber & Faber, 2006	David Robb
		James Robertson	*The Testament of Gideon Mack*	Hamish Hamilton, 2006	

(continued)

Year	Sponsor/ prize fund	Author	Title	Publisher	Judges
2007	Saltire Society, £5,000	Meg Bateman	*Soirbeas = Fair Wind*	Polygon, 2007	Allan Boyd
		Robert Crawford	*Scotland's Books: The Penguin History of Scottish Literature*	Penguin, 2007	Ian Campbell Douglas Gifford (chair)
		William Crawford	*The Last Mughal: The Fall of a Dynasty, Delhi 1857*	Bloomsbury, 2006	Ian MacDonald Joyce McMillan
		A. L. Kennedy	***Day***	**Jonathan Cape, 2007**	Ann Matheson
		Marista Leishman	*My Father: Reith of the BBC*	Saint Andrew Press, 2006	Marion Sinclair
		Andrew Marr	*A History of Modern Britain*	Macmillan, 2007	David Robb
		Iain Moireach	*Sniomh nan dual: 6 cluichean*	Acair, 2007	
		Don Paterson	*Orpheus*	Faber & Faber, 2006	
		Trevor Royle	*The Flowers of the Forest: Scotland and the First World War*	Birlinn, 2006	
2008	Scottish government, £5,000	Meaghan Delahunt	*The Red Book*	Granta, 2008	Allan Boyd
		James Kelman	***Kieron Smith, Boy***	**Hamish Hamilton, 2008**	Ian Campbell (chair) Douglas Gifford
		Mick Imlah	*The Lost Leader*	Faber & Faber, 2008	Ian MacDonald
		Màrtainn Macan t-saoir	*An latha as Fhaide*	CLÀR, 2008	Joyce McMillan
		James Meek	*We Are Now Beginning Our Descent*	Canongate, 2008	Ann Matheson Marion Sinclair, David Robb
		Andrew O'Hagan	*The Atlantic Ocean*	Faber & Faber, 2008	
		Ali Smith	*Girl Meets Boy*	Canongate, 2007	
2009	Homecoming Scotland, £10,000	James Buchan	*The Gate of Air*	MacLehose, 2008	Allan Boyd Ian Campbell
		Regi Claire	*Fighting It*	Two Ravens, 2009	Douglas Gifford (chair)
		Robert Crawford	***The Bard: Robert Burns, A Biography***	**Jonathan Cape, 2009**	Joyce McMillan
		Janice Galloway	*This Is Not about Me*	Granta, 2008	Ann Matheson
		A. L. Kennedy	*What Becomes*	Jonathan Cape, 2009	Marion Sinclair, David Robb
		John MacLeod	*When I Heard the Bell: The Loss of the Iolaire*	Birlinn, 2009	

Year	Award	Author	Title	Publisher	Judges
2010	Saltire Society, £5,000	Andrew Greig	At the Loch of the Green Corrie	Quercus, 2010	Allan Boyd
		David Greig	Dunsinane	Faber & Faber, 2010	Ian Campbell (chair)
		Robert Alan Jamieson	Da Happie Laand	Luath, 2010	Douglas Gifford
		Fionnlagh Macleòid	Gormshuil an Rìgh	CLÀR, 2010	Joyce McMillan
		Timothy Neat	Hamish Henderson: Vol. 2: Poetry Becomes People (1954–2002)	Polygon, 2009	Ann Matheson
					Marion Sinclair
		Don Paterson	Rain	Faber & Faber, 2009	David Robb
		Nicholas Phillipson	Adam Smith: An Enlightened Life	Allen Lane, 2010	
2011	Saltire Society, £5,000	**James Robertson**	**And the Land Lay Still**	**Hamish Hamilton, 2010**	Allan Boyd
		Alan Warner	The Stars in the Bright Sky	Jonathan Cape, 2010	Ian Campbell (chair)
		John Burnside	A Summer of Drowning	Jonathan Cape, 2011	Ann Matheson
		Alasdair Gray	**A Life in Pictures**	**Canongate, 2010**	Joyce McMillan
		Jackie Kay	Fiere	Picador, 2011	David Robb
		A. L. Kennedy	The Blue Book	Jonathan Cape, 2011	Claire Squires
		Somhairle MacGill-Eain	An Cuilithionn 1939: the Cuillin 1939 and Unpublished Poems	Association of Literary Studies, 2011	
		Ali Smith	There But For The	Hamish Hamilton, 2011	
		Don Paterson	Reading Shakespeare's Sonnets	Faber & Faber, 2010	
2012	Saltire Society, £5,000	Carol Ann Duffy	The Bees	Picador, 2011	Allan Boyd
		Kathleen Jamie	Sightlines	Sort Of, 2012	Ian Campbell (chair)
		James Kelman	**Mo Said She Was Quirky**	**Hamish Hamilton, 2012**	Ian MacDonald
		Aonghas MacNeacail	Dèanamh Gàire Ris A' Chloc: Dàin Ùr / Laughing at the Clock	Polygon, 2012	Ann Matheson
					Joyce McMillan
		Ewan Morrison	Tales from the Mall	Cargo, 2012	David Robb
		Alan Warner	The Deadman's Pedal	Jonathan Cape, 2012	Claire Squires
		Irvine Welsh	Skagboys	Jonathan Cape, 2012	

(continued)

Year	Sponsor/ prize fund	Author	Title	Publisher	Judges
2013	Saltire Society, £5,000	Kate Atkinson	Life after Life	Doubleday, 2013	Allan Boyd
		John Burnside	**Something Like Happy**	**Jonathan Cape, 2013**	Ian Campbell (chair)
		Julie Davidson	Looking for Mrs Livingstone	Saint Andrew Press, 2012	Ian MacDonald
		Gavin Francis	Empire Antarctica	Chatto and Windus, 2012	Ann Matheson
		Donnchadh Macgilliosa	Màiri Dhall agus Sgeulachdan	CLÀR, 2013	Joyce McMillan
		James Robertson	The Professor of Truth	Hamish Hamilton, 2013	David Robb
		Ali Smith	Artful	Hamish Hamilton, 2012	Claire Squires, Mark Wringe

Literary Book of the Year

Year	Sponsor/ prize fund	Author	Title	Publisher	Judges
2014	Saltire Society/ Creative Scotland, £2,000	Anne Donovan	Gone Are the Leaves	Canongate, 2014	Ian Campbell (chair)
		A. L. Kennedy	All the Rage	Jonathan Cape, 2014	Ian MacDonald
		Sally Magnusson	Where Memories Go	Two Roads, 2014	Ann Matheson
		Martin MacIntyre	Cala Bendita 'S a Bheannachdan	Acair, 2014	Joyce McMillan
		Rona Munro	The James Plays	Nick Hern Books, 2014	David Robb
		Ali Smith	**How To Be Both**	**Hamish Hamilton, 2014**	Claire Squires, Mark Wringe

Fiction Book of the Year

Year	Sponsor/ prize fund	Author	Title	Publisher	Judges
2015	Saltire Society/ Creative Scotland, £2,000	Kate Atkinson	God in Ruins	Doubleday, 2015	Ian Campbell (chair)
		Michel Faber	**The Book of Strange New Things**	**Canongate, 2014**	Hannah McGill
					Joyce McMillan
		Janice Galloway	Jellyfish	Freight Books, 2015	Ann Matheson
		Norma Nicleoid	An Dosan	Acair, 2015	Jenny Niven
		Andrew O'Hagan	The Illuminations	Faber & Faber, 2015	David Robb, David
		Irvine Welsh	A Decent Ride	Jonathan Cape, 2015	Robinson, Mark Wringe

Year	Organization	Authors	Titles	Publisher	Judges
2016	Saltire Society/ Creative Scotland, £2,000	Jenni Fagan James Kelman Kevin MacNeil **Graeme Macrae Burnett** Maggie O'Farrell Irvine Welsh	*The Sunlight Pilgrims* *Dirt Road* *The Brilliant Forever* ***His Bloody Project*** *This Must Be the Place* *The Blade Artist*	Windmill Books, 2016 Canongate, 2016 Birlinn, 2016 **Saraband, 2015** Headline, 2016 Jonathan Cape, 2016	Ian Campbell Ann Matheson Hannah McGill Joyce McMillan David Robinson, Mark Wringe
2017	Saltire Society/ Creative Scotland, £2,000	John Burnside **Angus Peter Campbell** Jason Donald James Kelman Bernard MacLaverty Denise Mina	*Ashland and Vine* ***Memory and Straw*** *Dalila* *That Was a Shiver and Other Stories* *Midwinter Break* *The Long Drop*	Jonathan Cape, 2017 **Luath, 2017** Jonathan Cape, 2017 Canongate, 2017 Jonathan Cape, 2017 Harvill Secker, 2017	Alan Bett Ian Campbell Ann Matheson Hannah McGill Joyce McMillan, Mark Wringe
2018	Saltire Society/ Creative Scotland, £2,000	**Leila Aboulela** Andrew Crumey Sally Magnusson Helen Sedgwick Manda Scott Irvine Welsh	***Elsewhere, Home*** *The Great Chain of Unbeing* *The Sealwoman's Gift* *The Growing Season* *A Treachery of Spies* *Dead Men's Trousers*	**Saqi Books, 2018** Dedalus, 2018 Two Roads, 2018 Harvill Secker, 2017 Transworld, 2018 Jonathan Cape, 2018	Ali Bowden Ken Cockburn Mark Wringe Rosemary Ward Shirley Whiteside Hamish Whyte
2019	Saltire Society/ Creative Scotland, £2,000	Leila Aboulela Damian Barr Polly Clark Lucy Ellmann Ruairidh MacIlleathain (Roddy MacLean) **Ewan Morrison**	*Bird Summons* *You Will Be Safe Here* *Tiger* *Ducks, Newburyport* *Còig Duilleagan na Seamraig (Five Leaves of the Shamrock)* ***Nina X***	Weidenfeld & Nicolson, 2019 Bloomsbury, 2019 Riverrun Books, 2019 Galley Beggar Press, 2019 CLÀR, 2019 **Fleet, 2019**	Valentina Bold (chair) Ali Bowden Ken Cockburn Alasdair McKillop Rosemary Ward

(continued)

Saltire Society First Book of the Year Award Judging Panel and Shortlist (winners in bold)

Year	Sponsor/prize fund	Author	Title	Publisher and year	Judging panel
1988	*The Scotsman*, £1,000	Ian Abbot	Avoiding the Gods	Chapman, 1988	Angus Calder
					Ian Campbel
		John Burnside	*The Hoop*	Carcanet, 1988	Douglas Gifford
		John J. Graham	*Shadowed Valley*	Shetland Publishing Company, 1987	Isobel Murray
					P. H. Scott (Chair)
		Robbie Kydd	*Auld Zimmery*	Mariscat Press, 1987	Alan Taylor
		Candia McWilliam	*A Case of Knives*	Bloomsbury, 1988	Derick Thomson
		Raymond Vettese	**The Richt Noise and ither Poems**	**Macdonald, 1988**	
1989	*The Scotsman*, £1,000	**Sian Hayton**	**Cells of Knowledge**	**Polygon, 1989**	Angus Calder
					Ian Campbell
		Roger Leitch	The Book of Sandy Stewart	Scottish Academic Press, 1988	Douglas Gifford
		Charles Palliser	The Quincunx	Canongate, 1989	Isobel Murray
					Paul H. Scott (Chair)
					Alan Taylor
1990	*The Scotsman*/Scottish Television, £1,500	Janice Galloway	*The Trick is to Keep Breathing*	Polygon, 1989	Angus Calder
		Gordon Legge	*The Shoe*	Polygon, 1989	Ian Campbell
		Harry Tait	**The Ballad of Sawney Bain**	**Polygon, 1989**	Douglas Gifford
					Isobel Murray
					Paul H. Scott (Chair)
					Alan Taylor
1991	*The Scotsman*/Scottish Television, £1,500	Elspeth Barker	*O Caledonia*	Hamish Hamilton, 1991	Angus Calder
		A. L. Kennedy	**Night Geometry and The Garscadden Trains**	**Polygon, 1990**	Ian Campbell
					Douglas Gifford
		Elizabeth Burns	*Ophelia and Other Poems*	Polygon, 1991	Isobel Murray
		David S. Mackenzie	*The Truth of Stone*	Mainstream, 1991	Paul H. Scott (Chair)
					Alan Taylor
					Derick Thomson

Year	Publisher/Prize	Author	Title	Publisher, Year	Judges
1992	*The Scotsman*/Scottish Television, £1,500	**Jackie Kay** Bridget Penney Harry Smart **Crisdean Whyte**	***Adoption Papers*** *Honeymoon with Death* *Pierrot* ***Uirsgeul = Myth***	**Bloodaxe, 1991** Polygon, 1991 Faber & Faber, 1991 **Gairm, 1991**	Angus Calder Ian Campbell Douglas Gifford Isobel Murray Paul H. Scott (Chair) Alan Taylor Derick Thomson
1993	*The Scotsman*/Scottish Television, £1,500	**Ian Bell** Andrew Marr Don Paterson James D. Ross Irvine Welsh	***Dreams of Exile: Robert Louis Stevenson, A Biography*** *The Battle for Scotland* *Nil Nil* *Musick Fyne* *Trainspotting*	**Mainstream, 1992** Penguin, 1992 Faber & Faber, 1993 The Mercat Press, 1993 Secker & Warburg, 1993	Angus Calder Ian Campbell Douglas Gifford Isobel Murray Paul H. Scott (Chair) Alan Taylor Derick Thomson
1994	*The Scotsman*/Scottish Television, £1,500	Andrew Cowan **Andrew Crumey** Timothy Neat	*Pig* ***Music in a Foreign Language*** *Part Seen, Part Imagined*	Michael Joseph, 1994 **Dedalus, 1994** Canongate, 1994	Angus Calder Ian Campbell Douglas Gifford Joyce McMillan Isobel Murray Paul H. Scott (Chair) Derick Thomson
1995	Gairm Publishers, £1,500	Meg Henderson Eric Lomax Lindsay Paterson **Ali Smith** Alan Warner	*Finding Peggy* *The Railway Man – Cape* *The Autonomy of Modern Scotland* ***Free Love*** *Morvern Callar*	Corgi, 1994 Jonathan Cape, 1995 Edinburgh University Press, 1994 **Virago, 1995** Jonathan Cape, 1995	Angus Calder Ian Campbell Douglas Gifford (Chair) Joyce McMillan Isobel Murray Derick Thomson

(continued)

Year	Sponsor/prize fund	Author	Title	Publisher and year	Judging panel
1996	Royal Mail/ Post Office, £1,500	**Kate Clanchy** Alan Clew Des Dillon Chris Dolan Andrew O'Hagan	***Slattern*** *A Child of Air* *Me and Ma Gal* *Poor Angels* *The Missing*	**Chatto & Windus, 1995** Headline Review, 1995 Argyll, 1995 Polygon, 1995 Picador, 1995	Angus Calder Ian Campbell (Chair) Douglas Gifford Joyce McMillan Isobel Murray Derick Thomson
1997	Royal Mail/ Post Office, £1,500	Julian D'Arcy Anne MacLeod Roddy Lumsden **Robin Robertson** Ruth Thomas	*Scottish Skalds and Sagamen* *Standing by Thistles* *Yeah Yeah Yeah* ***A Painted Field*** *Sea Monster Tattoo*	Tuckwell Press, 1996 Scottish Cultural Press, 1997 Bloodaxe, 1997 **Picador, 1997** Polygon, 1997	Angus Calder Ian Campbell Douglas Gifford (Chair) Joyce McMillan Isobel Murray Derick Thomson
1998	Royal Mail/ Post Office, £1,500	Laura Hird **Dennis O'Donnell** Ken Cockburn Donald S. Murray Gillian Ferguson Christopher Wallace	*Nail and Other Stories* ***Two Clocks Ticking*** *Souvenirs and Homelands* *Special Deliverance* *Air for Sleeping Fish* *The Pied Piper's Poison*	Rebel Inc, 1997 **Curly Snake, 1997** Scottish Cultural Press, 1998 Scottish Cultural Press, 1997 Bloodaxe, 1997 Flamingo, 1998	Allan Boyd Ian Campbell (Chair) Douglas Gifford Alison Lumsden Joyce McMillan Isobel Murray Iain Crichton Smith (Gaelic advisor)
1999	Royal Mail/ Post Office, £1,500	Regi Claire Toni Davidson **Michel Faber** Gregor Lamb	*Inside-Outside* *Scar Culture* ***Some Rain Must Fall*** *Langskaill*	Scottish Cultural Press, 1998 Rebel Inc, 1999 **Canongate, 1998** Byrgisey, 1998	Allan Boyd Ian Campbell Douglas Gifford (Chair) Alison Lumsden Joyce McMillan Isobel Murray

Year	Prize	Author	Title	Publisher	Judges
2000	Royal Mail/Post Office, £1,500	Leila Aboulela **Douglas Galbraith** Maggie Graham Helena McEwen Donald MacDonald	*The Translator* *The Rising Sun* *Sitting among the Eskimos* *The Big House* *Smuaintean fo Éiseabhal/Thoughts Under Easaval*	Polygon, 1999 **Picador, 2000** Review, 2000 Bloomsbury, 2000 Birlinn, 2000	Allan Boyd Ian Campbell (Chair) Douglas Gifford Alison Lumsden Joyce McMillan Isobel Murray
2001	Royal Mail/Post Office (Consignia), £1,500	Beatrice Colin Linda Cracknell **Meaghan Delahunt** Suhayl Saadi Raymon Soltysek	*Nude Untiled* *Life Drawing* **In the Blue House** *The Burning Mirror* *Occasional Demons*	Toby Press, 2000 11:9, 2000 **Bloomsbury, 2001** Polygon, 2001 11:9, 2000	Allan Boyd Ian Campbell Douglas Gifford (Chair) Alison Lumsden Joyce McMillan Isobel Murray
2002	Royal Mail/Post Office (Consignia), £1,500	Michael Mail **Liam McIlvanney** Zoë Strachan **Louise Welsh**	*Coralena* **Burns the Radical** *Negative Space* **The Cutting Room**	Scribner, 2002 **Tuckwell Press, 2002** Picador, 2002 **Canongate, 2002**	Allan Boyd Ian Campbell (Chair) Douglas Gifford Alison Lumsden Joyce McMillan Isobel Murray Ian MacDonald (Gaelic advisor)
2003	Royal Mail/Post Office, £1,500	**Mártainn Mac an t- Saoir** Ian McDonough David Nicol Anna Smith	**Ath-Aithne** *Clan MacHine* *The Fundamentals of New Caledonia* *Spit against the Wind*	**Clár, 2003** Chapman, 2002 Luath Press, 2003 Review, 2003	Allan Boyd Ian Campbell Douglas Gifford (Chair) Alison Lumsden Joyce McMillan Isobel Murray

(continued)

Year	Sponsor/prize fund	Author	Title	Publisher and year	Judging panel
2004	Royal Mail/ Post Office, £1,500	Rhona Cameron	*Nineteen Seventy-Nine, A Big Year in a Small Town*	Ebury Press, 2003	Allan Boyd Ian Campbell (Chair) Douglas Gifford Alison Lumsden Joyce McMillan Isobel Murray Ian MacDonald (Gaelic advisor)
		Sophie Cooke	*The Glass House*	Arrow, 2004	
		Andrew Drummond	*An Abridged History*	Polygon, 2004	
		Peter Hill	***Stargazing***	**Canongate, 2003**	
		Rhona Rauszer	*Consider an Island / An t-Eilean sgitheanach*	Polygon, 2004	
2005	Royal Mail/ Post Office, £1,500	**John Aberdein**	***Amande's Bed***	**Thirsty Books, 2005**	Allan Boyd Ian Campbell Douglas Gifford (Chair) Joyce McMillan Isobel Murray Marion Sinclair
		Leanda De Lisle	*After Elizabeth: How King James of Scots Won the Crown of England in 1603*	Harper Collins, 2005	
		Jenny Erdal	*Ghosting*	Canongate, 2004	
		Alison Flett	*Whit Lasyz Ur Inty*	Edi Thirsty Books, 2004	
		Rodge Glass	*No Fireworks*	Faber and Faber, 2005	
		Wendy Moore	*The Knife Man: The Extraordinary Life and Times of John Hunter, Father of Modern Surgery*	Bantam Press, 2005	
2006	Royal Mail/ Post Office, £1,500	Simon R. Biggam	*These Are Only Words*	Chroma, 2006	Allan Boyd Ian Campbell (Chair) Douglas Gifford Ian MacDonald Joyce McMillan Ann Matheson Marion Sinclair David Robb
		Maggie Fergusson	***George MacKay Brown: The Life***	**John Murray, 2006**	
		Alice Greenway	*White Ghost Girls*	Atlantic, 2006	
		Jane Harri	*The Observations*	Faber & Faber, 2006	
		Alison Miller	*Demo*	Hamish Hamilton, 2005	

2007	Royal Mail/ Post Office, £1,500	Angus Dunn **Mark McNay** Stef Penney Remzije Sherifi and Robert Davidson	*Writing in the Sand* ***Fresh: A Novel*** *The Tenderness of Wolves* *Shadow Behind the Sun*	Luath Press, 2006 **Canongate, 2007** Quercus, 2006 Sandstone, 2007	Allan Boyd Ian Campbell Douglas Gifford (Chair) Ian MacDonald Joyce McMillan Ann Matheson Marion Sinclair David Robb
2008	Royal Mail/ Post Office, £1,500	Elaine di Rollo D. C. Jackson David Knowles Simon Kövesi Shona MacLean Andrea McNicoll	*The Peachgrower's Almanac* *The Wall* *Meeting the Jet Man* *James Kelman* *The Redemption of Alexander Seaton* *Moonshine in the Morning*	Chatto & Windus, 2008 Faber & Faber, 2008 Two Ravens Press, 2008 Manchester University Press, 2007 Quercus, 2008 Alma Books, 2008	Allan Boyd Ian Campbell (Chair) Douglas Gifford Ian MacDonald Joyce McMillan Ann Matheson Marion Sinclair David Robb
2009	Royal Mail/ Post Office, £1,500	**Andy Nicholl** Jason Donald Sarah Gabriel Alison Lang Kirsten McKenzie **Eleanor Thom**	***The Good Mayor*** *Chokechain* *Eating Pomegranates* *Cainnt na Cailege Caillte* *Chapel at the Edge of the World* ***The Tinkin***	**Black & White, 2008** Jonathan Cape, 2009 Jonathan Cape, 2009 Clàr, 2009 John Murray, 2010 **Duckworth, 2009**	Allan Boyd Ian Campbell Douglas Gifford (Chair) Joyce McMillan Ann Matheson Marion Sinclair David Robb

(continued)

Year	Sponsor/prize fund	Author	Title	Publisher and year	Judging panel
2010	Royal Mail/ Post Office, £1,500	**Simon Hall**	***The History of Orkney Literature***	**John Donald, 2010**	Allan Boyd Ian Campbell (Chair) Douglas Gifford Joyce McMillan Ann Matheson Marion Sinclair David Robb
		Margaret Macaulay	*The Prisoner of St Kilda: The True Story of the Unfortunate Lady Grange*	Luath Press, 2009	
		Emily Mackie	*And This is True*	Sceptre, 2010	
		Màiri E. NicLeòid	*A' Ghlainne: agus Sgeulachdan Eile*	Clàr, 2009	
		Donald Paterson	*Homecomings*	Two Ravens Press, 2010	
		Sue Peebles	***The Death of Lomond Friel***	**Chatto & Windus, 2010**	
2011	The Saltire Society, £1,500	Karin Altenberg	*Island of Wings*	Quercus, 2011	Allan Boyd Ian Campbell (Chair) Ann Matheson Joyce McMillan David Robb Claire Squires
		Alison Irvine	*This Road Is Red*	Luath Press, 2011	
		Simon Stephenson	*Let Not the Waves of the Sea*	John Murray, 2012	
		Luke Williams	***The Echo Chamber***	**Hamish Hamilton, 2011**	
2012	The Saltire Society, £1,500	Maighread A. Challan	*Air Bilean an t-Sluaigh: Sealladh air Leantalachd Beul-Aithris Ghàidhlig Uibhist a Tuath*	Queens University Press, 2012	Allan Boyd Ian Campbell (Chair) Ian MacDonald Joyce McMillan Ann Matheson David Robb Claire Squires
		Sarah Fraser	***The Last Highlander: Scotland's Most Notorious Clan-Chief, Rebel and Double Agent***	**Harper Press, 2012**	
		Kerry Hudson	*Tony Hogan Bought Me an Ice Cream*	Chatto & Windus, 2012	

Year	Prize	Author	Book	Publisher	Judges
2013	The Saltire Society, £1,500	Moira McPartlin	*Float Before He Stole My Ma*	Fledgling Press, 2012	Allan Boyd
		Wayne Price	*The Incomers Furnace*	Freight Books, 2012	Ian Campbell (Chair)
		Elizabeth Reeder	*Ramshackle*	Freight Books, 2012	Ian MacDonald
		Tim Armstrong	***Air Cuan Dubh Drilseach***	**Clàr, 2013**	Joyce McMillan
		Eunice Buchanan	***As Far as I Can See***	**Kettillonia, 2012**	Ann Matheson
		Vicky Jarrett	*Nothing Is Heavy*	Linen Press, 2012	David Robb
		Kellan Macinnes	*Caleb's List*	Luath Press, 2013	Claire Squires
		Malcolm Mackay	*The Necessary Death of Lewis Winter*	Mantle, 2013	Mark Wringe
2014	Tamdhu Speyside Single Malt Whisky, £2,000	**Niall Campbell**	***Moontide***	**Bloodaxe Books, 2014**	Ian Campbell (Chair)
		Kate Horsley	*The Monster's Wife*	Barbican Press, 2014	Ian MacDonald
		Kirsty Logan	*The Rental Heart*	Salt, 2014	Hannah McGill
		Anneliese Mackintosh	*Any Other Mouth*	Freight Books, 2014	Joyce McMillan
		Mary F. McDonough	*The Last Pair of Ears*	Gadfly Editions, 2014	Ann Matheson
		Kirsty Wark	*The Legacy of Elizabeth Pringle*	Two Roads, 2014	David Robb
					Claire Squires
					Mark Wringe
2015	Saltire Society/ Creative Scotland, £2,000	Peter Geoghegan	*The People's Referendum*	Luath, 2014	Ian Campbell (Chair)
		Audrey Henderson	*Airstream*	Homebound Publications, 2014	Hannah McGill
		Helen McClory	***On the Edges of Vision***	**Queen's Ferry Press, 2015**	Joyce McMillan
		Fiona Rintoul	*The Leipzig Affair*	Aurora Metro, 2014	Ann Matheson
		Michael F. Russell	*Lie of the Land Sixty*	Polygon, 2015	Jenny Niven
		Malachy Tallack	*Degrees North*	Polygon, 2015	David Robb
					David Robinson
					Mark Wringe

(continued)

Year	Sponsor/prize fund	Author	Title	Publisher and year	Judging panel
2016	Saltire Society/ Creative Scotland, £2,000	Claire Askew	*This Changes Things*	Bloodaxe Books, 2016	Ian Campbell
		Isabel Buchanan	*Trials: On Death Row in Pakistan*	Jonathan Cape, 2016	Hannah McGill
					Joyce McMillan
		Martin MacInnes	*Infinite Ground*	Atlantic Books, 2016	Ann Matheson
		Chitra Ramaswamy	**Expecting: The Inner Life of Pregnancy**	**Saraband, 2016**	David Robinson (Chair)
					Mark Wringe
2017	Saltire Society/ Creative Scotland, £2,000	**Ever Dundas**	**Goblin**	**Saraband, 2017**	Alan Bett
		Kate Hunter	*The Caseroom*	Fledgling Press, 2017	Ian Campbell
		Sandra Ireland	*Beneath the Skin*	Polygon, 2016	Ann Matheson
		Anna Pia	*Language of My Choosing*	Luath, 2017	Hannah McGill
		Ross Sayers	*Mary's the Name*	Cranachan Publishing, 2017	Joyce McMillan
		Daniel Shand	*Fallow*	Sandstone Press, 2016	Mark Wringe
2018	Saltire Society/ Creative Scotland, £2,000	Alex Boyd	*St Kilda: The Silent Islands*	Luath Press, 2018	Alan Bett
		Mick Kitson	**Sal**	**Canongate, 2018**	Anna Day
		Calum L. MacLeòid	*A' Togail an t-Sràbain*	CLÀR, 2017	Laura Waddell
		Christina Neuwirth	*Amphibian*	Speculative Books, 2018	Louise Welsh
2019	Saltire Society/ Creative Scotland, £2,000	Alan Brown	*Overlander: Bikepacking Coast to Coast Across the Heart of the Highlands*	Saraband, 2019	Elenor Collins
					Vineet Lal
		Fraser MacDonald	*Escape from Earth*	Profile Books, 2019	Andrés N. Ordorica
		Clare Hunter	**Threads of Life**	**Hodder & Stoughton, 2019**	Laura Waddell
		Angela Meyer	*A Superior Spectre*	Contraband, 2019	Louise Welsh
		Stephen Rutt	**The Seafarers: A Journey Among Birds**	**Elliott & Thompson Limited, 2019**	

NOTES

Introduction

1 My role at the Society is discussed in more detail in the following article: Stevie Marsden and Claire Squires, 'The first rule of judging club...: Inside the Saltire Society Literary Awards', *Journal of Cultural Analysis and Social Change* 4, no. 2 (2019): 1–14, http://www.lectitopublishing.nl/Article/Detail/the-first-rule-of-judging-club-inside-the-saltire-society-literary-awards-6354 (accessed 17 August 2020).
2 The Booker Prize has had a number of monikers since its founding in 1969, depending on lead sponsors at the time. From 1969 to 2001, it was the Booker-McConnell Prize (although was commonly referred to as simply 'the Booker'). Between 2001 and 2019, it was the Man Booker, following the addition of the Man Group as sponsor. However, in early 2019, the Man Group announced it would be the last year they sponsor the prize, and so from 2020 onwards, the prize would be sponsored by the charitable organisation Crankstart with the prize henceforth being referred to as 'The Booker Prize'. Accordingly, the prize will be referred to as the Booker Prize throughout this book, regardless of the point in time at which the prize is being discussed.
3 Richard Todd, *Consuming Fictions: The Booker Prize and Fiction in Britain Today* (London: Bloomsbury, 1996), 10.
4 James F. English, 'Consuming fictions: The Booker Prize and fiction in Britain today', *Modern Fiction Studies*, 45, no. 2 (1999): 529–33 (530).
5 Ibid., 530.
6 James F. English, *The Economy of Prestige: Prizes, Awards, and the Circulation of Cultural Value* (London: Harvard University Press, 2005).
7 Pierre Bourdieu, 'The forms of capital', in *Handbook of Theory of Research for the Sociology of Education*, edited by J. E. Richardson, translated by Richard Nice (New York: Greenwood Press, 1986), 241–58.
8 Nina Power, 'Cultural capital', in *The Encyclopedia of Literary and Cultural Theory*, edited by M. Ryan (Malden, MA: Wiley, 2011), doi:10.1002/9781444337839.wbelctv3c011.
9 Ibid.
10 Bourdieu, 'The forms of capital', 243.
11 Ibid., 243.
12 Ibid., 247.
13 Ibid., 248.
14 Ion Trewin, 'Martyn Goff obituary', *Guardian*, 26 March 2015, https://www.theguardian.com/books/2015/mar/26/martyn-goff (accessed 17 August 2020).

15 English, *Economy of Prestige*, 127.
16 Ibid., 123.
17 For more, see ibid., 207–8.
18 Ibid., 10–11.
19 Ibid., 26.
20 Claire Squires, *Marketing Literature: The Making of Contemporary Writing in Britain* (Hampshire: Palgrave Macmillan, 2007a), 2.
21 Claire Squires, 'Book marketing and the book prize', in *Judging a Book by Its Cover*, edited by N. Matthews and N. Moody (Hampshire: Ashgate, 2007b), 73.
22 Ibid., 76.
23 Squires, *Marketing Literature*, 37.
24 Ibid., 101.
25 Beth Driscoll, *The New Literary Middlebrow: Tastemakers and Reading in the Twenty-First Century* (London: Palgrave Macmillan, 2014).
26 Ibid., 120.
27 Ibid., 121.
28 Ibid., 150–51.
29 Ibid., 122.
30 Sharon Norris, 'The Booker Prize: A Bourdieusian perspective', *Journal for Cultural Research* 10, no. 2 (2006a): 139–58 (140, 141).
31 Ibid., 141.
32 Alexandra Dane, *Gender and Prestige in Literature: Contemporary Australian Book Culture* (London: Palgrave Macmillan), 124.
33 Driscoll, *The New Literary Middlebrow*, 128.
34 Ibid., 151.
35 Richard Todd, 'How has the Booker Prize changed since 1996?', in *Fiction and Literary Prizes in Great Britain*, edited by Wolfgang Görtschacher and Holger Klein, with Claire Squires (Vienna: Praesens, 2006), 8–20.
36 Sharon Norris, 'Recontextualising the Booker', in *Fiction and Literary Prizes in Great Britain*, edited by Wolfgang Görtschacher and Holger Klein, with Claire Squires (Vienna: Praesens, 2006), 20–37 (32).
37 Sharon Norris, 'Scots and the Booker', in *Fiction and Literary Prizes in Great Britain*, edited by Wolfgang Görtschacher and Holger Klein, with Claire Squires (Vienna: Praesens, 2006), 37–52.
38 Graham Huggan, *The Postcolonial Exotic* (Oxon: Routledge, 2001), 106.
39 Huggan notes that 'the company, initially formed in 1834 to provide distributional services on the sugar-estates of Demerara (now Guyana), achieved rapid prosperity under a harsh colonial regime', *Postcolonial Exotic*, 107. This is further evidenced by Natalie Hopkinson who observes that 'the company's domination of the economic and political life was so complete that the colony became acidly referred to as "Booker's Guiana"'. Natalie Hopkinson, 'The Booker Prize's bad history', *New York Times*, 18 October 2017, https://www.nytimes.com/2017/10/17/opinion/man-booker-bad-history.html (accessed 17 August 2020).
40 Jonathan Taylor, 'The Man Booker back story', The Booker Prizes, https://thebookerprizes.com/author/man-booker-back-story (accessed 17 August 2020).
41 Huggan, *The Postcolonial Exotic*, 111.
42 Luke Strongman, *The Booker Prize and the Legacy of Empire* (New York: Rodopi, 2002), x.

43 See Stevie Marsden, 'Why I'm done with the Man Booker Prize and you should be too', *Medium*, 10 July 2018, https://medium.com/@steviemarsden/why-im-done-with-the-man-booker-prize-and-you-should-be-too-ad0057b95baf; Stevie Marsden, 'How the Man Booker fiction prize became stacked in favour of the big publishers', *Conversation*, 29 July 2015, https://theconversation.com/how-the-man-booker-fiction-prize-became-stacked-in-favour-of-the-big-publishers-45344; Stevie Marsden, 'The Man Booker Prize still has a long way to go before it is truly inclusive', *Conversation*, 14 October 2015, https://theconversation.com/the-man-booker-prize-still-has-a-long-way-to-go-before-it-is-truly-inclusive-49157; Sam Jordison, 'What happened?', *Times Literary Supplement*, 25 October 2019, https://www.the-tls.co.uk/articles/what-happened-booker-prize-ellmann/ (accessed 17 August 2020).
44 Strongman, *The Booker Prize*, xii.
45 See Driscoll, *The New Literary Middlebrow*; Squires, 'Book marketing and the book prize'.
46 Anna Auguscik, *Prizing Debate. The Fourth Decade of the Booker Prize and the Contemporary Novel in the UK* (Bielefeld: Transcript, 2017), 327.
47 Gillian Roberts, *Prizing Literature: The Celebration and Circulation of National Culture* (Toronto: University of Toronto Press, 2011), 4.
48 Ibid., 5.
49 Danielle Fuller, 'Listening to the readers of "Canada Reads"', *Canadian Literature* no. 193 (Summer 2007): 11–34; Danielle Fuller and DeNel Rehberg Sedo, 'A reading spectacle for the nation: The CBC and "Canada Reads"', *Journal of Canadian Studies* 40, no. 1 (Winter 2006): 5–36; Anouk Lang, '"A book that all Canadians should be proud to read": Canada Reads and Joseph Boyden's *Three Day Road*', *Canadian Literature* no. 215 (Winter 2012): 120–36; DeNel Rehberg Sedo, '"Richard & Judy's Book Club" and "Canada Reads": Readers, books and cultural programming in a digital era', *Information, Communication and Society* 11, no. 2 (2012): 188–206.
50 Beth Driscoll, 'Twitter, literary prizes and the circulation of capital', 103–19, and 'Making the list: The value of prizes for women writers in the construction of educational reading lists', 127–140, in *By the Book? Contemporary Publishing in Australia* (Melbourne: Monash University Press, 2013).
51 Dane, *Gender and Prestige in Literature*, 136.
52 Emmett Stinson, 'Small publishers and the emerging network of Australian literary production', *Australian Humanities Review* no. 59 (2016a): 23–43. Emmett Stinson, 'Small publishers and the Miles Franklin Award', in *The Return of Print? Contemporary Australian Publishing*, edited by A. Mannion and E. Stinson (Melbourne: Monash University, 2016b), 137–49.
53 This award, which is funded by donations from publishers and booksellers, comes with a €25,000 cash prize and, according to the Peace Prize Foundation, acts 'as a symbol of an entire industry's unique dedication to peace'. 'The Peace Prize of the German book trade', http://www.friedenspreis-des-deutschen-buchhandels.de/445943/ (accessed 17 August 2020). Britta Scheideler, 'Von Konsens zu Kritik: Der Friedenspreis des Deutschen Buchhandels', *50 Jahre Frankfurter Buchmesse: 1949–1999* (Berlin: Suhrkamp Verlag, 1999), 46–88.
54 Marie-Françoise Cachin and Sylvie Ducas-Spaes, 'The Goncourt and the Booker: A tale of two prizes', *Logos* 14, no. 2 (2003): 85–94. Sylvie Ducas, *La littérature, à quel(s) prix?* (Paris: La Découverte, 2013).

55 Edward Mack, *Manufacturing Modern Japanese Literature* (London: Duke University Press, 2010).
56 Alicia Joy, 'A brief history of Japan's most prestigious literary award, The Akutagawa Prize', *Culture Trip*, 21 September 2016, https://theculturetrip.com/asia/japan/articles/a-brief-history-of-japans-most-prestigious-literary-award-the-akutagawa-prize/ (accessed 17 August 2020).
57 Mack, *Manufacturing Modern Japanese Literature*, 6.
58 Yoshio Iwamoto, 'The Nobel Prize in Literature, 1967–1987: A Japanese view', *World Literature Today* 62, no. 2 (Spring 1988): 217–21.
59 Susan Pickford, 'The Booker and the Prix Goncourt: A case study of award-winning novels in translation', *Book History* no. 14 (2011): 221–40, 221.
60 Melanie Ramdarshan Bold and Corinna Norrick-Rühl, 'The Independent Foreign Fiction Prize and Man Booker International Prize merger', *Logos* 28, no. 3 (2017): 7–24. doi: https://doi.org/10.1163/1878-4712-11112131
61 Todd, *Consuming Fictions*, 134.
62 Claire Squires, 'A common ground? Book prize culture in Europe', *Public* 11, no. 4 (2004): 39.
63 Ibid., 39.
64 Casanova's work is used while bearing in mind the criticism *The World Republic of Letters* has received. Such criticisms will be considered and dealt with in more detail when Casanova is applied in later chapters of the book.
65 Pascale Casanova, *The World Republic of Letters*, translated by Malcolm DeBevoise (Cambridge: Harvard University Press, 2007), xii.
66 Ibid., 3.
67 Ibid.
68 Ibid.
69 'The James Tait Black Prize', University of Edinburgh, 14 August 2019, https://www.ed.ac.uk/events/james-tait-black/about/book (accessed 17 August 2020).
70 'Jenny Uglow wins the Hawthornden Prize for Literature 2018', *Faber*, 12 September 2018, https://www.faber.co.uk/blog/jenny-uglow-wins-the-hawthornden-prize-for-literature-2018/ (accessed 17 August 2020).
71 'History of the awards', Scottish Mortgage Investment Trust Book Awards, 5 December 2013, https://web.archive.org/web/20131205063655/http://www.scottishbookawards.com/about-the-award/history-of-the-awards/ (accessed 17 August 2020).
72 'Obituary of Prof S G Checkland', *Times*, 27 March 1986.
73 Sarah Ferrell, 'Bookshelf on Scotland and Audubon', *New York Times*, 27 July 1980, 13.
74 National Book League, *Guide to Literary Prizes: Grants and Awards in Britain and Ireland 1986* (London: National Book League and Society of Authors, 1986), 31.
75 Ibid.
76 Ibid.
77 Ibid.
78 Ibid.
79 Book Trust, *Guide to Literary Prizes: Grants and Awards in Britain and Ireland 1986* (London: Book Trust, 1992/93), 29.
80 Ibid., 41.
81 Ibid.

82 'History of the awards', Scottish Mortgage Investment Trust Book Awards, 5 December 2013, http:/www.scottishbookawards.com/about-the-award/history-of-the-awards/, available via Internet Archive, https://web.archive.org/web/20131205063655/http://www.scottishbookawards.com/about-the-award/history-of-the-awards/ (accessed 20 July 2020).
83 David Robinson, 'Debut novels on shortlist for top award', *Scotsman*, 10 May 2002, 8.
84 There is currently little published about the history of the SAC Children's Book Award, the introduction of Royal Mail as a sponsor and its handover to the Scottish Book Trust. This would be a fruitful area for further examination.
85 Phil Miller, 'New sponsor announced for £30,000 book awards', *Herald* (Glasgow), 6 March 2009, 11.
86 Book Trust, *Guide to Literary Prizes*, 23.
87 'Book prize's happy ending', *Herald*, 19 July 1997, 3.
88 Vivienne Nicoll, 'McVitie's defends decision to abandon literary award', *Scotsman*, 24 March 1997, 3.
89 Alexander Linklater, 'The end for Stakis Award', *Herald*, 19 January 1999, 1.
90 Ibid.
91 Squires, *Marketing Literature*, 4.

Chapter 1. The History of the Saltire Society

1 Saltire Society, *Saltire Society Annual Report, 1939–1940* (Edinburgh: Saltire Society, 1940), 2.
2 Ibid.
3 Ibid.
4 McCulloch illustrates how many of the writers who were involved in the founding years of the Society, namely George Malcolm Thomson, Andrew Dewar Gibb, Hugh MacDiarmid, Edwin Muir and Neil Gunn, had been writing about the sociopolitical problems Scotland faced during the 1920s and 30s. Margery Palmer McCulloch, 'Politics and society between the wars', *Scottish Modernism and Its Contexts 1918–1959* (Edinburgh: Edinburgh University Press, 2009), 100–3.
5 George Bruce, *'To Foster and Enrich': The First Fifty Years of the Saltire Society* (Edinburgh: Saltire Society, 1986), 12–13.
6 The name originally proposed for the Society – the 'Saltoun Society' – is likely a reference to the Scottish writer, patriot and book collector Andrew Fletcher of Saltoun. Given Fletcher's political activity and anti-union position, it is interesting that his name would be suggested as the title for the Society, which would eventually pride itself on being apolitical and independent. However, in 1988, the Society established the 'Andrew Fletcher of Saltoun Award', an annual award which recognises 'outstanding achievements in the fields of science, arts and public life'. The Society claims this award 'celebrates the legacy of Andrew Fletcher of Saltoun, a seventeenth century Scottish writer and politician and a keen patron of the arts during his lifetime'. John Robertson, 'Fletcher, Andrew, of Saltoun (1653?–1716)', Scottish patriot, political theorist, and book collector', *Oxford Dictionary of National Biography*, 23 September 2004, https://www-oxforddnb-com.ezproxy3.lib.le.ac.uk/view/10.1093/ref:odnb/9780198614128.001.0001/odnb-9780198614128-e-9720 (accessed 15 July 2020). The Saltire Society, 'The 2018 Fletcher of Saltoun Awards announced', The Saltire

Society, September 2018, https://www.saltiresociety.org.uk/news/2018/09/22/the-2018-fletcher-of-saltoun-awards-announced (accessed 15 July 2020).
7   Bruce, *To Foster and Enrich*, 12–13.
8   'The Saltire Society, Perth Conference, 1947', 3–4. Edinburgh, National Library of Scotland (NLS), Acc. 9393, File No. 342.
9   Ibid.
10 Iain Paul, 'The Saltire Society: A short account of the first ten years', *Scotland's Magazine*, 1947, 6.
11 For more on this, see Vanessa Thorpe, 'Unsung women emerge from the footnotes of history', *Guardian*, 22 September 2018, https://www.theguardian.com/books/2018/sep/22/unsung-women-emerge-from-footnotes-of-history (accessed 29 July 2020).
12 See Stevie Marsden, 'Why women don't win literary awards: The Saltire Society Literary Awards and implicit stereotyping', *Women: A Cultural Review* 30, no. 1 (2019): 43–65, doi:10.1080/09574042.2018.1561047
13 The Saltire Society, 'Saltire Society Annual Report, 1939'. Edinburgh, National Library of Scotland (NLS), Acc. 9393, File No. 16.
14 Ibid., 8.
15 Ibid.
16 Saltire Society, *Saltire Society Annual Report, 1945–46* (Edinburgh: Saltire Society, 1946), 1.
17 Saltire Society, *Saltire Society Annual Report 1941–42* (Edinburgh: Saltire Society, 1942), p. 3.
18 Ibid., 3.
19 Agnes Mure Mackenzie, 'The Saltire Society: Its background and purpose', *Aberdeen University Review* 30, no. 90 (1944): 240.
20 *Scottish Journal* (1952–54) was one of several post-war magazines published by Glasgow-based publisher William MacLellan. Like the magazines and journals that had existed in the 1920s, such as *Chapbook*, *Scottish Nation* and *Scots Magazine* (all edited and contributed to by Hugh MacDiarmid), *Scottish Journal* 'confirmed [...] how a Scottish-based magazine and publisher with a declared Scottish agenda was a necessary part of the cause of national cultural independence'. Peter Brooker and Andrew Thacker, 'Introduction', *The Oxford Critical and Cultural History of Modernist Magazines: Volume 1: Britain and Ireland 1880–1955* (Oxford: Oxford University Press, 2009), 709.
21 'The Saltire Society Conference', *Scottish Journal*, no. 7 (May–June 1953): 4.
22 Ibid.
23 Letter from Robert Hurd to William McLellan, 11 June 1953. Edinburgh, National Library of Scotland (NLS), Acc. 9393, File No. 347.
24 'The Saltire Society', *Scottish Journal*, no. 11 (November–December 1953): 6.
25 Cullen of Whitekirk, *Report of the Saltire Commission* (Edinburgh: Saltire Society, 2011), 3.
26 Ibid., 9.
27 Ibid., 10.
28 Catriona M. MacDonald, *Unionist Scotland 1800–1997* (Edinburgh: John Donald, 1998), 103.
29 T. M. Devine, *The Scottish Nation: 1700–2007* (London: Penguin, 2006), 267.
30 Michael Lynch, *Scotland: A New History* (London: Pimlico, 1992), 424.
31 Ibid., 435.

32 Robert Rait and George S. Pryde, *Scotland* (London: Ernest Benn, 1934), 141.
33 Bruce, *To Foster and Enrich*, 12–13.
34 Ibid., 12.
35 George McKechnie, *The Best Hated Man: Intellectuals and the Conditions of Scotland between the Wars* (Argyll: Argyll, 2013), 213.
36 It is worth noting that McKechnie relies on Bruce's short history of the Saltire Society '*To Foster and Enrich…*', a document which, while useful in some respects, relies heavily on anecdotal oral histories with little original sourcing or citation, making much of the story it tells difficult to verify.
37 George Malcolm Thomson, *Caledonia or the Future of the Scots* (London: Kegan Paul, Trench, Trubner, 1927), 66.
38 Ibid., 7–9.
39 Saltire Society, *Saltire Society Annual Report 1938–39* (Edinburgh: Saltire Society, 1939), 2.
40 Thomson, *Caledonia or the Future of the Scots*, 60–61.
41 D. Finkelstein and A. McCleery, *The Edinburgh History of the Book, Volume 4: Professionalism and Diversity, 1880–2000* (Edinburgh: Edinburgh University Press, 2007), 441.
42 McCulloch, 'Politics and society between the wars', 95.
43 C. M. Grieve, *Albyn or Scotland and the Future* (London: Kegan Paul, Trench, Trubner, 1927), 43.
44 Ibid., 5.
45 George Blake, 'Literary tendencies in modern Scotland', *Library Review* 3, no. 2 (1931): 63–66 (64).
46 Edwin Muir, *Scottish Journey* (London: William Heinemann, 1935), 3.
47 Rait and Pryde, *Scotland*, 141.
48 McCulloch, 'Politics and society between the wars', 94.
49 Ibid., 95.
50 John Foster, 'The twentieth century, 1914–1979', in *The New Penguin History of Scotland*, edited by Robert Allen Houston and William Knox (London: Penguin Books, 2002), 417–94, 443.
51 Richard Finlay, 'Modern times (1914–) general', in *Oxford Companion to Scottish History*, edited by Michael Lynch (Oxford: Oxford University Press, 2011), 150–53 (151).
52 Ibid., 151.
53 Writing in the *Bulletin of Scottish Politics* in 1981, Christopher Harvie also notes that other organisations committed to the preservation and development of Scottish culture, such as the 'Association for the Preservation of Rural Scotland […] the Scottish Travel Association […] the SNDC [Scottish National Development Council], the National Trust for Scotland, and the Scottish Youth Hostels Association' were also founded throughout the 1930s. Christopher Harvie, 'Labour and Scottish government: The age of Tom Johnstone', *Bulletin of Scottish Politics*, no. 2 (Spring 1981): 1–21 (6).
54 Michael Gardiner, *Modern Scottish Culture* (Edinburgh: Edinburgh University Press, 2005), 56.
55 The Saltire Society, AGM, 28 June 1944. Edinburgh, National Library of Scotland (NLS), Acc. 9393, File No. 16.
56 Ibid.
57 Allan Ramsay, *Poems Epistles, Fables, Satires, Elegies & Lyrics* (Edinburgh: Oliver & Boyd for Saltire Society, 1940); James Hogg, *Selected Poems of James Hogg*, ed. J. W. Oliver (Edinburgh: Oliver & Boyd for Saltire Society, 1940); James A. Bowie, *The Basis*

of Reconstruction (Edinburgh: Oliver & Boyd for Saltire Society, 1941); Alan Riach, *Building Scotland: A Cautionary Guide* (Edinburgh: C. J. Cousland and Sons for Saltire Society, 1941); Thomas Urquhart, *Selections from Sir Thomas Urquhart of Cromarty*i, ed. John Purves (Edinburgh: Oliver & Boyd for Saltire Society, 1942); *Four Scottish Poems of the 16th Century*, ed. John W. Oliver (Edinburgh: Saltire Society, 1943); *Mally Le:, To Which Is Added Three Folk Songs*, ed. John W. Oliver (Edinburgh: Saltire Society, 1944); William Dunbar, *Seasonal Poems*, ed. John W. Oliver (Edinburgh: Saltire Society, 1944); John Lorne Campbell, *Gaelic in Scottish Education and Life: Past, Present and Future* (Edinburgh: W. & A.K. Johnston for Saltire Society, 1945); Isabella Burns, *The Marriage of Robin Redbreast and the Wren* (Edinburgh: Saltire Society, 1945); Robert Hurd and Andrew Philip, *Planning and Building Post-War Scotland* (Edinburgh: Saltire Society, 1945); *Songs of the '45*, ed. John W. Oliver (Edinburgh: Saltire Society, 1945); *Six Scottish Poems of the Nineteenth Century*, ed. John W. Oliver (Edinburgh: Saltire Society, 1946); *Whuppity Stoorie*, ed. John W. Oliver (Edinburgh: Saltire Society, 1946); *Scottish Children's Rhymes and Lullabies*, ed. Joan Hassall (Edinburgh: Saltire Society, 1948); Robert O. Dougan, *The Scottish Tradition in Photography* (Edinburgh: Thomas Nelson & Sons for Saltire Society, 1949); William Beattie, *The Scottish Tradition in Printed Books* (Edinburgh: Thomas Nelson & Sons for Saltire Society, 1949); John Lorne Campbell, *Gaelic in Scottish Education and Life: Past, Present and Future* (Edinburgh: W. & A. K. Johnston for Saltire Society, 1950); *Scotland on Freedom: From an Anonymous Chronicle of About 1460*, ed. Ages Mure Mackenzie (Edinburgh: Saltire Society, 1950); Peter Frederick Anson, *Scots Fisherfolk* (Banff: Banffshire Journal for Saltire Society, 1950); *Rashie Coat*, ed. Joan Hassall (Edinburgh: R. and R. Clark for Saltire Society, 1951); Robert Hurd and Andrew Philip, *Gladstone's Land: the Story of an Old Edinburgh House* (Edinburgh: National Trust for Saltire Society, 1952); *Scottish Pageant*, ed. Agnes Mure Mackenzie (Edinburgh: Oliver & Boyd for Saltire Society, 1952); *The Bruce: A Selection*, ed. Alexander Kinghorn (Edinburgh: Oliver & Boyd for Saltire Society, 1960); *Old Highland Tartans: Early Tartans, Spinning Implements, Dye Samples, Illustrations of Highland Dress, Manuscripts, etc.* (Edinburgh: Saltire Society, 1965).

58 The *Saltire Review* was a triannual journal founded by the Society. According to the first issue, the purpose of the journal was to 'fill the gap in the cultural life of the country left by the unhappy demise of such monthlies as *The Scots Review* [...] like its predecessors it [sought] to be Scottish in orientation while avoiding parochialism'. The first edition of *Saltire Review* was edited by Alexander Scott, and its advisory board included Neil M. Gunn, Eric Linklater, Compton MacKenzie, Agnes Mure Mackenzie and Naomi Mitchison. The *Saltire Review* was published until 1961, at which point the Society decided to rebrand the journal, calling it the *New Saltire*. The *New Saltire* was edited by the literary agent Gordon Giles and Michael Scott-Moncrieff. Alexander Scott, 'Editorial', *Saltire Review* 1, no. 1 (1954): 6.

59 Alistair McCleery, 'Conglomerates', in *The Edinburgh History of the Book in Scotland: Volume 4, Professionalism and Diversity 1880–2000*, edited by David Finkelstein and Alistair McCleery (Edinburgh: Edinburgh University Press, 2007), 348–52 (348).

60 Oliver & Boyd Ltd. Agreements and Agencies. Edinburgh, National Library of Scotland (NLS), Acc. 5000, File No. 92.

61 Ibid.

62 Alistair McCleery, 'Scottish papermills', in *The Edinburgh History of the Book in Scotland: Volume 4, Professionalism and Diversity 1880–2000*, edited by David Finkelstein and Alistair McCleery (Edinburgh: Edinburgh University Press, 2007), 97–107 (97–99).

63 Saltire Society, *Saltire Society Annual Report, 1941–42* (Edinburgh: Saltire Society, 1942), 5.
64 Ibid.
65 Publication Secretary Notes, 1949. Edinburgh, National Library of Scotland (NLS), Acc. 9393, File No. 6.
66 Minutes of Meeting of the Saltire Society Publications Committee, 22 February 1966. Edinburgh, National Library of Scotland (NLS), Acc. 9393, File No. 938.
67 Michael Gardiner, 'Towards a post-British theory of modernism: Speech and vision in Edwin Morgan', *Pretexts: Literary and Cultural Studies* 11, no. 2 (2002): 133–46 (135).
68 Eleanor Bell and Linda Gunn, *The Scottish Sixties: Reading, Rebellion, Revolution?* (Amsterdam: Rodopi, 2013).
69 Gerard Carruthers, 'Scottish literature: Second renaissance', in *The Cambridge History of Twentieth-Century English Literature*, edited by Laura Marcus and Peter Nicholls (Cambridge: Cambridge University Press, 2004), 668–85.
70 Alasdair Gray, James Kelman and Tom Toremans, 'An interview with Alasdair Gray and James Kelman', *Contemporary Literature* 44, no. 4 (2003): 564–86 (569).
71 Douglas Gifford, 'Breaking boundaries: From modern to contemporary in Scottish fiction', *The Edinburgh History of Scottish Literature, Volume 3: Modern Transformations*, edited by Ian Brown, Thomas Owen Clancy, Susan Manning and Murray Pittock (Edinburgh: Edinburgh University Press, 2007), 237–53 (237).
72 Ibid.
73 Neil Davidson, *The Origins of Scottish Nationhood* (London: Pluto, 2000), 1.
74 Ibid.
75 Despite a majority vote (51.6 per cent) in favour of devolution in Scotland's 1979 referendum, the Act was not passed due to the lack of a registered electorate turnout of less than 40 per cent (32.9 per cent).
76 Gifford, 'Breaking boundaries', 237.
77 T. M. Devine, *Scotland and the Union, 1707–2007* (Edinburgh: Edinburgh University Press, 2008), 146–47.
78 'A new voice in Scotland: Political parties? Trade unions?' Edinburgh, National Library of Scotland (NLS), Acc. 10347, File No. 115.
79 General Election Results, 9 June 1983, House of Commons Public Information Office Factsheet, 22, June 1984. General Election Results, 11 June 1987, House of Commons Public Information Office Factsheet, 47, June 1987. General Election Results, 9 April 1992, House of Commons Public Information Office Factsheet, 61, 1993.
80 Ian Macwhirter, *Road to Referendum* (Glasgow: Cargo, 2014), 42.
81 Carruthers, 'Scottish literature', 668.
82 Ibid.
83 Paul Henderson Scott, 'A new sang: Devolution and development', 1977. Edinburgh, National Library of Scotland (NLS), Acc. 10347, File No. 115.
84 A. C. Davis, 'A manifesto for the arts in Scotland: Conference', 21 March 1979. Edinburgh, National Library of Scotland (NLS), Acc. 10347, File No. 115.
85 'Scottish Independence Referendum', 29 February 2016, https://www.gov.uk/government/topical-events/scottish-independence-referendum/about#how-was-the-result-decided (accessed 20 July 2020).
86 'Leading writers put forward a philosophical slant on the referendum question', *Herald*, 18 July 2014, 6.

87 Ibid.
88 Stevie Marsden, private notes.
89 'Peter Geoghegan, *The People's Referendum: Why Scotland Will Never Be the Same Again* (Luath Press £9.99)', *Scottish Review of Books*, 26 January 2015, https://www.scottishreviewofbooks.org/free-content/peter-geoghegan-the-people-s-referendum-why-scotland-will-never-be-the-same-again-luath-press-9-99/ (accessed 20 July 2020).
90 'Saltire Society Literary Awards: Non Fiction', *Books from Scotland*, November 2015, https://booksfromscotland.com/2015/11/saltire-society-literary-awards-non-fiction/ (accessed 29 July 2020).
91 '*This Is Scotland: A Country in Words and* Pictures by Daniel Gray and Alan McCredie (Luath Press)', *Scottish Review of Books*, 6 November 2014, https://www.scottishreviewofbooks.org/free-content/this-is-scotland-a-country-in-words-and-pictures-by-daniel-gray-and-alan-mccredie-luath-press/ (accessed 29 July 2020).
92 'Open Project Funding August 2019–March 2020', *Creative Scotland*, 1 April 2020, https://www.creativescotland.com/funding/archive/open-project-funding (accessed 29 July 2020).
93 Just as this book was going to press, it was announced that the 2020 Saltire Society Literary Awards would not be going ahead due to an unsuccessful bid to Creative Scotland. This is the first year since 1982 that it has not conferred its literary awards.

Chapter 2. The Saltire Society Scottish Book of the Year

1 The Saltire Society's first 'Housing Commendation' was given to 'Houses at Milton, Bowling, Dunbartonshire' in 1937, with subsequent awards being made in 1938 ('Westquarter, Stirlingshire') and 1939 ('Houses at Alyth, Perthshire'). The Society's housing awards developed from an 'area of interest of the earliest meetings in connection with architecture' and were to focus on 'housing the people'. Similarly to the book commendations, the 'Housing Design Award', as it came to be known during this period, is 'lapsed for the period of the 1939–1945 war'. George Bruce, *'To Foster and Enrich': The First Fifty Years of the Saltire Society* (Edinburgh: Saltire Society, 1986), 56, 59.
2 Saltire Society, *Saltire Society Annual Report 1937* (Edinburgh: Saltire Society, 1937), 5.
3 Bruce, *To Foster and Enrich*, 26.
4 Saltire Society, *Saltire Society Annual Report, 1937–1938* (Edinburgh: Saltire Society, 1938), 17.
5 Ibid.
6 *Saltire Society Annual Report 1937*, 7.
7 Saltire Society, *Saltire Society Annual Report, 1936–1937* (Edinburgh: Saltire Society, 1937), 2.
8 'Prize novel award to Neil Gunn', *Evening Telegraph*, 3 May 1938, 9.
9 Alastair Cording, 'The plays of Robert McLellan', in *Robert McLellan: Playing Scotland's Story*, edited by Colin Donati (Edinburgh: Luath Press, 2013), 431.
10 Ibid..
11 'Books of today', *Western Morning News*, 6 June 1944, 2.
12 James A. Bowie, *The Future of Scotland: A Survey of the Present Position with Some Proposals for Future Policy* (London: W. & R. Chambers, 1939), 6.

13 Saltire Society, *Saltire Society Annual Report 1939–40* (Edinburgh: Saltire Society, 1938), 2.
14 'No title', *Aberdeen Press and Journal*, 25 August 1937, 13.
15 Valerie Holman, 'Carefully concealed connections: The ministry of information and British publishing', *Book History* no. 8 (2005): 208.
16 David McKetterick, 'The Roberts years', *A History of Cambridge University Press: Volume 3, New Worlds for Learning, 1873–1972* (Cambridge: Cambridge University Press, 2004), 286.
17 Minutes of Meeting of Publications Committee of the Saltire Society held in Edinburgh on 7 October 1953, Edinburgh, National Library of Scotland (NLS), Acc. 9393, File No. 937.
18 Minutes of Meeting of Publications Committee of the Saltire Society held in Glasgow on 8 February 1954, Edinburgh, National Library of Scotland (NLS), Acc. 9393, File No. 937.
19 Minutes of Meeting of Publications Committee of the Saltire Society held in Edinburgh on 22 June 1954, Edinburgh, National Library of Scotland (NLS), Acc. 9393, File No. 937.
20 Ibid.
21 Ibid.
22 Ibid.
23 The £500 award was 'made possible by the munificence of the Scottish Arts Council' after the funding from Pauline Niven came to an end. For more on this, see 'Frederick Niven Award', *Books in Scotland* no. 15 (1984): 2; 'Frederick Niven', *Encyclopaedia Britannica*, 27 March 2020, http://www.britannica.com/biography/Frederick-John-Niven (accessed 31 July 2020).
24 Ibid.
25 Minutes of Meeting of Publications Committee of the Saltire Society held in Edinburgh, 16 December 1954. Edinburgh, National Library of Scotland (NLS), Acc. 9393, File No. 937.
26 Minutes of Meeting of Publications Committee of the Saltire Society held in Glasgow, 22 March, 1955. Edinburgh, National Library of Scotland (NLS), Acc. 9393, File No. 937.
27 Unfortunately, all references made to Hogben in the Society's records do not offer a first name or initial, so his exact identity and expertise remain a mystery.
28 Pierre Bourdieu, 'The forms of capital', in *Handbook of Theory of Research for the Sociology of Education*, edited by J. E. Richardson, translated by Richard Nice (New York: Greenwood Press, 1986), 248.
29 'Saltire scheme', *Scotsman*, 19 October 1955.
30 Saltire Society, *Saltire Society Annual Report, 1955–1956* (Edinburgh: Saltire Society, 1956), 6.
31 Minutes of Meeting of Publications Committee of the Saltire Society held in Edinburgh, 29 January 1957. Edinburgh, National Library of Scotland (NLS), Acc. 9393, File No. 937.
32 Minutes of Meeting of Publications Committee of the Saltire Society held in Glasgow, 6 November 1957. Edinburgh, National Library of Scotland (NLS), Acc. 9393, File No. 937.
33 F. I. G. Rawlins, 'The architecture of Scottish post-reformation churches, 1560–1843 by George Hay', *Studies in Conservation* 3, no. 3 (April 1958): 142.

NOTES

34. Saltire Society, *Saltire Society Annual Report 1957–1958* (Edinburgh: Saltire Society, 1958), 10.
35. Saltire Society, *Saltire Society Annual Report 1958–1959* (Edinburgh: Saltire Society, 1959), 11.
36. Paul Henderson Scott, interview with Stevie Marsden, 6 March 2013.
37. Paul Henderson Scott, 'Behind the awards', *Books in Scotland* no. 37 (1991): 1.
38. Scott, interview with Marsden, 6 March 2013.
39. Mark W. Rectanus, 'Redefining culture, absolutely', *Culture Incorporated Book: Museums, Artists, and Corporate Sponsorships* (Minneapolis: University of Minnesota Press, 2002), 61.
40. Beth Driscoll, *The New Literary Middlebrow: Tastemakers and Reading in the Twenty-First Century* (London: Palgrave Macmillan, 2014), 131.
41. Letter from Gordon P. Fenton (assistant public relations officer, Royal Bank of Scotland) to Paul Henderon Scott, 18 August 1981. Edinburgh, National Library of Scotland (NLS), Acc. 9393, File No. 153.
42. Press release announcing the 'Saltire Society and Royal Bank Scottish Literary Award', 3 November 1981. Edinburgh, National Library of Scotland (NLS), Acc. 9393, File No. 153.
43. Letter from Paul Scott to Thomas Crawford; J. A. Ford; Edwin Morgan; Dr Anne Smith, 29 September 1981. Edinburgh, National Library of Scotland (NLS), Acc. 9393, File No. 153.
44. Ibid.
45. Ibid.
46. Ibid.
47. Letter enclosing description of 'new Scottish Book Award' and request for nominations (commencing October 1982) from Paul Scott to R. Knox, *Aberdeen Press and Journal*; Duncan Glen, *Akros*; Joy Hendry, *Chapman*; Glen Murray, *Cencrastus*; John Fowler, *Glasgow Herald*; J. K. Annand, *Lallans*; Mr McDonald, *Lines Review*; Dr Anne Smith, *Literary Review*; James Campbell, *New Edinburgh Review*; Tom Crawford, *Scottish Literary Journal*; M. Lindsay, *Scottish Review*; J. Seaton, *Scotsman*; Clive Sandground, *Sunday Standard*, 23 September 1981. Edinburgh, National Library of Scotland (NLS), Acc. 9393, File No. 153.
48. Letter from John Arnott, senior producer talks and features (BBC Radio) to Paul Henderson Scott, 19 October 1981. Edinburgh, National Library of Scotland (NLS), Acc. 9393, File No. 153.
49. Ibid.
50. Claire Squires, 'The review and the reviewer', in *Contemporary Publishing and the Culture of Books*, edited by Alison Baverstock and Richard Bradford (Abingdon: Routledge, 2020), 121.
51. Scott, 'Behind the awards', 1991, 2.
52. Douglas Gifford, 'The Saltire shortlists', *Books in Scotland* no. 40 (Winter 1991): 3.
53. 'The Saltire Society/Royal Bank of Scotland Literary Award – Nominations for 1987'. Edinburgh, National Library of Scotland (NLS), Acc. 10504, File No. 15a.
54. Nominations for the Book of the Year Award, 1990 and Nominations for the Book of the Year Award 1991. Edinburgh, National Library of Scotland (NLS), Acc. 11714, File No. 23.
55. Nominations for the Book of the Year Award 1996. Edinburgh, National Library of Scotland (NLS), Acc. 11714, File No. 25.

56 Nominations for the Book of the Year Award 1998. Edinburgh, National Library of Scotland (NLS), Acc. 11828, File No. 58.
57 Saltire Society Scottish Book of the Year Award 2010: Call for Nominations. Saltire Society, Private Archives.
58 Saltire Society Literary Awards 2015: Entry Form. Saltire Society, Private Archives.
59 The Saltire Society and the Royal Bank of Scotland: Launch of Literary Award, 17 November 1981. Edinburgh, National Library of Scotland (NLS), Acc. 9393, File No. 153.
60 Ibid.
61 Although the Society's official press release for the first award notes that Crawford, Daiches, Ford, Morgan, Scott and Smith were the members of the first judging panel, both Ian Campbell and Douglas Gifford have indicated in interviews and public speeches that they were members of the first Book of the Year Award panel. However, a letter from Scott addressed to Campbell and Gifford and sent in January 1983 indicates that this was in fact the time at which Campbell and Gifford were invited to join the panel. Letter from Paul Henderson Scott to Angus Calder, Ian Campbell, Douglas Gifford, Alan Massie, Isobel Murray, 14 January 1983. Edinburgh, National Library of Scotland (NLS), Acc. 9393, File No. 154.
62 The Saltire Society and the Royal Bank of Scotland: Launch of Literary Award, 17 November 1981. Edinburgh, National Library of Scotland (NLS), Acc. 9393, File No. 153.
63 'New Scottish Book Award', *Daily Telegraph (Northern Edition)*, 18 November 1981, 14; 'Scottish Book of the Year', *Books in Scotland* no. 9 (1981–82): 3; 'The Saltire Society and the Royal Bank of Scotland are launching an annual award for the Scottish Book of the Year', *Business and Finance in Scotland* 8, no. 6 (December 1981): 8.
64 Letter from A. Fairly to Saltire Society, 20 November 1981. Edinburgh, National Library of Scotland (NLS), Acc. 9393, File No. 153.
65 Letter from Marion Muir to Saltire Society, 26 November 1981. Edinburgh, National Library of Scotland (NLS), Acc. 9393, File No. 153.
66 The full list of recipients of this letter from Scott, 10 August 1982: J. K. Annand; Thomas Crawford; David Daiches; Callum McDonald, editor, *Lines Review*; James Allan Ford; John Fowler, literary editor, *Glasgow Herald*; Duncan Glen, editor *Akros*; Cuthbert Graham, contributor *Aberdeen Press and Journal*; Joy Hendry, editor, *Chapman*; R. B. Jeffrey, literary editor, *Sunday Standard*; Maurice Lindsay, editor, *Scottish Review*; Allan Massie, literary critic, *Scotsman*; Edwin Morgan; Glen Murray, editor, *Cencrastus*; James Seaton, literary editor, *Scotsman*; Ann Smith; Norman Wilson, editor, *Books in Scotland*. Letter requesting nominations for the Book of the Year Award. Edinburgh, National Library of Scotland (NLS), Acc. 9393, File No. 153.
67 Scott had also written to the literary editors and critics of many of these publications before the announcement of the award in September 1981 to ask if they would be willing to nominate books for the first award in October 1982. The recipients of this initial letter from Scott included R. Knox, features editor, *Aberdeen Press and Journal*; Duncan Glen, editor, *Akros*; Joy Hendry, editor, *Chapman*; Glen Murray, editor, *Cencrastus*; John Fowler, literary editor, *Glasgow Herald*; J. K. Annand, editor, *Lallans*; Mr McDonald, *Lines Review*; Dr Anne Smith, editor, *Literary Review*; James Campbell, editor, *New Edinburgh Review*; Tom Crawford, editor, *Scottish Literary Journal*; M. Lindsay, editor, *Scottish Review*; J. Seaton, literary editor, *Scotsman*; Clive Sandground, features

editor, *Sunday Standard*. Letter enclosing description of the Book of the Year Award and request for nominations. Edinburgh, National Library of Scotland (NLS), Acc. 9393, No. 153.
68   Ibid.
69   Letter from Norman Wilson to Paul Henderson Scott, 27 September 1982. Edinburgh, National Library of Scotland (NLS), Acc. 9393, File No. 153.
70   Letter from Sheila G. Hearn, executive editor, *Cencrastus*, to Paul Henderson Scott, 29 September 1982. Edinburgh, National Library of Scotland (NLS), Acc. 9393, File No. 153.
71   While they missed out on winning, or being shortlisted for, the Society's inaugural Book of the Year Award, Angus Calder, F. R. Hart and J. B. Pick did receive Scottish Arts Council Book Awards which came with a £600 prize in 1982. 'Scottish book awards', *Books in Scotland* no. 10 (Spring 1982): 3.
72   Draft press release and letter from Gordon Fenton to Paul Henderson Scott, 3 November 1981. Edinburgh, National Library of Scotland (NLS), Acc. 9393, File No. 153.
73   Letter from Thomas Crawford to Paul Henderson Scott, 11 August 1982. Edinburgh, National Library of Scotland, Acc. 9393, File No. 153.
74   Letter from Edwin Morgan to Paul Henderson Scott, 13 October 1982. Edinburgh, National Library of Scotland (NLS), Acc. 9393, File No. 153.
75   Press release: The Saltire Society and Royal Bank Scottish Literary Award, 13 October 1982. Edinburgh, National Library of Scotland (NLS), Acc. 9393, File No. 153.
76   Letter from Paul Scott sent to the publishers John Calder, Michael Joseph, Cambridge University Press, John Murray, Canongate and Paul Harris Publishing, 1 October 1982. Edinburgh, National Library of Scotland (NLS), Acc. 9393, File No. 153.
77   Letter from Paul Scott sent to J. K. Annand, Tom Crawford, David Daiches, McDonald, James Ford, John Fowler, Duncan Glen, Cuthbert Graham, Joy Hendry, Robert Jeffrey, Maurice Lindsay, Allan Massie, Edwin Morgan, Glen Murray, James Seaton, Ann Smith, Norman Wilson, 10 August 1982. Edinburgh, National Library of Scotland (NLS), Acc. 9393, File No. 153.
78   Letter from Norman Wilson to Paul Scott, 27 September 1982. Edinburgh, National Library of Scotland (NLS), Acc. 9393, File No. 153.
79   Letter from Cuthbert Graham to Paul Henderson Scott, 13 September 1982. Edinburgh, National Library of Scotland (NLS), Acc. 9393, File No. 153.
80   Cuthbert Graham, 'Macbeth – as Thorfinn the Mighty', *Aberdeen Press and Journal*, 8 May 1982, 8.
81   Letter from Cuthbert Graham to Paul Henderson Scott, 13 September 1982. Edinburgh, National Library of Scotland (NLS), Acc. 9393, File No. 153.
82   Ibid.
83   Stevie Marsden, 'Why women don't win literary awards: The Saltire Society Literary Awards and implicit stereotyping', *Women: A Cultural Review* 30, no. 1 (2019): 43–65. doi:10.1080/09574042.2018.1561047
84   Press release: The Saltire Society and Royal Bank Scottish Literary Award, 16 November 1982. Edinburgh, National Library of Scotland (NLS), Acc. 9393, File No. 153.
85   Ibid.
86   Ibid.
87   Ibid.

88 Ibid.
89 Ibid.
90 '"Lanark" author wins new award', *Glasgow Herald*, 17 November 1982.
91 'Scottish book award', *Retail Newsagent London*, 1 January 1983.
92 Bruce, *To Foster and Enrich*, 16.
93 'The Waverley column', *Edinburgh Evening News*, 17 November 1982.
94 Ibid.
95 Ibid.
96 Letter from Paul Henderson Scott to Angus Calder, Ian Campbell, Douglas Gifford, Alan Massie, Isobel Murray, 14 January 1983. Edinburgh, National Library of Scotland (NLS), Acc. 9393, File No. 154.
97 Although Campbell stepped down as the chair of the Society's Literary Awards panel in 2015, he remained an active member as a judge.
98 Selected works by Campbell, Gifford and Murray include Ian Campbell et al., *Collected Letters of Thomas and Jane Welsh Carlyle, Vols 1–42* (Durham: Duke University Press, 1973 to present); Ian Campbell (ed.), *Nineteenth-Century Scottish Fiction Critical Essays* (Manchester: Carcanet Press, 1979); Ian Campbell, *Kailyard* (Edinburgh: Ramsay Head Press, 1981); Douglas Gifford, *Dear Green Place? The Novel in the West of Scotland* (Glasgow: Third Eye Centre, 1985); Douglas Gifford and Dorothy McMillan, *History of Scottish Women's Writing* (Edinburgh: Edinburgh University Press, 1997); Douglas Gifford et al., *Scottish Literature in English and Scots* (Edinburgh: Edinburgh University Press, 2002); Isobel Murray (ed.), *Complete Shorter Fiction Oscar Wilde* (Oxford: Oxford University Press, 1980); Isobel Murray, *Jessie Kesson: Writing Her Life: A Biography* (Edinburgh: Canongate, 2000); Isobel Murray (ed.), *Beyond This Limit: Selected Shorter Fiction of Naomi Mitchison* (Glasgow: Kennedy and Boyd, 2008); Isobel Murray, *Scottish Novels of the Second World War* (Edinburgh: Word Power Books, 2011).
99 Angus Calder, *People' War: Britain 1939–1945* (London: Cape, 1969); Angus Calder, *Revolving Culture: Notes from the Scottish Republic* (London: I.B. Tauris, 1994). Calder was also nominated for the 1982 Scottish Book of the Year Award for his book *Revolutionary Empire: The Rise of the English-Speaking Empires from the Fifteenth Century to the 1780s* (London: Cape, 1981).
100 James Allan Ford's novels include *Brave White Flag* (London: Hodder & Stoughton, 1961); *Judge of Men* (London: Hodder & Stoughton, 1968); *Mouth of Truth* (London: Gollancz, 1972); *Season of Escape* (London: Hodder & Stoughton, 1963); *A Statue for a Public Place* (London: Hodder & Stoughton, 1965).
101 'Obituary: Capital novelist James Allan Ford was a man of many talents', *Scotsman*, 30 April 2009, http://www.scotsman.com/lifestyle/capital-novelist-james-allan-ford-was-a-man-of-many-talents-1-1205011 (accessed 31 July 2020).
102 Scott interview with Marsden, 6 March 2013.
103 Driscoll, *The New Literary Middlebrow*, 127.
104 Letter from M. G. Keohane, head of group public relations, to Paul Henderson Scott, 11 May 1987. Edinburgh, National Library of Scotland (NLS), Acc. 9393, File No. 156.
105 Letter from David Daiches to Michael Herries, chairman at RBS, 7 July 1987. Edinburgh, National Library of Scotland, Acc. 9393, File No. 156.
106 Letter from Sir Michael Herries to David Daiches, 16 July 1987. Edinburgh, National Library of Scotland (NLS), Acc. 9393, File No. 156.

107 Ibid.
108 Letter from Paul Henderson Scott to Randal Allan, *Scotsman*, 2 December 1987. Edinburgh, National Library of Scotland (NLS), Acc. 9393, File No. 156.
109 Ibid.
110 Ibid.
111 Ibid.
112 Ibid.
113 Ibid.
114 Rob McKenna, 'Murder choice for McVitie's Prize', *Herald*, 1 December 1995, 5; Lynne Robertson, 'McIlvanney wins award', *Herald*, 28 November 1996, 9; 'Literary prizes', *New Straits Times*, 3 May 1993, 35.
115 The reputation and public profile of the Saltire Society was a particularly hot topic among the Society's council and public relations and publicity committee more generally during this period. Minutes from a meeting of the public relations and publicity committee held on Wednesday, 8 April 1987, show that the Society was keen to 'examine the public image of the Saltire Society fifty years after its inception' and 'improve contacts between the Society and Press/Media'. Although Scott was not present for this meeting, the minutes of the meeting were circulated among all other committees, including the Book of the Year Award panel. Further, Scott did attend a later meeting of the public relations and publicity committee, 1 February 1988, indicating that he was conscious of the determined efforts being made by the Society to assure its public profile. Minutes of Public Relations and Publicity Committee Meeting, 8 April 1987, 1 February 1988. Edinburgh, National Library of Scotland (NLS), Acc. 10347, File No. 116.
116 The way in which the cultural capital of the Society's Literary Awards has been perceived and demonstrated is discussed in Chapters 5 and 6 of this book.
117 Letter from Paul Scott to Angus Calder, Ian C., Douglas Gifford, Isobel Murray, Derick Thomson and Alan Taylor. Edinburgh, National Library of Scotland (NLS), Acc. 10347, File No. 21.
118 Ibid.
119 Letter from Paul Henderson Scott to Ian Thomson, *Scotsman*, 30 May 1988. Edinburgh, National Library of Scotland (NLS), Acc. 10347, File No. 21.
120 Letter from Simon Berry, *Scotsman*, to Paul Henderson Scott, 9 December 1988. Edinburgh, National Library of Scotland (NLS), Acc. 10347, File No. 21.
121 Ibid.
122 Driscoll, *The New Literary Middlebrow*, 135.
123 Letter from Paul Henderson Scott to Literary Award Panel Members, 21 December 1988. Edinburgh, National Library of Scotland (NLS), Acc. 10347, File No. 21.
124 Ibid.
125 Letter from Derick Thomson to Paul Henderson Scott, 31 December 1988. Edinburgh, National Library of Scotland (NLS), Acc. 10347, File No. 21.
126 Letter from Isobel Murray to Paul Henderson Scott, 9 January 1989. Edinburgh, National library of Scotland (NLS), Acc. 10347, File No. 21.
127 Letter from Angus Calder to Paul Henderson Scott, 12 January 1989. Edinburgh, National Library of Scotland (NLS), Acc. 10347, File No. 21.
128 Letter from Paul Henderson Scott to the Literary Awards Judging Panel, 1 March 1989. Edinburgh, National Library of Scotland (NLS), Acc. 10347, File No. 21.

129 On average there has usually been only two or three judges who can read Gaelic on the panel over the years.
130 Stevie Marsden, *The Saltire Society Book Awards Schema: Report* (Edinburgh: Saltire Society, 2017).
131 In 2014 the Saltire Society, in partnership with the Scottish Poetry Library, founded the Poetry Book of the Year Award. In its first year, the award – which is awarded to new collections of poetry by Scottish-born authors, authors of Scottish descent or authors living in Scotland – was adjudicated by Dr Robyn Marsack, the former director of the Scottish Poetry Library (2000–2015) and poet, writer and professor emeritus at the University of Stirling, Rory Watson. In 2015, Dorothy McMillan, senior lecturer in English literature at the University of Glasgow, joined Marsack and Watson as the third member of the panel. Prior to 2014, poetry books nominated for the Society's Book of the Year Award or First Book of the Year Award were judged alongside all other entries for these awards. In 2013, the Society also founded a Publisher of the Year Award for publishers whose headquarters are based in Scotland. Between 2013 and 2015, the award was judged by CEO of Publishing Scotland, Marion Sinclair; acting head of literature, languages and publishing at Creative Scotland, Aly Barr; literary agent Jenny Brown; Professor Claire Squires, director of the Stirling Centre for International Publishing and Communication, University of Stirling; the award-winning independent bookseller Roz de la Hay; and the CEO of New Writing North, Claire Malcolm.
132 Letter from Paul Henderson Scott to Members of the Saltire Society Book of the Year Judging Panel, 1 March 1989. Edinburgh, National Library of Scotland (NLS), Acc. 10347, File No. 21.
133 Ibid.
134 Letter from Angus Calder to Paul Henderson Scott, 7 March 1989. Edinburgh, National Library of Scotland (NLS), Acc. 10347, File No. 21.
135 Ibid.
136 Letter from Isobel Murray to Paul Henderson Scott, 10 March 1989. Edinburgh, National Library of Scotland (NLS), Acc. 10347, File No. 21.
137 Letter from Ian Campbell to Paul Henderson Scott, 8 March 1989. Edinburgh, National Library of Scotland (NLS), Acc. 10347, File No. 21.
138 Letter from Paul Henderson Scott to Sorley McLean, 11 January 1991. Edinburgh, National Library of Scotland (NLS), Acc. 10504, File No. 15.
139 Although there is evidence that a number of the Society's Literary Award ceremonies were recorded and broadcast by STV, only one archived recording, of the 1995 ceremony, has been traced within the STV footage archives.
140 Letter from Ian Campbell to Kathleen Munro, 14 January 1993. Edinburgh, National Library of Scotland (NLS), Acc. 11259, File No. 24.
141 Letter from Gus MacDonald, managing director, STV, to Magnus Linklater, *Scotsman*, and Arnold Kemp, *Herald*, 3 February 1994. Edinburgh, National Library of Scotland (NLS), Acc. 11374, File No. 12.
142 Letter from Magnus Linklater to Paul Henderson Scott, 15 February 1994. Edinburgh, National Library of Scotland (NLS), Acc. 11374, File No. 12.
143 Ibid.
144 Letter from Paul Scott to Magnus Linklater, *Scotsman* and David Whitton, STV, 9 March 1994. Edinburgh, National Library of Scotland (NLS), Acc. 11374, File No. 12.

145 Ibid.
146 Ibid.
147 Letter from Derick Thomson to Kathleen Munro, 14 March 1994. Edinburgh, National Library of Scotland (NLS), Acc. 11374, File No. 12.
148 Ibid.
149 Letter from David Whitton, head of public affairs, STV, to Paul Henderson Scott, 29 July 1994. Edinburgh, National Library of Scotland (NLS), Acc. 11374, File No. 12.
150 Ibid.
151 Letter from Paul Henderson Scott to Douglas Gifford, 12 June 1995. Edinburgh, National Library of Scotland (NLS), Acc. 11714, File No, 24.
152 Letter from Kathleen Munro to Douglas Gifford, 5 January 1996. Edinburgh, National Library of Scotland (NLS), Acc. 11714, File No. 25.
153 Nominations for the 1995 Saltire Society Book of the Year Award. Edinburgh, National Library of Scotland (NLS), Acc. 11714, File No. 24.
154 Nominations for the 1996 Saltire Society Book of the Year Award. Edinburgh, National Library of Scotland (NLS), Acc. 11714, File No. 25.
155 Letter from Ian Campbell to Kathleen Munro, 4 November 1996. Edinburgh, National Library of Scotland (NLS), Acc. 11714, File No. 25.
156 Ibid.
157 Claire Squires, 'Book marketing and the book prize', in *Judging a Book by Its Cover*, edited by N. Matthews and N. Moody (Hampshire: Ashgate, 2007), 87.
158 Letter from Steven Malcolm, deputy promotions manager, *Scotsman*, to Kathleen Munro, 3 March 2000. Edinburgh, National Library of Scotland (NLS), Acc. 12393, File No 84.
159 Press release: 'Advocates Open New Chapter with Saltire Book of the Year Sponsorship', 14 October 2004. Edinburgh, National Library of Scotland (NLS), Acc. 13219, File No 23.
160 Letter from Bruce McKain, director of public affairs at Faculty of Advocates, to Michael Hance, director of Saltire Society, 16 April 2004. Edinburgh, National Library of Scotland (NLS), Acc. 13219, File No 23.
161 'The Scottish Book of the Year axed' (2008). Edinburgh, National Library of Scotland (NLS), Acc. 13517, File No 31.
162 Press release: Saltire Society Literary Awards 2009, 30 November. Saltire Society, Private Archives.
163 'All write for year of homecoming', 28 November 2008. Saltire Society, Private Archives.
164 Autumn appeal, 2010. Saltire Society, Private Archives.
165 This £10,000 budget for the award was illustrated in information materials provided to potential sponsors for the 2010 Book of the Year Award. The breakdown of this sum was detailed as follows: preparation in the run up to the award ceremony, £1,500; a proportion of the cost of the award ceremony, £1,500; production of publicity material for the shortlisted books and winning book, £2,000; prize to winning author, £5,000.
166 Figures provided by the Saltire Society. Saltire Society, Private Archives.
167 'Saltire Society literature brief 2011'. Saltire Society, Private Archives.
168 Cullen of Whitekirk, 'Saltire Society report of the Saltire Commission', January 2011, 10, www.saltiresociety.org.uk/Downloads/Saltire-CommIssion-Report.pdf (accessed 31 July 2020).

169 Ibid., 3.
170 Ibid., 4.
171 The Scottish Mortgage Investment Trust, managed by Baillie Gifford, is a Scottish investment management company well known for its sponsorship of the arts, particularly literary festivals. In 2019, Baillie Gifford sponsored venues and events at a range of UK literary festivals, including *Hay Festival*, *Borders Book Festival*, *Edinburgh international Book Festival* and *The Times and Sunday Times Cheltenham Literature Festival*. Since 2015, Baillie Gifford has also been the title sponsor of a non-fiction award. Formerly known as the Samuel Johnson Prize, the winner of the annual Baillie Gifford Prize receives £50,000.
172 Derek is an anonymous pseudonym for the publisher interviewed by the author on 25 February 2015.

Chapter 3. The Saltire Society First Book of the Year Award

1 Letter from PHS to Angus Calder, Ian C, Douglas Gifford, Isobel Murray, Derick Thomson, Alan Taylor, Monday, 15 February 1988. Edinburgh, National Library of Scotland (NLS), Acc. 10347, File No. 21.
2 Letter from Isobel to Paul Henderson Scott, Tuesday, 16 February 1988. Edinburgh, National Library of Scotland (NLS), Acc. 10347, File No. 21.
3 Catherine Lockerbie, 'Nonplussed Bruce wins Saltire Book Prize', *Scotsman*, 1 December 1999, 4.
4 Letter from Kathleen Austin to the editor of *Citizen*, 19 April 1988. Edinburgh, National Library of Scotland (NLS), Acc. 10504, File No. 15.
5 Letter from Kathleen Austin to Barbara Thomson, information officer at SAC, 19 April 1988. Edinburgh, National Library of Scotland (NLS), Acc. 10504, File No. 15.
6 The Scottish Book Marketing Group originated from the Scottish Publishers Association (founded in 1973) which became the Scottish Publishers Association in 1986 and has been known as Publishing Scotland since 2007.
7 Letter from Lorraine Fannin to Paul Henderson Scott, 19 May 1988. Edinburgh, National Library of Scotland (NLS), Acc. 10347, File No. 21.
8 *Scotsman*, 2 November 1988, 7.
9 'An A–Z of Scottish writers', *Scotsman*, 30 December 1995, 15.
10 The Saltire Society Best First Book Nominations 1988. Edinburgh, National Library of Scotland (NLS), Acc. 10347, File No. 21.
11 Simon Berry, 'Title fight for Scottish talent', *Scotsman*, 17 October 1988, 15.
12 Ibid.
13 Angus Calder, 'The dream ticket that shows where Scots should be going', *Scotsman*, 1988, 11.
14 Letter from Alan Taylor to Paul Henderson Scott, 20 October 1989. Edinburgh, National Library of Scotland (NLS), Acc. 10504, File No. 15.
15 Ibid.
16 Ibid.
17 Such movement of books between categories has always been an option for the Society's Literary Award judges, with the judges reserving the right to recommend a book to another panel or category if they felt it was necessary, and while this has happened with books being recommended by the judges of the Book of the Year

Award to the History of Research Book of the Year Award, the Literary Awards judging panel has never 'upgraded' a first book from the First Book of the Year Award to the Book of the Year Award.
18. Letter from Isobel Murray to Paul Henderson Scott, 22 October 1989. Edinburgh, National Library of Scotland (NLS), Acc. 10504, File No. 15.
19. Ibid.
20. Ibid.
21. Ibid.
22. Letter from Paul Henderson Scott to Sian Hayton, 4 January 1990. Edinburgh, National Library of Scotland (NLS), Acc. 10504, File No. 15.
23. Ibid.
24. Letter from Sian Hayton to Kathleen Austin, 12 January 1990. Edinburgh, National Library of Scotland (NLS), Acc. 10504, File No. 15.
25. B. Bell, S. W. Brown, W. McDougall (eds), 'Publishing policies: The literary culture', in *The Edinburgh History of the Book in Scotland, Volume 4: Professionalism and Diversity 1880– 2000* (Edinburgh: Edinburgh University Press, 2007), 184.
26. Saltire Society Literary Awards press release, 31 January 1991. Edinburgh, National Library of Scotland (NLS), Acc. 10504, File No. 15.
27. Miriam Elizaebth Burstein, 'The Ballad of Sawney Bain', The Little Professor, 29 December 2015, https://littleprofessor.typepad.com/the_little_professor/2015/12/the-ballad-of-sawney-bain.html (accessed 2 August 2020).
28. Saltire Society Literary Awards press release, 31 January 1991. Edinburgh, National Library of Scotland (NLS), Acc. 10504, File No. 15.
29. 'Kaunda lives on family support', *Times*, 8 February 1992, 20.
30. Letter from Paul Henderson Scott to Isobel Murray, 9 January 1992. Edinburgh, National Library of Scotland (NLS), Acc. 10890, File No. 28.
31. Ibid.
32. Letter from Simon Forrest (STV) to Paul Henderson Scott, 2 January 1992. Edinburgh, National Library of Scotland (NLS), Acc. 10890, File No. 28.
33. Ibid.
34. Sunny Singh, 'As the first black woman to win the Booker Prize, Bernardine Evaristo deserved to win alone', gal-dem, 15 October 2019, https://gal-dem.com/as-the-first-black-woman-to-win-the-booker-prize-bernardine-evaristo-deserved-to-win-alone/ (accessed 2 August 2020).
35. Indeed, Singh founded the Jhalak Prize which is open to 'entries published in the UK by writers of colour [including] (and not limited to) fiction, non-fiction, short stories, graphic novels, poetry, children's books, YA, teen and all other genres. The prize is also open to self-published writers.' Following the publication of the *Writing the Future: Black and Asian Writers and Publishers in the UK Market Place* report in 2015, which indicated that publishing and writing in the UK had in fact become less inclusive since the publication of a similar report in 2006, Singh has said that this is where the inspiration for the Jhalak Prize came from, stating that 'I knew for a fact that one of the easiest ways to disrupt publishing, is to have a prize'. Myesha Munro, 'Sunny Singh talks about the turbulent first few years of the Jhalak Prize', Oxford Student, 30 May 2020, https://www.oxfordstudent.com/2020/05/30/sunny-singh-talks-about-the-turbulent-first-few-years-of-the-jhalak-prize/ (accessed 3 August 2020).
36. Letter from Ian Campbell to Kathleen Munro, 26 January 1993. Edinburgh, National Library of Scotland (NLS), Acc. 11259, File No. 24.

37 Letter from Magnus Linklater to Paul Henderson Scott, 23 June 1993. Edinburgh, National Library of Scotland (NLS), Acc. 11259, File No. 25.
38 Letter from Ian Scott to Eddie Bell, chief executive of HarperCollins, 17 May 1996. Edinburgh, National Library of Scotland (NLS), Acc. 11828, File No. 51.
39 Letter from Eddie Bell, executive chairman of Harper Collins, to Ian Scott, 19 June 1996. Edinburgh, National Library of Scotland (NLS), Acc. 11828, File No. 51.
40 Letter from Honor Wilson-Fletcher, PR and publicity manager of Waterstones, to Ian Scott, 23 April 1996. Edinburgh, National Library of Scotland (NLS), Acc. 11828, File No. 51.
41 It just so happened that Scott's search for sponsorship corresponded with a brief recession in the UK book trade following the breakdown of the Net Book Agreement (NBA) in 1995. The NBA had allowed publishers to set minimum prices for books, but when this option was removed, 'consumer spending on books bottomed out in the spring of 1996'. Giles Clark and Angus Phillips, 'The reshaping of retail', *Inside Book Publishing* (London: Routledge, 2014), 35.
42 Letter from D. Ainslie Thin, James Thin Books, to Ian Scott, 17 April 1996. Edinburgh, National Library of Scotland (NLS), Acc. 11828, File No. 51.
43 Letter from Kathleen Munro to Martin Cummins, Scottish Post Office Board, 1 July 1996. Edinburgh, National Library of Scotland (NLS), Acc. 11828, File No. 51.
44 Ibid.
45 Letter from Kathleen Munro to Martin Cummins, 5 August 1996. Edinburgh, National Library of Scotland (NLS), Acc. 11828, File No. 51.
46 Ibid.
47 Letter from Martin Cummins to Kathleen Munro, 22 October 1996. Edinburgh, National Library of Scotland (NLS), Acc. 11828, File No. 51.
48 Ibid.
49 Letter from Kathleen Munro to Martin Cummins, 23 October 1996. Edinburgh, National Library of Scotland (NLS), Acc. 11828, File No. 51.
50 Saltire Society Literary Awards press release, 21 October 1996. Edinburgh, National Library of Scotland (NLS), Acc. 11828, File No. 51.
51 Nick Thorpe, 'Every story in the book makes a wide-ranging Saltire list complete', *Scotsman*, 26 October 1996, 3.
52 Saltire Society First Book of the Year Award press release (n.d.). Edinburgh, National Library of Scotland (NLS), Acc. 11714, File No. 25.
53 Ibid.
54 Murray Ritchie, 'Man who made the Post Office patron of the arts', *Glasgow Herald*, 16 March 1987, 17.
55 'Saltire Society Book Award final judging meeting', 4 November 1996. Edinburgh, National Library of Scotland (NLS), Acc. 11714, File No. 25.
56 Ibid.
57 Letter from Ian Campbell to Kathleen Munro, 4 November 1996. Edinburgh, National Library of Scotland (NLS), Acc. 11714, File No. 25.
58 Ibid.
59 Letter from Kathleen Munro to Douglas Gifford, 2 July 1997. Edinburgh, National Library of Scotland (NLS), Acc. 11991, File No. 16
60 Ibid.
61 Letter from Kathleen Munro to Douglas Gifford, 20 October 1997. Edinburgh, National Library of Scotland (NLS), Acc. 11991, File No. 16.

62 Letter from Kathleen Munro to Martin Cummins, 21 March 2000. Edinburgh, National Library of Scotland (NLS), Acc. 12393, File No. 84.
63 Letter from Martin Cummins to Kathleen Munro, 12 April 2000. Edinburgh, National Library of Scotland (NLS), Acc. 12393, File No. 84.
64 Hugh Macdonald, 'Outsider joins the in-crowd; Hugh MacDonald interviews this year's Saltire winner, Ronald Frame, and profiles the successful debut-novel and non-fiction writers', *Herald*, 1 December 2000, 21.
65 'Obituary: Douglas Galbraith, author whose life was devastated by the loss of his children', *Scotsman*, 7 May 2018, https://www.scotsman.com/news/obituary-douglas-galbraith-author-whose-life-was-devastated-loss-his-children-1429787 (accessed 3 August 2020).
66 'U.K.'s Post Office will change its name to Consignia in March', *Wall Street Journal*, 10 January 2001, http://www.wsj.com/articles/SB979075589579344054 (accessed 31 July 2020).
67 'Billboard', *Herald*, 7 November 2001, 15.
68 Mary Fagan, 'Consignia name in lost post as Royal Mail returns', *Telegraph*, 9 June 2002, http://www.telegraph.co.uk/finance/2764832/Consignia-name-lost-in-post-as-Royal-Mail-returns.html (accessed 31 July 2020).
69 Letter from Kathleen Munro to Ian Campbell, 8 January 2002. Edinburgh, National Library of Scotland (NLS), Acc. 12256, File No. 36.
70 Email correspondence between Isobel Murray and K Munro, 5 February 2002. Edinburgh, National Library of Scotland (NLS), Acc. 12256, File No. 38.
71 Raymond Duncan, 'Titans of writing win Saltire Awards; Life achievement honour for Morgan and Jenkins', *Herald*, 29 November 2003, 7.
72 Saltire Society 2010 annual finances. Saltire Society, Private Archives.
73 'Saltire Society Literary Awards call for judges', Saltire Society, July 2018, http://www.saltiresociety.org.uk/Downloads/Literary_Awards/Saltire_Society_Literary_Awards_call_for_Judges.pdf (accessed 3 August 2020).
74 Ibid.
75 Hannah McGill, 'Darren McGarvey's poverty safari omission gives pause for thought', *Herald*, 6 November 2018, https://www.heraldscotland.com/opinion/17203384.omission-of-darren-mcgarveys-poverty-safari-omission-gives-pause-for-thought/?ref=twtrec. (accessed 3 August 2020).
76 Ibid.
77 Ibid.
78 Ibid.
79 https://twitter.com/lokiscottishrap/status/1059914597619122176
80 Beth Driscoll, *The New Literary Middlebrow: Tastemakers and Reading in the Twenty-First Century* (London: Palgrave Macmillan, 2014), 120.

Chapter 4. 'WHAT'S THIS GOT TO DO WITH SCOTLAND?'

1 Alison Sheppard, 'The Saltire Society: Retrospect and intentions', Saltire Society Perth Conference Report 1947. Edinburgh, National Library of Scotland (NLS), Acc. 9393, File No. 342.
2 Neil Davidson, *The Origins of Scottish Nationhood* (London: Pluto Press, 2000), 22.
3 T. S. Eliot, 'Was there a Scottish literature?', *Athenaeum*, 1 August 1919, 680–81.

4   Edwin Muir, *Scott and Scotland: The Predicament of the Scottish Writer* (London: George Routledge, 1936), 15.
5   Alan Bold, *Modern Scottish Literature* (London: Longman, 1983), 1.
6   Liam Connell, 'Modes of marginality: Scottish literature and the uses of postcolonial theory', *Comparative Studies of South Asia, Africa and the Middle East* 23, nos 1&2 (2003): 52.
7   Alex Thomson, 'You can't get there from here': Devolution and Scottish literary history', *International Journal of Scottish Literature* no. 3 (Autumn/Winter 2007): 5, www.ijsl.stir.ac.uk/issue3/thomson.htm (accessed 31 July 2020).
8   John Hutchison, 'Cultural nationalism and moral regeneration', in *Nationalism*, edited by John Hutchison and Anthony D. Smith (Oxford: Oxford University Press, 1994), 123.
9   Ibid., 123.
10 Minutes of Meeting of Publications Committee of the Saltire Society held in Glasgow, 8 February 1954. Edinburgh, National Library of Scotland (NLS), Acc. 9393, File No. 937.
11 Letter from Paul Henderson Scott to Thomas Crawford, J. A. Ford, Edwin Morgan, Dr Anne Smith, 29 September 1981. Edinburgh, National Library of Scotland (NLS), Acc. 9393, File No. 153.
12 Saltire Society Literary Awards entry form 2015. Saltire Society, Private Archives.
13 Douglas Gifford, 'The Saltire shortlists', *Books in Scotland* no. 40 (Winter 1991): 1.
14 Ibid.
15 Ibid.
16 Ibid.
17 Kevin Williamson, 'The Man Booker Prize & 44 years of institutionalised anti-Scottish racism', *Bella Caledonia*, 26 July 2012, https://bellacaledonia.org.uk/2012/07/26/the-man-booker-prize-44-years-of-institutionalised-anti-scottish-racism/ (accessed 31 July 2020).
18 Ibid.
19 Ibid.
20 Ibid.
21 Alan Bissett, 'The unnoticed bias of the Booker Prize', *Guardian*, 27 July 2012, https://www.theguardian.com/books/booksblog/2012/jul/27/booker-prize-bias-english (accessed 31 July 2020).
22 Sharon Norris, 'Scots and the Booker', in *Fiction and Literary Prizes in Great Britain*, edited by Wolfgang Görtschacher and Holger Klein, with Claire Squires (Vienna: Praesens, 2006), 46.
23 Ibid.
24 Ibid.
25 *Guide to Literary Prizes: Grants and Awards in Britain and Ireland 1982* (London: National Book League and Society of Authors, 1982).
26 Ibid.
27 *Guide to Literary Prizes: Grants and Awards in Britain and Ireland 1988* (London: National Book League and Society of Authors, 1988), 27.
28 Saltire Society Literary Award judge interviewed by Stevie Marsden, 2 April 2014.
29 Ibid.
30 Ibid.
31 Norris, 'Scots and the Booker', 49.
32 Ibid.

33 Saltire Society Literary Award judge, 2014.
34 Gillian Roberts, *Prizing Literature* (Toronto: Toronto University Press, 2011), 3.
35 Ibid., 4.
36 Saltire Society Literary Award judge, 2014.
37 Alistair Macleod, 'My favourite place: Deep roots on Cape Breton', *Star*, 14 June 2013, http://www.thestar.com/news/insight/2012/06/30/my_favourite_place_deep_roots_on_cape_breton.html (accessed 31 July 2020).
38 Saltire Society Literary Award judge interviewed by Stevie Marsden, 16 April 2014.
39 Although the Book of the Year Award was expanded into new categories in 2014 and 2015, for the purposes of accuracy, this count includes all relevant data for the Society's Book of the Year Award from 1982 to 2014 and also includes figures for the Poetry, Fiction and Non-Fiction Book of the Year Awards from 2014 to 2018.
40 Sir David Robert Gilmour fourth baronet is the son of Ian Gilmour, baron of Cragimillar, and Lady Caroline Margaret Montagu-Douglas-Scott, the youngest daughter of the eighth duke of Buccleuch.
41 It is worth noting that, in some cases, it may be difficult to ascertain if some authors and their books do traverse more than criteria from the information available online (via publisher profiles, interviews and author social media), since it may be difficult to confirm if they are Scottish-born, or still live in Scotland as well as writing Scottish content. While this analysis has endeavoured to provide the most up-to-date and comprehensive data available at the time of publication, it should be taken as indicative of trends in the Society's Literary Awards, as opposed to unvarying rubrics.
42 Like Gilmour, Tennant is a descendant of Scottish nobility. Her father was Christopher Tennant, second baron of Glenconner, and her mother was Elizabeth Lady Glenconner.
43 It is worth noting that it was difficult to confirm why two authors – Simon R. Biggam and Sarah Gabriel, shortlisted for the First Book of the Year Award in 2006 and 2009, respectively – were eligible for the award. Biggam's debut thriller novel, *These Are Only Words*, was published by Scottish publisher Black and White Publishing and was also subsidised by an SAC grant. Likewise, Gabriel's book *Eating Pomegranates*, a memoir about her mother's death from breast cancer and the author's own battle with the illness (published by Jonathan Cape, 2009), does not have any Scottish content, and newspaper articles have stated that Gabriel lived in Oxford at the time of publication, with one review of *Eating Pomegranates* stating that she is English. Accordingly, Gabriel was included within the count for authors who are 'Scottish-born' as it seems the most likely reason why she was in fact eligible for the award.
44 Stevie Marsden, 'How the Man Booker fiction prize became stacked in favour of the big publishers', *Conversation*, 29 July 2015, https://theconversation.com/how-the-man-booker-fiction-prize-became-stacked-in-favour-of-the-big-publishers-45344 (accessed 7 August 2020).
45 The central belt is the most populated area of Scotland.
46 Natasha Onwuemezi, 'Saraband to move to Manchester', 28 February 2017, https://www.thebookseller.com/news/saraband-move-manchester-496346 (accessed 7 August 2020).
47 Natasha Onwuemezi, 'James Kelman signs with Canongate', Bookseller, 13 October 2015, http://www.thebookseller.com/news/booker-prizewinner-james-kelman-joins-canongate-314309 (accessed 31 July 2020).

48 Miha Kovač and Claire Squires, 'Scotland and Slovenia: Making books in wee lands', *Logos* 25, no. 4 (2014): 15.
49 Paul is an anonymous pseudonym for a publisher interviewed by Stevie Marsden on 26 June 2014.
50 'About', Gutter, 9 September 2014, http://www.guttermag.co.uk/ (accessed 15 May 2015).
51 Ibid.
52 Ibid.
53 Ibid.
54 Carol is an anonymous pseudonym for the publisher interviewed by the author on 25 February 2015.
55 Ibid.
56 Alan Taylor, 'Case of the vanishing publishers', *Scotsman*, 18 November 1997, 17.
57 Ibid.
58 Ibid.
59 Ibid.
60 Pascale Casanova, *The World Republic of Letters*, translated by Malcolm DeBevoise (Cambridge: Harvard University Press, 2007), 34.
61 Roberts, *Prizing Literature*, 17.
62 Alan Bold, *Modern Scottish Literature* (London: Longman, 1983), 1.
63 Katie Trumpener, 'Annals of ice: Formations of empire, place and history in John Galt and Alice Munro', in *Scottish Literature and Postcolonial Literature: Comparative Texts and Critical Perspectives*, edited by M. Gardiner and G. Macdonald (Edinburgh: Edinburgh University Press, 2011), 43.
64 Ibid.
65 Danielle Fuller and DeNel Rehberg Sedo, 'A reading spectacle for the nation: The CBC and "Canada Reads"', *Journal of Canadian Studies* 40, no. 1 (Winter 2006): 7.
66 Benedict Anderson, *Imagined Communities: Reflections on the Origin and Spread of Nationalism* (London: Verso, 2006), 6.
67 Casanova, *The World Republic of Letters*, 39.
68 'The Saltire Society Perth Conference, 1947', 3–4. Edinburgh, National Library of Scotland (NLS) Acc. 9393, File No. 342.
69 Ibid.
70 Beth Driscoll, 'Contemporary Australian literary culture', *Oxford Research Encyclopedia of Literature*, 28 June 2017, https://oxfordre.com/literature/view/10.1093/acrefore/9780190201098.001.0001/acrefore-9780190201098-e-153 (accessed 10 August 2020).
71 Ibid.
72 George Malcolm Thomson, *Caledonia or the Future of the Scots* (London: Kegan Paul, Trench, Trubner, 1927), 60.
73 Driscoll, 'Contemporary Australian literary culture'.
74 Roberts, *Prizing Literature*, 17.
75 John Hutchison and Anthony D. Smith (eds), *Nationalism* (Oxford: Oxford University Press, 1994), 124.
76 Besides the Saltire Society Literary Awards, there are also the Scottish Children's Book Awards organised by the Scottish Book Trust annually. These awards include categories for readers aged 3–7, 8–11 and 12–16 years and are voted for by 'children and young people across Scotland'. To be eligible, authors and illustrators must

reside in Scotland. Helen Croney, '2013 Scottish Children's Book Awards – Shortlist announced', 18 June 2013, http://www.scottishbooktrust.com/blog/2013/06/2013-scottish-childrens-book-awards-shortlist-announced (accessed 31 July 2020).

Chapter 5. Noticing Talent

1. Dani Garavelli, 'Writing the wrongs in literary prize land', *Scotsman*, 19 December 2019, https://www.scotsman.com/news/opinion/columnists/dani-garavelli-writing-the-wrongs-in-literary-prize-land-1-5064671 (accessed 31 July 2020).
2. Stevie Marsden, 'Why women don't win literary awards: The Saltire Society Literary Awards and implicit stereotyping', *Women: A Cultural Review* 30, no. 1 (2019): 43–65, doi: 10.1080/09574042.2018.1561047
3. Garavelli, 'Writing the wrongs in literary prize land'.
4. Ibid.
5. See, for example, Phil Miller, 'Kelman takes top literary prize as Saltire awards get £25,000 boost', *Herald*, 29 November 2008, 3; Phil Miller, 'Saltire Society revamp in bid to inspire debate in run-up to independence poll', *Herald*, 15 November 2012, 5; Phil Miller, 'Saltire Society announces poetry and fiction prizes', *Herald*, 3 March 2014, 3; Brian Ferguson, 'Irvine Welsh and James Kelman up for Saltire Literary Award', *Scotsman*, 20 October 2016.
6. Rosalind Porter and Joshua Knelman, *Four Letter Word: New Love Letters* (London: Chatto & Windus, 2007), 250.
7. 'Third triumph for Dutch Wordsmith', *Aberdeen Press and Journal*, 13 April 1998, 8.
8. Ibid.
9. Alexander Linklater, 'Word on the street', *Herald*, 21 May 1999, 23.
10. 'The canons', Canongate, https://canongate.co.uk/collections/the-canons/ (accessed 31 July 2020).
11. Stephen Naysmith, 'Prize hopes for Scots publisher', *Sunday Herald*, 12 November 2000, 10.
12. 'Foot notes', *Sunday Herald*, 19 November 2000, 10.
13. Jenny Jackson, 'A study in contradictions', *Ottawa Citizen*, 10 November 2002, C13.
14. 'Five are shortlisted for £15,000 literary award', *Scotsman*, 4 April 2006.
15. Lynsey Bews, 'Michel Faber wins Saltire Book of the Year Award', *Press Association Scotland Newswire*, 26 November 2015.
16. Alison Flood, 'Michel Faber's space missionary joins MR Carey's zombies on Arthur C Clarke shortlist', *Guardian*, 8 April 2015.
17. 'James Kelman', *BBC*, September 2004, https://www.bbc.co.uk/programmes/profiles/5SBCngLClyJs30G03BtvS6m/james-kelman (accessed 31 July 2020).
18. D. Rowbotham, 'A fierce Scottish pride during some lean times', *Courier Mail*, 28 September 1985.
19. 'Better late than never', *Scotland on Sunday*, 20 March 1994.
20. 'The Booker Prize 1989', The Booker Prizes, https://thebookerprizes.com/booker-prize/1989 (accessed 31 July 2020).
21. Jospeh Connolly, 'My own little list of Booker disaffection', *Times*, 21 October 1989.
22. Ibid.
23. Mary McGlynn, '*How Late It Was, How Late* and literary value', in *The Edinburgh Companion to James Kelman*, edited by Scott Hames (Edinburgh: Edinburgh University Press, 2010), 20–30 (20).

24 Zoe Heller, 'A tissue of truths: Zoe Heller talks to Kazuo Ishiguro whose novel, *The Remains of the Day*, was awarded this year's Booker Prize', *Independent*, 28 October 1989, 36.
25 Daniel Johnson, 'Is this book too shocking to win?', *Times*, 6 September 1994.
26 Shawn Pogatchnik, '*How Late It Was, How Late* wins Britain's top literary prize', *Associated Press*, 11 October 1994.
27 Annalena McAfee, 'Judges split as Kelman wins Booker', *Financial Times*, 12 October 1994, 12.
28 'Diary', *Sunday Times*, 23 October 1994.
29 Rob Scully, '*Four Weddings* wins Writers' Guild Prize', *Press Association*, 3 October 1994.
30 Phil Miller, 'Kelman picks up Scottish novel of the year award', *Herald*, 20 June 2009, 3.
31 Paul Dalgarno, 'Prize fighter; he might be the British hope for the Booker International, but don't go thinking James Kelman has joined the establishment', *Herald*, 25 April 2009, 20.
32 'First book takes prize', *Mail on Sunday*, 5 April 1992, 5.
33 Alice Thomson, 'Generation X', *Times*, 17 July 1993.
34 Jasper Rees, 'Suffering from second novel syndrome? You are not alone', *Telegraph*, 4 September 1999, https://www.telegraph.co.uk/culture/4718323/Suffering-from-second-novel-syndrome-You-are-not-alone.html (accessed 2 August 2020).
35 Catherine Lockerbie, 'Prizes that wrap up the truly gifted', *Scotsman*, 20 December 1997, 16.
36 Erica Wagner, '*The Master* is head of serious shortlist', *Times*, 22 September 2004, 10.
37 Meghan O'Rouke, 'England, England: Grant's best young British novelists, 2003', *Slate*, 3 June 2003, https://slate.com/culture/2003/06/granta-s-best-of-young-british-novelists.html (accessed 2 August 2020).
38 David Robinson, 'A L Kennedy takes award with plea for access to books', *Scotsman*, 1 December 2007, 9.
39 Ibid.
40 'Kennedy secures Costa Book Award', *BBC*, 22 January 2008, http://news.bbc.co.uk/1/hi/entertainment/7201911.stm (accessed 2 August 2020).
41 'Literature: English', *Britannica Book of the Year 2009* (London: Encyclopaedia Britannica, 2009), 255.
42 For more see 'Welcome', Lannan, 6 February 2002, https://lannan.org/about (accessed 2 August 2020).
43 'Austria: Austrian state prize for European literature to A. L. Kennedy', *US Fed News*, 22 October 2007.
44 'Schottische Autorin A.L. Kennedy mit Eifel-Literaturpreis geehrt', *Swiss News Agency*, 8 June 2008.
45 Alison Flood and Mark Brown, 'Man Booker shortlist 2016: tiny Scottish imprint sees off publishing giants', *Guardian*, 13 September 2016, https://www.theguardian.com/books/2016/sep/13/man-booker-shortlist-2016-announced-graeme-macrae-burnet-deborah-levy (accessed 2 August 2020).
46 'A L Kennedy receives prestigious Heine Prize of Dusseldorf', 2016, https://warwick.ac.uk/newsandevents/pressreleases/al_kennedy_receives/ (accessed 2 August 2020).
47 Ibid.

48 Stuart Jeffries, 'A grim delight', *Guardian*, 24 January 2008, https://www.theguardian.com/books/2008/jan/24/costabookawards2007.costabookaward (accessed 2 August 2020).
49 Alison Daniels, 'Pen and paper prescribe the perfect tonic', *Scotsman*, 11 June 1994.
50 Rosemary Goring, 'Ali Smith "blessed" by book of year award', *Herald*, 7 June 2002, 10.
51 Michelle Pauli, 'Ali Smith hits the shortlists again', *Guardian*, 2 May 2006, https://www.theguardian.com/books/2006/may/02/jamestaitblackprize.awardsandprizes (accessed 2 August 2020).
52 Mike Wade, 'Poet triumphs over illness and writer's block to win', *Times*, 21 June 2008, 28.
53 Emma Higginbotham, 'Ali Smith at Winter Wordfest', *Cambridge Evening News*, 24 November 2011.
54 'About the prize', The Goldsmiths Prize 2020, 28 January 2013, https://www.gold.ac.uk/goldsmiths-prize/about/ (accessed 2 August 2020).
55 Joanna Kavenna, '*Autumn* by Ali Smith review – A beautiful, transient symphony', 12 October 2016, https://www.theguardian.com/books/2016/oct/12/autumn-ali-smith-review (accessed 2 August 2020).
56 Smith's publisher, the Penguin Random House imprint Hamish Hamilton, was alerted to the cover misprint via a reader on Twitter. I have been unable to find this Twitter exchange from 2016. However, I would like to thank the bookseller and literary prize scholar Will Smith for informing me of this anecdote about the cover misprint and resultant Twitter exchange.
57 'David Walliams, Tim Peake and Philip Pullman shortlisted for British Book Awards', *Belfast Telegraph*, 15 March 2018, https://www.belfasttelegraph.co.uk/entertainment/news/david-walliams-tim-peake-and-philip-pullman-shortlisted-for-british-book-awards-36710904.html (accessed 2 August 2020).
58 '2018 book prize shortlist', The Orwell Prize, https://www.orwellfoundation.com/book-title/winter/ (accessed 2 August 2020).
59 Alison Flood, 'Ali Smith novel could be first to win Orwell Prize in a decade after making shortlist', *Guardian*, 18 May 2018, https://www.theguardian.com/books/2018/may/18/ali-smith-novel-could-be-first-to-win-orwell-prize-in-a-decade-after-making-shortlist (accessed 2 August 2020).
60 The Orwell Foundation, 'Orwell Prize longlists for political writing and political fiction 2020', 8 April 2020, https://www.orwellfoundation.com/the-orwell-foundation/news-events/news-events/news/orwell-prize-longlists-political-writing-political-fiction-2020/ (accessed 11 August 2020).
61 'Ali Smith', The Royal Society of Literature, 6 May 2016, https://rsliterature.org/fellow/ali-smith-3/ (accessed 2 August 2020).
62 '2015 New Year's honours list. Order of the Companions of Honour: Members of the Order of the Companions of Honour', January 2015, https://assets.publishing.service.gov.uk/government/uploads/system/uploads/attachment_data/file/393780/New_Years_Honours_2015_Queens_List.pdf (accessed 2 August 2020).
63 'Ali Smith CBE', Anglia Ruskin University, 26 August 2020, https://aru.ac.uk/graduation-and-alumni/honorary-award-holders2/ali-smith (accessed 2 August 2020).

64 'Region's successes to inspire next generation at graduation', University of East Anglia, 8 June 2016, https://www.uea.ac.uk/about/-/region-s-successes-set-to-inspire-next-generation-at-uea-graduation (accessed 2 August 2020).
65 'Press office: Honorary degrees celebrate excellence', Newcastle University, 17 July 2019, https://www.ncl.ac.uk/press/articles/latest/2019/07/honorarydegrees2019/ (accessed 2 August 2020).
66 Claire Squires, 'Book marketing and the book prize', in *Judging a Book by Its Cover*, edited by N. Matthews and N. Moody (Hampshire: Ashgate, 2007), 71–83 (73).
67 Michel Faber, *The Fahrenheit Twins* (Edinburgh: Canongate, 2006).
68 Michel Faber, *Under the Skin* (Edinburgh: Canongate, 2014).
69 Ibid.
70 '*The Book of Strange New Things*: Michel Faber', Canongate, 6 July 2014, https://canongate.co.uk/books/2209-the-book-of-strange-new-things/ (accessed 2 August 2020).
71 Colleen Kennedy-Karpat and Eric Sandberg, 'Adaptation and systems of cultural value', in *Adaptation, Awards Cultures, and the Value of Prestige*, edited by Colleen Kennedy-Karpat and Eric Sandberg (London: Palgrave Macmillan, 2017), 4.
72 James Kelman, *How Late It Was, How Late* (London: Secker & Warburg, 1994).
73 James Kelman, *A Disaffection* (London: Secker & Warburg, 1999).
74 James Kelman, *Kieron Smith, Boy* (London: Hamish Hamilton, 2009).
75 Nicky Agate, 'Arts: Author, academic, outcast; James Kelman is an acclaimed author abroad. But in his native Scotland he's still a pariah', *Independent*, 18 July 1998.
76 Francisco Garcia, ' "Scottish writers are superior by far": James Kelman on the Booker, class and literary elitism', 13 March 2019, https://www.newstatesman.com/james-kelman-booker-winner-how-late-it-was-25-years-interview (accessed 11 August 2020).
77 Ibid.
78 Stuart Wavell, 'Scots bewail 4,000-expletive blot on the national character', *Sunday Times*, 16 October 1994.
79 Kelman, *Kieron Smith, Boy*.
80 James Kelman, *The Busconductor Hines* (Edinburgh: Polygon, 2007).
81 A. L. Kennedy, *Night Geometry and the Garscadden Trains* (London: Vintage, 2004).
82 A. L. Kennedy, *Serious Sweet* (London: Vintage, 2017).
83 'The Little Snake: A. L. Kennedy', 1 August 2018, https://canongate.co.uk/books/2498-the-little-snake/ (accessed 2 August 2020).
84 Ali Smith, *Free Love and Other Stories* (London: Virago, 2002).
85 Ibid.
86 Ali Smith, *How To Be Both* (London: Penguin, 2015).
87 Dalya Alberge, 'A.L. Kennedy's tale of war and redemption pips Stalin to take £25,000 Costa Prize', *Times*, 23 January 2008, https://www.thetimes.co.uk/article/al-kennedys-tale-of-war-and-redemption-pips-stalin-to-take-pound25000-costa-prize-dr30zx8k68m (accessed 2 August 2020).
88 Stevie Marsden and Claire Squires, 'The first rule of judging club…: Inside the Saltire Society Literary Awards', *Journal of Cultural Analysis and Social Change* 4, no. 2 (2019): 1–14 (6). http://www.lectitopublishing.nl/Article/Detail/the-first-rule-of-judging-club-inside-the-saltire-society-literary-awards-6354.
89 Ibid.
90 A. L. Kennedy, *On Writing* (London: Jonathan Cape, 2013), 339–40.

91 Ibid., 355–56.
92 A. L. Kennedy, email correspondence with the author, 2019.
93 Ibid.
94 Ibid.
95 Michel Faber, email correspondence with the author, 2019.
96 Ibid.
97 Ann Matheson, interview with the author, 2014.
98 I was present at this awards ceremony, but it was also covered by a number of news outlets and blogs, such as Dustin Kurtz, 'The grand tradition of starving Scottish authors', Melville House, 3 December 2012, https://www.mhpbooks.com/the-grand-tradition-of-starving-scottish-authors/ (accessed 12 August 2020).
99 Tom Gatti, 'I've been homeless myself: you start thinking, "I'm not entitled": Novelist Anna Burns on winning the Booker Prize', *New Statesman*, 24 October 2018, https://www.newstatesman.com/culture/books/2018/10/i-ve-been-homeless-myself-you-start-thinking-i-m-not-entitled-novelist-anna (accessed 12 August 2020).
100 Authors' Licensing and Collecting Society (ALCS), *2018 Authors' Earnings: A Survey of UK Writers* (London: ALCS, 2018), 3.
101 Michel Faber, email correspondence with the author, 2019.

Chapter 6. Not Your Typical Book Award

1 James F. English, *The Economy of Prestige: Prizes, Awards, and the Circulation of Cultural Value* (London: Harvard University Press, 2005), 62.
2 Ibid.
3 Ibid., 199.
4 Pascale Casanova, *The World Republic of Letters*, translated by Malcolm DeBevoise (Cambridge: Harvard University Press, 2007), 147.
5 Examples of the kind of controversy surrounding the Nobel Prize in Literature include the debates surrounding the Swedish Academy's decision to award the singer/songwriter Bob Dylan in 2016 (with a number of cultural commentators saying Dylan should not have received the accolade) and the postponement of the 2018 award due to allegations of sexual harassment and abuse. Anna North, 'Opinion: Why Bob Dylan shouldn't have gotten a Nobel', *New York Times*, 13 October 2016, https://www.nytimes.com/2016/10/13/opinion/why-bob-dylan-shouldnt-have-gotten-a-nobel.html (accessed 13 August 2020); Bijan Stephen, 'Bob Dylan is a legend, but he doesn't deserve his Nobel Prize', *Vice News*, 13 October 2016, https://www.vice.com/en_us/article/wjpqnm/bob-dylan-is-a-legend-but-he-doesnt-deserve-his-nobel-prize (accessed 13 August 2020). Andrew Brown, 'The ugly scandal that cancelled the Nobel Prize', *Guardian*, 17 July 2018, https://www.theguardian.com/news/2018/jul/17/the-ugly-scandal-that-cancelled-the-nobel-prize-in-literature (accessed 12 August 2020).
6 Bali Sahota, 'Review of Pascale Casanova, *The World Republic of Letters*, trans. M. B. DeBevoise', *Bryn Mawr Review of Comparative Literature*, 6, no. 2 (2007): 1–6 (2).
7 Christopher Prendergast, 'Negotiating world literature', *New Left Review* no. 8 (2001): 100–21, 106.
8 Ibid.
9 Beth Driscoll, *The New Literary Middlebrow: Tastemakers and Reading in the Twenty-First Century* (London: Palgrave Macmillan, 2014), 122.
10 Ibid.

11 Ibid., 134.
12 Juliette Garside, 'Top writers' agent slams Scotland's book award', *Sunday Herald*, 21 November 2001, 7.
13 Ibid.
14 Ibid.
15 Ibid.
16 Ibid.
17 '"Visionary and Profound" poetry collection is 2016 Saltire Book of the Year', Creative Scotland, 24 November 2016, https://www.creativescotland.com/what-we-do/latest-news/archive/2016/11/visionary-and-profound-poetry-collection-is-2016-saltire-book-of-the-year (accessed 2 August 2020).
18 The Saltire Society, 'Report of the trustees and unaudited financial statements for the year ended 31 March 2017', https://www.saltiresociety.org.uk/about-us/annual-accounts/ (accessed 2 August 2020).
19 David MacDonald Graham, 'Saltire Society: What defines the best? The experience of being a shadow fiction judge for the Saltire Society', University of Stirling, 30 November 2017, http://www.publishing.stir.ac.uk/tag/saltire-society/ (accessed 2 August 2020).
20 Driscoll, *The New Literary Middlebrow*, 127.
21 Colleen Kennedy-Karpat and Eric Sandberg, 'Adaptation and systems of cultural value', in *Adaptation, Awards Cultures, and the Value of Prestige*, edited by Colleen Kennedy-Karpat and Eric Sandberg (London: Palgrave Macmillan, 2017), 3.
22 Ibid.
23 Ibid., 3–4.
24 Press release: 2015 Saltire Literary Awards open for nominations. Saltire Society, Private Archives.
25 See, for example, David Robinson, 'Glasgow writer wins prestigious book prize', *Scotsman*, 1 December 2000, 1; C. Dennier, 'Glaswegian patter sets tone for visit of top theatre troupe', *Aberdeen Press and Journal*, 2 May 2002; 'Debut novel is cutting edge for award-winning writer', *Evening News* (Edinburgh), 13 November 2002, 25; Brian Ferguson, 'Gaelic science fiction novel wins literary prize', *Scotsman*, 15 November 2013; Phil Miller, 'A L Kennedy wins Saltire Award', *Herald*, 1 December 2007, 5; Phil Miller, 'Burnside work names Book of the Year', *Herald*, 15 November 2013; Nicola Macbeath, 'Aberdeen academic receives Saltire Society book award', *Aberdeen Press and Journal*, 13 November 2014, 8.
26 Rosemary Goring, 'Last word', *Herald*, 25 November 2006, 12.
27 Ibid.
28 Rosemary Goring, 'Prize's reputation is dimmed', *Herald*, 1 December 2004, 8.
29 Richard Holloway, interview by Stevie Marsden, 13 June 2014.
30 Carol is an anonymous pseudonym for the publisher interviewed by the author on 25 February 2015.
31 Derek is an anonymous pseudonym for the publisher interviewed by the author on 6 February 2015.
32 'The Man Booker effect', The Man Booker Prize, 13 November 2012, http://themanbookerprize.com/news/2012/11/13/man-booker-effect (accessed 4 August 2020).
33 Claire Squires, 'Literary prizes and awards', in *A Companion to Creative Writing*, edited by G. Harper (Oxford: Wiley-Blackwell, 2013), 296. doi:10.1002/9781118325759.ch19.

34. 'Booker Prize 2012: Sales for all the winners and the 2012 shortlist, including Hilary Mantel', *Guardian*, 10 October 2012, http://www.theguardian.com/news/datablog/2012/oct/10/booker-prize-2012-winners-sales-data (accessed 4 August 2020).
35. Ibid.
36. Vinay Menon, 'The Giller effect', *Toronto Star*, 15 December 2015, https://www.thestar.com/entertainment/books/2013/11/01/the_giller_effect.html (accessed 4 August 2020).
37. English, *The Economy of Prestige*, 231.
38. Publisher interviewed by Stevie Marsden, 27 January 2015.
39. Publisher interviewed by Stevie Marsden, 7 March 2014.
40. Ibid.
41. While this was a period of significant change to the Society's Literary Awards, it is nonetheless useful to consider the data available for this period.
42. Accessed via Nielsen Bookscan.
43. In December 2014, for example, the *Bookseller* reported that 'sales for the week of Christmas were at their highest since 2010. In the final week of the year (Nielsen week 52) just under £50m (£49.87m) was spent in the seven days ending 27th December. This is up 32.4% in value on the same week last year when £37.7m was spent during Christmas week.' John Lewis, 'Print market solid in 2014', *Bookseller*, 30 December 2014, http://www.thebookseller.com/news/print-market-solid-2014 (accessed 4 August 2020). It was also reported in 2015 that 'Christmas presents accoun[t] for 30% of all the books we buy'. Jeremy Howell, 'Super Thursday: Opening the books on Christmas sales', *BBC News*, 8 October 2015, https://www.bbc.co.uk/news/business-34463922 (accessed 4 August 2020).
44. '*On the Edges of Vision* wins Saltire First Book of the Year Award!', Schietree, 27 November 2015, https://schietree.wordpress.com/2015/11/27/on-the-edges-of-vision-wins-saltire-first-book-of-the-year-award/ (accessed 4 August 2020).
45. @HelenMcClory, Twitter, 27 November 2015, https://twitter.com/HelenMcClory/status/670164536058494976 (accessed 4 August 2020).
46. '*Empire Antarctica* named Scottish Book of the Year', *BBC News*, 3 November 2013, https://www.bbc.co.uk/news/uk-scotland-24778681 (accessed 4 August 2020).
47. 'Authors shortlisted for literary awards', *Herald*, 28 August 2013, 5. See also Phil Miller, 'New sponsor announced for £30,000 book awards', *Herald*, 6 March 2009, 11; Lori Reid, 'Writer "honoured" to win top book award', *Aberdeen Press and Journal*, 20 June 2009, 20; Calum Ross, 'Author in running for prize with portrait of bankrupt city', *Aberdeen Press and Journal*, 19 March 2010, 7; 'Scots writers view for £30,000 book prize', *Herald*, 19 March 2010, 11; 'Write prescription', *Metro*, 4 November 2013, 5.
48. English, *The Economy of Prestige*, 63.
49. John Atkinson, *The Oscars Book* (Hertfordshire: Pocket Essentials, 2005), 8.
50. Ibid., 8.
51. Kate Mosse, 'History', The Women's Prize for Fiction, 9 March 2013, https://www.womensprizeforfiction.co.uk/about/history (accessed 4 August 2020).
52. 'About the Prize', Hyundai Mercury Prize, 7 August 2016, https://www.mercuryprize.com/about-the-prize (accessed 4 August 2020).
53. Lewis Knight, 'Mercury Prize 2019: What time are the awards tonight and how to watch in the UK', *Mirror*, 19 September 2019, https://www.mirror.co.uk/tv/tv-news/mercury-prize-2019-what-time-20096150 (accessed 4 August 2020).

54 'About us: Welcome to the BRITAwards 2020 with Mastercard', 10 December 2019, https://www.brits.co.uk/about-us (accessed 4 August 2020).
55 Pierre Bourdieu, *The Field of Cultural Production* (Cambridge: Polity Press, 1993), 42.
56 David Savran, *Highbrow/Lowdown: Theater, Jass and the Making of the New Middle Class* (Ann Arbor: University of Michigan Press, 2009), 223.
57 Ibid., 224.
58 Ibid.
59 Ibid. Savran here quotes from David Swartz, *Culture & Power: The Sociology of Pierre Bourdieu* (London: University of Chicago Press, 1997), 84.
60 Alexandra Dane, *Gender and Prestige in Literature* (Switzerland: Palgrave Macmillan, 2020), 124.
61 Graham Huggan, *The Postcolonial Exotic* (Oxon: Routledge, 2001), 119.
62 Ibid., 121.
63 Sharon Norris, 'The Booker Prize: A Bourdieusian perspective', *Journal for Cultural Research* 10, no. 2 (2006a): 139–58 (141). doi:10.1080/14797580600624752.
64 Huggan, *The Postcolonial Exotic*, 119.
65 Emmett Stinson, 'Small publishers and the Miles Franklin Award', in *The Return of Print? Contemporary Australian Publishing*, edited by Aaron Mannion and Emmett Stinson (Victoria: Monash University Press), http://books.publishing.monash.edu/apps/bookworm/view/The+Return+of+Print%3F%3A+Contemporary+Australian+Publishing/204/Text/12_chapter07.html.
66 Ibid.
67 Driscoll, *The New Literary Middlebrow*, 128.
68 Ibid., 129.
69 English, *The Economy of Prestige*, 65.
70 'About the Prize', Hyundai Mercury Prize.
71 'Not the Booker Prize', *Guardian*, https://www.theguardian.com/books/series/not-the-booker-prize (accessed 4 August 2020).
72 Harry Phillips and Patricia Bostian, 'Avoid fallacies of inconsistency', *The Purposeful Argument: A Practical Guide*, 2nd edition (Stamford: Cengage Learning, 2016), 129.
73 See, for example, Jonathan Baron and John T. Jost, 'False equivalence: Are Liberals and Conservatives in the United States equally biased?', *Perspectives on Psychological Science* 14, no. 2 (2019): 292–303, doi:10.1177/1745691618788876; Bob Garfield, 'False equivalence: how "balance" makes the media dangerously dumb', *Guardian*, 11 October 2013, https://www.theguardian.com/commentisfree/2013/oct/11/false-equivalence-balance-media (accessed 4 August 2020).
74 Jason Cowley, 'And the winner is?', *Observer*, 22 October 2006, https://www.theguardian.com/books/2006/oct/22/bookerprize2006.bookerprize (accessed 4 August 2020).
75 Benjamin Black, 'The Doge's Dagger', *Times*, 24 July 2010, 50–51.
76 Alex Marshall, 'Graphic novel in running for Man Booker Prize for first time', *New York Times*, 23 July 2018, https://www.nytimes.com/2018/07/23/books/booker-prize-graphic-novel-ondaatje.html (accessed 4 August 2020).
77 Further examples include Zoe Paskett, 'Turner Prize 2019: Everything you need to know about the contemporary art prize', 10 September 2019, https://www.standard.co.uk/go/london/arts/turner-prize-2019-artists-shortlist-exhibition-winners-a4233151.html (accessed 4 August 2020); Philip Kennicott, 'The most prestigious U.K. art award went to all four finalists. And that's a loss',

Washington Post, 4 December 2019, https://www.washingtonpost.com/entertainment/museums/the-real-turner-art-prize-is-the-aesthetic-riddle-we-pondered-along-the-way/2019/12/04/b5f2236e-16b9-11ea-9110-3b34ce1d92b1_story.html (accessed 4 August 2020).

78   Matthew Collings, 'Second front: The art of prize fighting – With this year's Turner Prize winner to be announced tonight, Matthew Collings applauds an event that may not always represent the cutting edge of modern art, but which offers all of us a chance to share the fun', *Guardian*, 28 November 1995.

79   William Feaver, 'Art: Tired Turner needs a tonic', *Observer*, 31 October 1993.

80   Tim Atkin, 'Food & Drink: Booker in the cooker – The Glenfiddich can be every bit as tough and rewarding as its most famous literary equivalent', *Guardian*, 27 April 1991.

81   Will Smith, '"Has anybody heard of it?!!!" The Constable Trophy for northern writers and its prize environment', *Journal of Cultural Analysis and Social Change* 4, no. 2 (2019): 13.

82   'Peru's *Vargas Llosa* wins Nobel Literature Prize', *EFE World News Service*, 7 October 2010.

83   Scott Roxborough, 'Oscars: How "Les Miserables" and "Atlantics" explore class strife', *Hollywood Reporter*, 26 December 2019, https://www.hollywoodreporter.com/news/how-les-miserables-atlantics-french-helmers-explored-class-strife-1263481 (accessed 5 August 2020).

84   Ida Lim, 'Malaysia's 2019 achievements, and how the 2020 bar got set higher', *Malay Mail*, 31 December 2019, https://www.malaymail.com/news/malaysia/2019/12/31/malaysias-2019-achievements-and-how-the-2020-bar-got-set-higher/1823420 (accessed 5 August 2020).

85   Stephen Bissett, 'Don't try this at home! The Australian stunt team behind Mel Gibson's *Hacksaw Ridge* take out TOP honours in industry's Oscars equivalent', *MailOnline*, 20 May 2017, https://www.dailymail.co.uk/tvshowbiz/article-4524548/Hacksaw-Ridge-stunt-team-industry-honours.html (accessed 5 August 2020).

86   Karen Price, 'Iwan me both – Wales' Olivier Award winners', *WalesOnline*, 8 May 2010, https://www.walesonline.co.uk/lifestyle/showbiz/iwan-both---wales-olivier-1916693 (accessed 5 August 2020).

87   '"The Oscars equivalent for neuroscience" comes to *LaLa Land*', *Cision PR Newswire*, 28 February 2019, https://www.prnewswire.com/news-releases/the-oscars-equivalent-for-neuroscience-comes-to-lala-land-300804093.html (accessed 5 August 2020).

88   Henry Hepburn, 'Award-winning head voices her fears for school-leavers', tes, 26 October 2012, https://www.tes.com/news/award-winning-head-voices-her-fears-school-leavers (accessed 5 August 2020).

89   Senior Master Sgt. Kevin Wagner, 'ACT nabs honors in European military's Oscars equivalent', Aviano Air Base, 11 May 2011, https://www.aviano.af.mil/News/Articles/News-Display/Article/280931/act-nabs-honors-in-european-militarys-oscars-equivalent/ (accessed 5 August 2020).

90   John Street, '"Showbusiness of a serious kind": A cultural politics of the arts prize', *Media Culture Society* 27, no. 6 (2005): 819–40 (819).

Conclusion

1   James F. English, 'Winning the culture game: Prizes, awards, and the rules of art', *New Literary History* 33, no. 1 (2002): 109–35 (109).

BIBLIOGRAPHY

'About', *Gutter Magazine*, 9 September 2014, http://www.guttermag.co.uk/ (accessed 15 May 2015).

'About the prize', Hyundai Mercury Prize, 7 August 2016, https://www.mercuryprize.com/about-the-prize (accessed 4 August 2020).

'About us: Welcome to the BRITAwards 2020 with Mastercard', 10 December 2019, https://www.brits.co.uk/about-us (accessed 4 August 2020).

Aikman, William. 'Fletcher, Andrew, of Saltoun (1653?–1716)', *Oxford Dictionary of National Biography*, 23 September 2004, https://www-oxforddnb.com.ezproxy3.lib.le.ac.uk/view/10.1093/ref:odnb/9780198614128.001.000 1/odnb-9780198614128-e-1012165 (accessed 7 July 2020).

Alison Lumsden interviewed by Stevie Marsden, 16 April 2014.

Allan Boyd interviewed by Stevie Marsden, 2 April 2014.

'An A–Z of Scottish writers', *Scotsman*, 30 December 1995: 15.

Anderson, Benedict. *Imagined Communities: Reflections on the Origin and Spread of Nationalism*. London: Verso, 2006.

Atkin, Tim, 'Food & Drink: Booker in the cooker – The Glenfiddich can be every bit as tough and rewarding as its most famous literary equivalent', *Guardian*, 27 April 1991.

Atkinson, John. *The Oscars Book*. Hertfordshire: Pocket Essentials, 2005.

Auguscik, Anna. *Prizing Debate. The Fourth Decade of the Booker Prize and the Contemporary Novel in the UK*. Bielefeld: Transcript, 2017.

'Authors shortlisted for literary awards', *Herald*, 28 August 2013, 5.

Baverstock, Alison and Richard Bradford. *Contemporary Publishing and the Culture of Books*. Abingdon: Routledge, 2020.

Bell, Eleanor, and Linda Gunn. *The Scottish Sixties: Reading, Rebellion, Revolution?* Amsterdam: Rodopi, 2013.

Berry, Simon. 'Title fight for Scottish talent', *Scotsman*, 17 October 1988, 15.

'Billboard', *Herald*, 7 November 2001, 15.

Bissett, Alan. 'The unnoticed bias of the Booker Prize', *Guardian*, 27 July 2012, https://www.theguardian.com/books/booksblog/2012/jul/27/booker-prize-bias-english (accessed 9 July 2020).

Bissett, Stephen. 'Don't try this at home! The Australian stunt team behind Mel Gibson's *Hacksaw Ridge* take out TOP honours in industry's Oscars equivalent', *MailOnline*, 20 May 2017, https://www.dailymail.co.uk/tvshowbiz/article-4524548/Hacksaw-Ridge-stunt-team-industry-honours.html (accessed 5 August 2020).

Black, Benjamin. 'The doge's dagger', *Times*, 24 July 2010, 50–51.

Blake, George. 'Literary tendencies in modern Scotland', *Library Review* 3, no. 2 (1931): 63–66.

Bold, Alan. *Modern Scottish Literature*. London: Longman Group, 1983.
'Book prize's happy ending', *Herald*, 19 July 1997, 3.
The Book Trust. *The Book Trust Guide to Literary Prizes, Grants and Awards in Britain and Ireland*. London: Book Trust in Association with the Society of Authors, 1988.
'Booker Prize 2012: Sales for all the winners and the 2012 shortlist, including Hilary Mantel', *Guardian*, 10 October 2012, http://www.theguardian.com/news/datablog/2012/oct/10/booker-prize-2012-winners-sales-data (accessed 5 June 2013).
'Books of today', *Western Morning News*, 6 June 1944, 2.
The Book Trust. *The Book Trust Guide to Literary Prizes, Grants and Awards in Britain and Ireland*. London: Book Trust in Association with the Society of Authors, 1988.
Bourdieu, Pierre. 'The forms of capital', in *Handbook of Theory of Research for the Sociology of Education*, edited by J. E. Richardson, translated by Richard Nice. New York: Greenwood Press, 1986, 241–58.
———. *The Field of Cultural Production*. Cambridge: Polity Press, 1993.
Bowie, James A. *The Future of Scotland: A Survey of the Present Position with Some Proposals for Future Policy*. London: W. & R. Chambers, Ltd., 1939.
Brooker, Peter, and Andrew Thacker. 'Introduction', *The Oxford Critical and Cultural History of Modernist Magazines: Vol. 1: Britain and Ireland 1880–1955*. Oxford: Oxford University Press, 2009, 709.
Bruce, George. *'To Foster and Enrich': The First Fifty Years of the Saltire Society*. Edinburgh: Saltire Society, 1986.
Cachin, Marie-Françoise, and Sylvie Ducas-Spaes. 'The Goncourt and the Booker: A tale of two prizes', *Logos* 14, no. 2 (2003): 85–94.
Calder, Angus. 'The dream ticket that shows where Scots should be going', *Scotsman*, 2 October 1988, 11.
Carruthers, Gerard. 'Scottish literature: Second renaissance', in *The Cambridge History of Twentieth-Century English Literature*, edited by Laura Marcus and Peter Nicholls. Cambridge: Cambridge University Press, 2004, 668–85.
Casanova, P. *The World Republic of Letters*, translated by M. DeBevoise. Cambridge: Harvard University Press, 2007.
Clark, Giles, and Angus Phillips. *Inside Book Publishing*. London: Routledge, 2014.
Collings, Matthew. 'Second front: The art of prize fighting – With this year's Turner Prize winner to be announced tonight, Matthew Collings applauds an event that may not always represent the cutting edge of modern art, but which offers all of us a chance to share the fun', *Guardian*, 28 November 1995.
Connell, Liam. 'Modes of marginality: Scottish literature and the uses of postcolonial theory', *Comparative Studies of South Asia, Africa and the Middle East* 23, no. 1&2 (2003): 41–53.
Cording, Alastair. 'The plays of Robert McLellan', in *Robert McLellan: Playing Scotland's Story*, edited by Colin Donati. Edinburgh: Luath Press, 2013, 431–40.
Cowley, Jason. 'And the winner is?', *Observer*, 22 October 2006, https://www.theguardian.com/books/2006/oct/22/bookerprize2006.bookerprize (accessed 4 August 2020).
Croney, Helen. '2013 Scottish Children's Book Awards – Shortlist announced', Scottish Book Trust, 18 June 2013, http://www.scottishbooktrust.com/blog/2013/06/2013-scottish-childrens-book-awards-shortlist-announced (accessed 5 June 2015).
Cullen, William Douglas. *Report of the Saltire Commission*. Edinburgh: Saltire Society, 2011.
Dane, Alexandra. *Gender and Prestige in Literature*. Switzerland: Palgrave Macmillan, 2020.
Davidson, Neil. *The Origins of Scottish Nationhood*. London: Pluto Press, 2000.
Devine, T. M. *The Scottish Nation: 1700–2007*. London: Penguin, 2006.

———. *Scotland and the Union, 1707–2007*. Edinburgh: Edinburgh University Press, 2008.
Driscoll, Beth. 'Twitter, literary prizes and the circulation of capital', in *By the Book? Contemporary Publishing in Australia*, edited by Emmett Stinson. Melbourne: Monash University Press, 2013a, 103–19.
———. 'Making the list: The value of prizes for women writers in the construction of educational reading lists', in *By the Book? Contemporary Publishing in Australia*, edited by Emmett Stinson. Melbourne: Monash University Press, 2013b, 127–40.
———. *The New Literary Middlebrow: Tastemakers and Reading in the Twenty-First Century*. London: Palgrave Macmillan, 2014.
———. 'Contemporary Australian literary culture', *Oxford Research Encyclopedia of Literature*, 28 June 2017, https://oxfordre.com/literature/view/10.1093/acrefore/9780190201098.001.0001/acrefore-9780190201098-e-153 (accessed 10 August 2020).
Ducas, Sylvie. *La littérature, à quel(s) prix?* Paris: La Découverte, 2013.
Duncan, Raymond. 'Titans of writing win Saltire Awards; life achievement honour for Morgan and Jenkins', *Herald*, 29 November 2003, 7.
'*Empire Antarctica* named Scottish Book of the Year', *BBC News*, 3 November 2013, https://www.bbc.co.uk/news/uk-scotland-24778681 (accessed 4 August 2020).
English, James F. 'Consuming fictions: The Booker Prize and fiction in Britain today', *Modern Fiction Studies* 45, no. 2 (1999): 529–33.
———. 'Winning the culture game: Prizes, awards, and the rules of art', *New Literary History* 33, no. 1 (2002): 109–35.
———. *The Economy of Prestige: Prizes, Awards, and the Circulation of Cultural Value*. London: Harvard University Press, 2008.
Fagan, Mary. 'Consignia name in lost post as Royal Mail returns', *Telegraph*, 9 June 2002, http://www.telegraph.co.uk/finance/2764832/Consignia-name-lost-in-post-as-Royal-Mail-returns.html (accessed 20 April 2015).
Feaver, William. 'Art: Tired Turner needs a tonic', *Observer*, 31 October 1993.
Finkelstein, D., and A. McCleery. *The Edinburgh History of the Book, Volume 4: Professionalism and Diversity, 1880–2000*. Edinburgh: Edinburgh University Press, 2007.
Finlay, Richard. 'Modern times (1914–) general', in *Oxford Companion to Scottish History*, edited by Michael Lynch. Oxford: Oxford University Press, 2011, 150–53.
Foster, John. 'The twentieth century, 1914–1979', in *The New Penguin History of Scotland*, edited by Robert Allen Houston and William Knox. London: Penguin Books, 2002, 417–94.
'Frederick Niven', Encyclopaedia Britannica, http://www.britannica.com/biography/Frederick-John-Niven (accessed 8 July 2020).
'Frederick Niven Award', *Books in Scotland* no. 15 (1984): 2.
Frieden preis des Deutschen Buchhandels. 'About the Peace Prize', https://www.friedenspreis-des-deutschen-buchhandels.de/en/about-the-peace-prize (accessed 7 July 2020).
Fuller, Danielle. 'Listening to the readers of "Canada Reads"', *Canadian Literature* no. 193 (summer 2007): 11–34.
Fuller, Danielle, and DeNel Rehberg Sed. 'A reading spectacle for the nation: The CBC and "Canada Reads"', *Journal of Canadian Studies* 40, no. 1 (winter 2006): 5–36.
Gardiner, Michael. *Modern Scottish Culture*. Edinburgh: Edinburgh University Press, 2005.
———. 'Towards a post-British theory of modernism: Speech and vision in Edwin Morgan', *Pretexts: Literary and Cultural Studies* 11, no. 2 (2002): 133–46.

Garside, Juliette. 'Top writers' agent slams Scotland's book award', *Sunday Herald*, 25 November 2001, 7.
Gifford, Douglas. 'The Saltire shortlists', *Books in Scotland* no. 40 (winter 1991): 1–4.
———. 'Breaking boundaries: From modern to contemporary in Scottish fiction', in *The Edinburgh History of Scottish Literature, Volume 3*, edited by Ian Brown, Thomas Owen Clancy, Susan Manning and Murray Pittock. Edinburgh: Edinburgh University Press, 2007, 237–53.
Goring, Rosemary. 'Prize's reputation is dimmed', *Herald*, 1 December 2004, 8.
———. 'Last word', *Herald*, 25 November 2006, 12.
Graham, Cuthbert. 'Macbeth – As Thorfinn the Mighty', *Aberdeen Press and Journal*, 8 May 1982, 8.
Graham, David MacDonald. 'Saltire Society: What defines the best? The experience of being a shadow fiction judge for the Saltire Society', University of Stirling, 30 November 2017, http://www.publishing.stir.ac.uk/tag/saltire-society/ (accessed 2 August 2020).
Gray, A., J. Kelman and T. Toremans. 'An interview with Alasdair Gray and James Kelman', *Contemporary Literature* 44, no. 4 (2003): 564–86.
Grieve, C. M. *Albyn or Scotland and the Future*. London: Kegan Paul, Trench, Trubner, 1927.
Harvie, Christopher. 'Labour and Scottish government: The age of Tom Johnstone', *Bulletin of Scottish Politics* no. 2 (spring 1981): 1–21.
Hepburn, Henry. 'Award-winning head voices her fears for school-leavers', tes, 26 October 2012, https://www.tes.com/news/award-winning-head-voices-her-fears-school-leavers (accessed 5 August 2020).
'History of the awards', Scottish Mortgage Investment Trust Book Awards, 5 December 2013, https://web.archive.org/web/20131205063655/http://www.scottishbookawards.com/about-the-award/history-of-the-awards/ (accessed 20 July 2020).
Holman, Valerie. 'Carefully concealed connections: The Ministry of Information and British publishing', *Book History* no. 8 (2005): 197–226.
House of Commons Public Information Office. 'General Election Results', 9 June 1983, Factsheet No. 22, June 1984, https://www.parliament.uk/about/how/guides/factsheets/members-elections/m09/ (accessed 17 August 2020).
———. 'General Election Results', 11 June 1987, Factsheet No. 47, June 1987, https://www.parliament.uk/about/how/guides/factsheets/members-elections/m11/ (accessed 17 August 2020).
———. 'General Election Results', 9 April 1992, Factsheet No. 61, 1993, https://www.parliament.uk/about/how/guides/factsheets/members-elections/m13/ (accessed 17 August 2020).
Huggan, Graham. *The Postcolonial Exotic*. Oxon: Routledge, 2001.
Hutchison, John, and Anthony D. Smith (eds). *Nationalism*. Oxford: Oxford University Press, 1994.
Iwamoto, Yoshio. 'The Nobel Prize in Literature, 1967–1987: A Japanese view', *World Literature Today* 62, no. 2 (spring 1988): 17–221.
'The James Tait Black Prize', University of Edinburgh, 14 August 2019, https://www.ed.ac.uk/events/james-tait-black/about/book (accessed 17 August 2020).
'Jenny Uglow wins the Hawthornden Prize for Literature 2018', Faber, 12 September 2018, https://www.faber.co.uk/blog/jenny-uglow-wins-the-hawthornden-prize-for-literature-2018/ (accessed 17 August 2020).

Joy, A. 'A brief history of Japan's most prestigious literary award, The Akutagawa Prize', *Culture Trip*, 21 September 2016, https://theculturetrip.com/asia/japan/articles/a-brief-history-of-japans-most-prestigious-literary-award-the-akutagawa-prize/ (accessed 17 August 2020).

'Kaunda lives on family support', *Times*, 8 February 1992, 20.

Kennedy-Karpat, Colleen, and Eric Sandberg (eds). *Adaptation, Awards Cultures, and the Value of Prestige*. London: Palgrave Macmillan, 2017.

Knight, Lewis. 'Mercury Prize 2019: What time are the awards tonight and how to watch in the UK', *Mirror*, 19 September 2019, https://www.mirror.co.uk/tv/tv-news/mercury-prize-2019-what-time-20096150 (accessed 4 August 2020).

Kovač, M., and C. Squires. 'Scotland and Slovenia: Making books in wee lands', *Logos* 25, no. 4 (2014): 7–19.

'"Lanark" author wins new award', *Glasgow Herald*, 17 November 1982.

Lang, Anouk. '"A book that all Canadians should be proud to read": Canada reads and Joseph Boyden's *Three Day Road*', *Canadian Literature* no. 215 (winter 2012): 120–36.

Lim, Ida. 'Malaysia's 2019 achievements, and how the 2020 bar got set higher', *Malay Mail*, 31 December 2019, https://www.malaymail.com/news/malaysia/2019/12/31/malaysias-2019- achievements-and-how-the-2020-bar-got-set-higher/1823420 (accessed 5 August 2020).

'The list', *Herald*, 15 December 2001, 6.

'Literary prizes', *New Straits Times*, 3 May 1993, 35.

Lockerbie, Catherine. 'Nonplussed Bruce wins Saltire Book Prize', *Scotsman*, 1 December 1999, 4.

Lynch, Michael. *Scotland: A New History*. London: Pimlico, 1992.

McClory, Helen. '*On the Edges of Vision* wins Saltire First Book of the Year Award!', 27 November 2015, https://schietree.wordpress.com/2015/11/27/on-the-edges-of-vision-wins-saltire-first-book-of- the-year-award/ (accessed 4 August 2020).

MacDonald, Catriona M. *Unionist Scotland 1800–1997*. Edinburgh: John Donald, 1998.

Macdonald, Hugh. 'Outsider joins the in-crowd; Hugh MacDonald interviews this year's Saltire winner, Ronald Frame, and profiles the successful debut-novel and non-fiction writers', *Herald*, 1 December 2000, 21.

Mack, Edward. *Manufacturing Modern Japanese Literature*. London: Duke University Press, 2010.

Macleod, Alistair. 'My favourite place: Deep roots on Cape Breton', *Star*, 14 June 2013, http://www.thestar.com/news/insight/2012/06/30/my_favourite_place_deep_roots_on_cape_breton.html (accessed 5 June 2015).

Macwhirter, Ian. *Road to Referendum*. Glasgow: Cargo, 2014.

Maine, G. F. (ed.). *Scotland's Welcome 1938*. Glasgow: WM Collins and Sons, 1938.

'The Man Booker effect', The Man Booker Prize, 13 November 2012, http://themanbookerprize.com/news/2012/11/13/man-booker-effect (accessed 4 August 2020).

Marsden, S., and C. Squires. 'The first rule of judging club…: Inside the Saltire Society Literary Awards', *Journal of Cultural Analysis and Social Change* 4, no. 2 (2019): 1–14, doi:10.20897/jcasc/6354.

Marshall, Alex. 'Graphic novel in running for Man Booker Prize for first time', *New York Times*, 23 July 2018, https://www.nytimes.com/2018/07/23/books/booker-prize-graphic-novel- ondaatje.html (accessed 4 August 2020).

McKechnie, George. *The Best Hated Man: Intellectuals and the Conditions of Scotland between the Wars*. Argyll: Argyll, 2013.

McKenna, Rob. 'Murder choice for McVitie's Prize', *Herald*, 1 December 1995, 5.

McKetterick, David. 'The Roberts years', in *A History of Cambridge University Press, Volume 3, New Worlds for Learning, 1873–1972*. Cambridge: Cambridge University Press, 2004, 257–95.

Menon, V. 'The Giller effect', *Toronto Star*, 15 December 2015, https://www.thestar.com/entertainment/books/2013/11/01/the_giller_effect.html (accessed 12 February 2016).

Mosse, Kate. 'History', The Women's Prize for Fiction, 9 March 2013, https://www.womensprizeforfiction.co.uk/about/history (accessed 4 August 2020).

Muir, Edwin. *Scottish Journey*. London: William Heinemann, 1935.

———. *Scott and Scotland: The Predicament of the Scottish Writer*. London: George Routledge, 1936.

Mure Mackenzie, Agnes. 'The Saltire Society: Its background and purpose', *Aberdeen University Review* 30, no. 90 (1944): 240.

National Book League. *Guide to Literary Prizes: Grants and Awards in Britain and Ireland 1982*. London: National Book League and Society of Authors, 1982.

———. *Guide to Literary Prizes: Grants and Awards in Britain and Ireland 1988*. London: National Book League and Society of Authors, 1988.

'New Scottish book award', *Daily Telegraph* (Northern Edition), 18 November 1981, 14.

'No title', *Aberdeen Press and Journal*, 25 August 1937, 13.

'No title', *Scotsman*, 2 November 1988, 7.

Norris, Sharon. 'The Booker Prize: A Bourdieusian perspective', *Journal for Cultural Research* 10, no. 2 (2006a): 139–58 (141), doi:10.1080/14797580600624752.

———. 'Recontextualising the Booker', in *Fiction and Literary Prizes in Great Britain*, edited by Wolfgang Görtschacher and Holger Klein, with Claire Squires. Vienna: Praesens, 2006b, 20–37.

———. 'Scots and the Booker', in *Fiction and Literary Prizes in Great Britain*, edited by Wolfgang Görtschacher and Holger Klein, with Claire Squires. Vienna: Praesens, 2006c, 37–52.

'Not the Booker Prize', *Guardian*, https://www.theguardian.com/books/series/not-the-booker-prize (accessed 4 August 2020).

'Obituary: Capital novelist James Allan Ford was a man of many talents', *Scotsman*, 30 April 2009, http://www.scotsman.com/lifestyle/capital-novelist-james-allan-ford-was-a-man-of-many-talents-1-1205011 (accessed 21 February 2016).

Oliver and Boyd Ltd. Agreements and Agencies, Acc. 5000, File No. 92, National Library of Scotland, Edinburgh, Scotland.

'*On the Edges of Vision* wins Saltire First Book of the Year Award!', Schietree, 27 November 2015, https://schietree.wordpress.com/2015/11/27/on-the-edges-of-vision-wins-saltire-first-book-of-the-year-award/ (accessed 4 August 2020).

Onwuemezi, Natasha. 'James Kelman signs with Canongate', *Bookseller*, 13 October 2015, http://www.thebookseller.com/news/booker-prizewinner-james-kelman-joins-canongate-314309 (accessed 14 October 2015).

'"The Oscars equivalent for neuroscience" comes to *LaLa Land*', *Cision PR Newswire*, 28 February 2019, https://www.prnewswire.com/news-releases/the-oscars-equivalent-for-neuroscience-comes-to-lala-land-300804093.html (accessed 5 August 2020).

Palmer McCulloch, Margery. *Scottish Modernism and Its Contexts 1918–1959: Literature, National Identity and Cultural Exchange*. Edinburgh: Edinburgh University Press, 2009.

Paul, Iain. 'The Saltire Society: A short account of the first ten years', *Scotland's Magazine*, 1947.
'Peru's Vargas Llosa wins Nobel Literature Prize', *EFE World News Service*, 7 October 2010.
Phillips, Harry, and Patricia Bostian. 'Avoid fallacies of inconsistency', *The Purposeful Argument: A Practical Guide*, 2nd edition. Stamford: Cengage Learning, 2016.
Pickford, Susan. 'The Booker and the Prix Goncourt: A case study of award-winning novels in translation', *Book History* no. 14 (2011): 221–40.
Power, Nina. 'Cultural capital', in *The Encyclopedia of Literary and Cultural Theory*, edited by Michael Ryan. Malden, MA: Wiley, 2011, doi:10.1002/9781444337839.wbelctv3c011.
Prendergast, Christopher. 'Negotiating world literature', *New Left Review* no. 8 (2001): 100–21.
Press release: 2015 Saltire Literary Awards open for nominations. Saltire Society, Private Archives.
Price, Karen. 'Iwan me both – Wales' Olivier Award winners', *WalesOnline*, 8 May 2010, https://www.walesonline.co.uk/lifestyle/showbiz/iwan-both---wales-olivier-1916693 (accessed 5 August 2020).
'Prize Novel Award to Neil Gunn', *Evening Telegraph*, 3 May 1938, 9.
Rait, Robert, and George S. Pryde. *Scotland*. London: Ernest Benn, 1934.
Ramdarshan Bold, M., and C. Norrick-Rühl. 'The Independent Foreign Fiction Prize and Man Booker International Prize merger', *Logos* 28, no. 3 (2017): 7–24, doi:10.1163/1878-4712-11112131.
Rawlins, F. I. G. 'The architecture of Scottish post-Reformation churches, 1560–1843 by George Hay', *Studies in Conservation* 3, no. 3 (April 1958): 142.
Rehberg Sedo, DeNel. '"Richard & Judy's Book Club" and "Canada Reads": Readers, books and cultural programming in a digital era', *Information, Communication and Society* 11, no. 2 (2012): 188–206.
Richard Holloway interviewed by Stevie Marsden, 13 June 2014.
Ritchie, Murray. 'Man who made the post office patron of the arts', *Glasgow Herald*, 16 March 1987, 17.
Roberts, Gillian. *Prizing Literature: The Celebration and Circulation of National Culture*. Toronto: University of Toronto Press, 2011.
Robertson, John. 'Fletcher, Andrew, of Saltoun (1653?–1716), Scottish patriot, political theorist, and book collector', *Oxford Dictionary of National Biography*, 23 September 2004, https://www.oxforddnbcom.ezproxy3.lib.le.ac.uk/view/10.1093/ref:odnb/9780198614128.001.0001/odnb-9780198614128-e-9720 (accessed 15 July 2020).
Robertson, Lynne. 'McIlvanney wins award', *Herald*, 28 November 1996, 9.
Roxborough, Scott. 'Oscars: How 'Les Miserables' and 'Atlantics' explore class strife', *Hollywood Reporter*, 26 December 2019, https://www.hollywoodreporter.com/news/how-les-miserables-atlantics-french-helmers-explored-class-strife-1263481 (accessed 5 August 2020).
Sahota, Bali. 'Review of *Pascale Casanova, The World Republic of Letters*, trans. M. B. DeBevoise', *Bryn Mawr Review of Comparative Literature* 6, no. 2 (2007): 1–6.
'Saltire scheme', *Scotsman*, 19 October 1955.
'The Saltire Society', *Scottish Journal* no. 11 (November–December 1953): 5–6.
The Saltire Society. 'Report of the trustees and unaudited financial statements for the year ended 31 March 2017', https://www.saltiresociety.org.uk/about-us/annual-accounts/ (accessed 2 August 2020).
———. *The Saltire Society Annual Report, 1937*. Edinburgh: The Saltire Society, 1937.
———. *The Saltire Society Annual Report, 1937–1938*. Edinburgh: The Saltire Society, 1938.

———. *Saltire Society Annual Report 1938–39*. Edinburgh: The Saltire Society, 1939.
———. *The Saltire Society Annual Report, 1939–1940*. Edinburgh: The Saltire Society, 1940.
———. *Saltire Society Annual Report 1941–42*. Edinburgh: The Saltire Society, 1942.
———. *Saltire Society Annual Report, 1945–46*. Edinburgh: The Saltire Society, 1946.
———. *The Saltire Society Annual Report, 1955–1956*. Edinburgh: The Saltire Society, 1956.
———. *The Saltire Society Annual Report 1957–1958*. Edinburgh: The Saltire Society, 1958.
———. *The Saltire Society Annual Report 1958–1959*. Edinburgh: The Saltire Society, 1959.
The Saltire Society Archives, Acc. 9393, File No. 6, National Library of Scotland, Edinburgh, Scotland.
———, Acc. 9393, File No. 16, National Library of Scotland, Edinburgh, Scotland.
———, Acc. 9393, File No. 153, National Library of Scotland, Edinburgh, Scotland.
———, Acc. 9393, File No. 154, National Library of Scotland, Edinburgh, Scotland.
———, Acc. 9393, File No. 156, National Library of Scotland, Edinburgh, Scotland.
———, Acc. 9393, File No. 342, National Library of Scotland, Edinburgh, Scotland.
———, Acc. 9393, File No. 347, National Library of Scotland, Edinburgh, Scotland.
———, Acc. 9393, File No. 937, National Library of Scotland, Edinburgh, Scotland.
———, Acc. 9393, File No. 938, National Library of Scotland, Edinburgh, Scotland.
———, Acc. 10347, File No. 21, National Library of Scotland, Edinburgh, Scotland.
———, Acc. 10347, File No. 115, National Library of Scotland, Edinburgh, Scotland.
———, Acc. 10347, File No. 116, National Library of Scotland, Edinburgh, Scotland.
———, Acc. 10504, File No. 15, National Library of Scotland, Edinburgh, Scotland.
———, Acc. 10504, File No. 15a, National Library of Scotland, Edinburgh, Scotland.
———, Acc. 10890, File No. 28, National Library of Scotland, Edinburgh, Scotland.
———, Acc. 11259, File No. 24, National Library of Scotland, Edinburgh, Scotland.
———, Acc. 11259, File No. 25, National Library of Scotland, Edinburgh, Scotland.
———, Acc. 11374, File No. 12, National Library of Scotland, Edinburgh, Scotland.
———, Acc. 11714, File No. 23, National Library of Scotland, Edinburgh, Scotland.
———, Acc. 11714, File No. 24, National Library of Scotland, Edinburgh, Scotland.
———, Acc. 11714, File No. 25, National Library of Scotland, Edinburgh, Scotland.
———, Acc. 11828, File No. 51, National Library of Scotland, Edinburgh, Scotland.
———, Acc. 11828, File No. 58, National Library of Scotland, Edinburgh, Scotland.
———, Acc. 11991, File No. 16, National Library of Scotland, Edinburgh, Scotland.
———, Acc. 12256, File No. 36, National Library of Scotland, Edinburgh, Scotland.
———, Acc. 12256, File No. 38, National Library of Scotland, Edinburgh, Scotland.
———, Acc. 12393, File No. 84, National Library of Scotland, Edinburgh, Scotland.
———, Acc. 13219, File No. 23, National Library of Scotland, Edinburgh, Scotland.
———, Acc. 13517, File No. 31, National Library of Scotland, Edinburgh, Scotland.
'The Saltire Society conference', *Scottish Journal* no. 7 (May–June 1953): 4.
'The Saltire Society and The Royal Bank of Scotland are launching an annual award for the Scottish Book of the Year', *Business and Finance in Scotland* 8, no. 6 (December 1981): 8.
Savran, David. *Highbrow/Lowdown: Theater, Jass and the Making of the New Middle Class*. Ann Arbor: University of Michigan Press, 2009.
Scheideler, Britta. 'Von Konsens zu Kritik: Der Friedenspreis des Deutschen Buchhandels', *50 Jahre Frankfurter Buchmesse: 1949–1999*. Berlin: Suhrkamp Verlag, 1999, 46–88.
Scott, Alexander. 'Editorial', *Saltire Review* 1, no. 1 (1954): 6.
Scott, Paul Henderson. 'Behind the awards', *Books in Scotland* no. 37 (1991): 1–3.

———. Interview with Stevie Marsden, 6 March 2013.
'Scottish book award', *Retail Newsagent London*, 1 January 1983.
'Scottish book awards', *Books in Scotland* no. 10 (spring 1982): 3.
'Scottish Book of the Year', *Books in Scotland* no. 9 (1981–82): 3.
Smith, Will. ' "Has anybody heard of it?!!!" The Constable Trophy for northern writers and its prize environment', *Journal of Cultural Analysis and Social Change* 4, no. 2 (2019).
Squires, Claire. 'A common ground? Book prize culture in Europe', *Public* 11, no. 4 (2004): 37–48.
———. *Marketing Literature: The Making of Contemporary Writing in Britain*. Hampshire: Palgrave Macmillan, 2007a.
———. 'Book marketing and the Booker Prize', in *Judging a Book by Its Cover*, edited by N. Matthews and N. Moody. Hampshire: Ashgate, 2007b, 71–83.
———. 'Literary prizes and awards', in *A Companion to Creative Writing*, edited by G. Harper. Oxford: Wiley-Blackwell, 2013, doi:10.1002/9781118325759.ch19.
Stinson, E. 'Small publishers and the emerging network of Australian literary production', *Australian Humanities Review* no. 59 (2016a): 23–24.
———. 'Small publishers and the Miles Franklin Award', in *The Return of Print? Contemporary Australian Publishing*, edited by Aaron Mannion and Emmett Stinson. Victoria: Monash University Press, 2016b, http://books.publishing.monash.edu/apps/bookworm/view/The+Return+of+Print%3F%3A+Contemporary+Australian+Publishing/204/Text/12_chapter07.html (accessed 17 August 2020).
Street, John. ' "Showbusiness of a serious kind": A cultural politics of the arts prize', *Media Culture Society* 27, no. 6 (2005): 819–40.
Strongman, Luke. *The Booker Prize and the Legacy of Empire*. New York: Rodopi, 2002.
Taylor, Alan. 'Case of the vanishing publishers', *Scotsman*, 18 November 1997, 17.
Thomson, George Malcolm. *Caledonia or the Future of the Scots*. London: Kegan Paul, Trench, Trubner, 1927.
Thomson, Alex. ' "You can't get there from here": Devolution and Scottish literary history', *International Journal of Scottish Literature* no. 3 (autumn/winter 2007), www.ijsl.stir.ac.uk/issue3/thomson.htm (accessed 31 July 2020).
Thorpe, Nick. 'Every story in the book makes a wide-ranging Saltire list complete', *Scotsman*, 26 October 1996, 3.
Todd, Richard. *Consuming Fictions: The Booker Prize and Fiction in Britain Today*. London: Bloomsbury, 1996.
Trewin, Ion. 'Martyn Goff obituary', *Guardian*, 26 March 2015, https://www.theguardian.com/books/2015/mar/26/martyn-goff (accessed 17 August 2020).
Trumpener, Katie. 'Annals of ice: Formations of empire, place and history in John Galt and Alice Munro', in *Scottish Literature and Postcolonial Literature: Comparative Texts and Critical Perspectives*, edited by M. Gardiner and G. Macdonald. Edinburgh: Edinburgh University Press, 2011, 43–56.
'U.K.'s Post Office will change its name to Consignia in March', *Wall Street Journal*, 10 January 2001, http://www.wsj.com/articles/SB979075589579344054 (accessed 20 April 2015).
' "Visionary and Profound" poetry collection is 2016 Saltire Book of the Year', *Creative Scotland*, 24 November 2016, https://www.creativescotland.com/what-we-do/latest-news/archive/2016/11/visionary-and-profound-poetry-collection-is-2016-saltire-book-of-the-year (accessed 2 August 2020).

Wagner, Kevin. 'ACT nabs honors in European military's Oscars equivalent', Aviano Air Base, 11 May 2011, https://www.aviano.af.mil/News/Articles/News-Display/Article/280931/act-nabs-honors-in-european-militarys-oscars-equivalent/ (accessed 5 August 2020).
'The Waverley column', *Edinburgh Evening News*, 17 November 1982.
Williamson, Kevin. 'The Man Booker Prize & 44 years of institutionalised anti-Scottish racism', *Bella Caledonia*, 26 July 2012, https://bellacaledonia.org.uk/2012/07/26/the-man-booker-prize-44-years-of- institutionalised-anti-scottish-racism// (accessed 9 July 2020).

INDEX

adjudication 47–48, 61, 63, 65, 78, 137–38
awards ceremony 14, 55, 63, 66–67,
    81–83, 87–89, 127, 149, 153–56

BBC 28, 47, 49, 65, 69, 87
Booker Prize 1–9, 64, 70, 82, 100–101,
    104, 108, 111, 125, 126, 128–31,
    133–36, 140, 146–48, 150, 152, 157,
    159–65, 167, 170, 171
Bourdieu, Pierre 2–3, 41, 145, 158, 167

Campbell, Ian 49, 56, 59, 62, 63, 66–67,
    75, 82–83, 87–89, 100
Canada 8, 104–5, 110, 116–17
Canada Reads 9, 117
Canongate 113, 124, 132, 135, 141
capital
    forms of 3–6, 92, 145, 158
    intraconversion 4, 131, 132, 145, 150
Casanova, Pascale 10–11, 117, 146
Costa Book Awards. *See* Whitbread
    Book Awards
Creative Scotland 35–36, 70, 90, 99
cultural capital 3–4, 9, 17, 57, 122,
    136–37, 148, 150, 162, 167
cultural hierarchy/hierarchies 159

Driscoll, Beth 2, 6, 9, 45, 57, 60, 92,
    117–18, 147–48, 150, 161, 170

economic capital 3–4, 29, 73, 116, 122,
    141, 166, 169, 171
emotional capital 143
English, James F. 2–7, 57, 132, 145–47,
    150, 156, 161, 162, 165, 167

Faber, Michel 16, 69, 121–25, 129–33,
    139, 140–42, 154, 170

false equivalence 10, 163, 171
First World War 23, 24, 25, 32
Frederick Niven Award 40–41, 102

Gaelic 14, 61, 83, 89, 100, 102, 105, 155
Gaelic Books Council 89
gender 45, 121, 160
General Election
    1974 32
    1983 33
Gifford, Douglas 31, 48, 49, 53, 56, 59,
    63, 66, 75, 83, 87–88, 100, 102,
    134, 149
Goldsmiths Prize 130, 136, 154–55
Gray, Alasdair 10, 31, 41, 50–55, 101, 121,
    123, 125, 134, 148

Huggan, Graham 2, 7, 160–61

Indyref. *See* Scottish Independence
    Referendum

James Thin Books 83–84
journalistic capital 4–5, 66, 81, 92, 142,
    145, 148, 158, 171

Kay, Jackie 69, 81–82, 114, 121, 123
Kelman, James 9, 10, 16, 31, 80, 87,
    101–2, 113, 115, 121–23, 125–27,
    130–34, 140, 142, 151, 170
Kennedy, A. L. 16, 81, 83, 101, 114–15,
    121–23, 127–32, 134–35, 137–39,
    142, 150–51, 154, 170

literary prize hierarchy/hierarchies 64,
    142, 160, 163–64, 170

Mackenzie, Agnes Mure 37, 40, 42, 43, 46

INDEX

Man Booker Prize. *See* Booker Prize
Manifesto of the Arts in Scotland 33, 43
McVitie's Prize 13–14, 58–59, 65, 67, 73, 87, 102. *See also* Stakis Prize
Mercury Prize 157, 162, 164
Muir, Edwin 27, 37, 42–43, 98, 118

national capital 116, 170
nationality 7, 45, 103, 106, 141
national identity 16, 31–33, 97–99, 102, 104–5, 107–8, 116–19
National Library of Scotland 1, 28, 56, 88–89
Nobel Prize(s) 171
   for Literature 1, 9, 17, 145–46, 160, 165, 171
Norris, Sharon 2, 6, 7, 10, 101–3, 160

Oliver & Boyd 24, 29
Orange Prize 128, 129, 157. *See also* Women's Prize for Fiction
Oscars 17, 157, 165

paratextual 4, 17, 122, 130, 137, 154, 170
Polygon 80–81, 89, 113
postcolonial 7, 160
Post Office 84, 85, 86, 87, 88. *See also* Royal Mail
prize hierarchy/hierarchies 17, 64, 142, 160, 163, 164, 165, 169, 170
promotion 4, 5, 29, 43, 45, 55, 67, 85, 87, 135, 142, 158, 167, 171
Publications Committee (Saltire Society)
Publishing Scotland. *See* Scottish Publishers Association

RBS 44–46, 49, 50, 52, 54–55, 57–58, 73. *See also* Royal Bank of Scotland
Roberts, Gillian 8, 104, 116, 118, 170
Royal Bank of Scotland 44–46, 54–55, 58, 75. *See also* RBS
Royal Mail 13, 84, 88–89, 169. *See also* Post Office

Saltire Society, The
   membership 3, 23, 28–29
   publications 28, 29, 30, 35
   Publications Committee 30, 39–43

Scotsman 42, 44, 48–49, 51, 56, 58–63, 65, 67, 75–77, 79, 80, 82–83, 85–86, 88, 102, 126, 169
Scott, Paul Henderson 43, 49, 53–74, 75–76, 81, 83–85
Scottish Arts Council (SAC) 10, 12–13, 49, 65, 70, 76, 87, 102, 123–27, 129, 136
Scottish Independence Referendum
   1979 33
   2014 34, 35, 98
Scottish National Party (SNP) 32
Scottish Poetry Library 62, 71, 79
Scottish Publishers Association 50
Scottish Television (STV) 48, 63–66, 73, 79, 81–83, 85, 87, 169
Scottishness 16, 32, 97–99, 102–7, 109, 113–14, 116, 118, 122–23, 170
Second World War 23
Smith, Ali 16, 84, 103–4, 115, 121–24, 126, 129, 130–31, 135–36, 142, 153–55, 170
social capital 3, 39, 41, 57, 87, 92, 131, 169
sponsors 3, 4, 5, 10, 11, 48, 60, 63–66, 73, 75, 81, 83–85, 92, 151, 169
sponsorship 6, 14, 44–45, 57–60, 63, 65–68, 70, 78–79, 83–89, 92, 161, 163, 169
Squires, Claire 2, 4–6, 10, 15, 17, 48, 113, 130, 137, 138, 152
Stakis Prize 14, 87–88, 126–27. *See also* McVitie's Prize
Street, John 164
symbolic capital 9, 45, 57, 132, 150
symbolic violence 6–7, 159–62

terms of eligibility 7, 11, 16, 38, 65, 97, 99, 100, 102, 106–9, 118, 157, 163, 168, 170
Turner Prize 162, 164

Waterstones 84, 153
W H Smith 61
Whitbread Book Awards 60, 61, 124, 129, 131–32, 170
Women's Prize for Fiction 1, 16, 130, 136, 157, 167, 170

www.ingramcontent.com/pod-product-compliance
Lightning Source LLC
Chambersburg PA
CBHW021824300426
44114CB00009BA/313